PUBLICATIONS IN OPERATIONS RESEARCH

Operations Research Society of America

Editor for Publications in Operations Research
DAVID B. HERTZ

No. 1. QUEUES, INVENTORIES AND MAINTENANCE
Philip M. Morse

No. 2. FINITE QUEUING TABLES
L. G. Peck and R. N. Hazelwood

No. 3. EFFICIENCY IN GOVERNMENT THROUGH SYSTEMS ANALYSIS
Roland N. McKean

No. 4. A COMPREHENSIVE BIBLIOGRAPHY ON OPERATIONS RESEARCH*
Operations Research Group, Case Institute

No. 5. PROGRESS IN OPERATIONS RESEARCH, VOLUME I
Edited by Russell L. Ackoff

No. 6. STATISTICAL MANAGEMENT OF INVENTORY SYSTEMS*
Harvey M. Wagner

No. 7. PRICE, OUTPUT, AND INVENTORY POLICY*
Edwin S. Mills

No. 8. A COMPREHENSIVE BIBLIOGRAPHY ON OPERATIONS RESEARCH, 1957–1958*
Operations Research Group, Case Institute

No. 9. PROGRESS IN OPERATIONS RESEARCH, VOLUME II
David B. Hertz and Roger T. Eddison

No. 10. DECISION AND VALUE THEORY
Peter C. Fishburn

No. 11. HANDBOOK OF THE POISSON DISTRIBUTION
Frank A. Haight

No. 12. OPERATIONS RESEARCH IN SELLER'S COMPETITION: A STOCHASTIC MICROTHEORY
S. Sankar Sengupta

No. 13. BAYESIAN DECISION PROBLEMS & MARKOV CHAINS
J. J. Martin

No. 14. MATHEMATICAL MODELS OF ARMS CONTROL AND DISARMAMENTS:
APPLICATION OF MATHEMATICAL STRUCTURE IN POLITICS
Thomas L. Saaty

No. 15. FOURTH INTERNATIONAL CONFERENCE ON OPERATIONS RESEARCH
David B. Hertz and Jacques Melese

No. 16. PROGRESS IN OPERATIONS RESEARCH, VOLUME III
RELATIONSHIP BETWEEN OPERATIONS RESEARCH AND THE COMPUTER
J. S. Aronofsky

No. 17. INTRODUCTION TO SYSTEMS COST EFFECTIVENESS
Karl Seiler, III

No. 18. UTILITY THEORY FOR DECISION MAKING
Peter C. Fishburn

No. 19. THE IMPLEMENTATION OF OPERATIONS RESEARCH
Jan H. B. M. Huysmans

No. 20. THE CHALLENGE TO SYSTEMS ANALYSIS: PUBLIC POLICY AND SOCIAL CHANGE
Edited by Grace J. Kelleher

No. 21. QUANTITATIVE THEORIES IN ADVERTISING
A. G. Rao

No. 22. SIMULATION IN HUMAN SYSTEMS: DECISION MAKING IN PSYCHOTHERAPY
Richard Bellman and Charlene Paule Smith

* Out-of-print

SIMULATION IN HUMAN SYSTEMS:

Decision-Making in Psychotherapy

RICHARD BELLMAN
and
CHARLENE PAULE SMITH

University of Southern California
Los Angeles, California

A Wiley-Interscience Publication

John Wiley & Sons

New York • London • Sydney • Toronto

Library of Congress Cataloging in Publication Data:

Bellman, Richard Ernest, 1920-
Simulation in human systems.

(Operations Research Society of America. Publications
in operations research no. 22)
"A Wiley-Interscience publication."
1. Psychotherapy. 2. Decision-making. I. Smith,
Charlene Paule, joint author. II. Title. III. Series.
[DNLM: 1. Decision making. 2. Human engineering.
3. Models, Psychological. 4. Psychotherapy.
*M 420 B445s 1973]

RC480.5.B42   616.8′914   73-6654
ISBN 0-471-06414-9

Printed in the United States of America

10 9 8 7 6 5 4 3 2 1

to our parents

Jack and Alice Paule

John James and Pearl Saffian Bellman

PREFACE

This book has several objectives. The first of these is to illustrate certain contemporary mathematical concepts and methods applied to decision processes occurring in a human interaction system. A concurrent aim is to provide an introduction to the powerful and versatile technique of simulation. With this technique we shall construct and then study mathematical models of some initial psychotherapy interviews, first having discussed some important underlying conceptual structures in psychotherapy. Let us note here that, using our models, we are able to investigate the structure of any psychotherapy interview, or indeed any two-person interaction which has identifiable goals. Thus, not only are we free from ties to a particular psychiatric or psychological theory, but we may readily extend our structures into other areas where interviewing has a role to play. Finally, we wish to describe some of the ways in which computers may be employed to increase the effectiveness of simulation processes used for research and teaching.

The discussion will be expository, elementary and self-contained. We assume no previous familiarity with computers, simulations, psychotherapy, decision-making or systems theory. Their underlying mathematical structures and concepts will be identified and discussed in non-mathematical language.

This research was undertaken for a variety of reasons. Having studied and applied decision-making in the mathematical, engineering and business areas for a number of years, the time seemed ripe for an examination of decision-making in other domains. Secondly, we were interested in investigating how simulation as a technique for rational decision-making could be applied to areas in which qualitative features are the important ones. Decision-making in psychotherapy would seem to be as qualitative as one can get. Consequently, methods effective in this area would *ipso facto* prove useful in other areas involving human beings. Finally, since mental health is a problem of national concern, it was important to focus upon it all of the appropriate tools of modern technology at our command.

Our hope is that these efforts will form a base for further research and that they will provide useful tools for training and teaching and for interdisciplinary communication. What follows is an example of the use of modern systems analysis in one branch of the human sciences. It is designed in its treatment of highly qualitative and subjective matters to serve as a useful case study for all areas in which conventional quantitative methods are so difficult to employ.

We have aimed the book at specific audiences: engineers who wish to understand how the methodology of simulation is used in non-quantifiable areas; social scientists who wish to understand how the engineering technique of simulation may be useful to them; mathematicians and others concerned with the use of mathematics for carrying out rational decision-making processes; educators concerned with a computer assisted technique of programmed learning where real-time interaction is an important feature of reality; students of psychotherapy; and finally all those looking for theories and techniques for analyzing and teaching any purposeful two-person interaction, as for example those concerned with interviewing in any field.

Let us briefly indicate the organization and contents of the volume. The first chapter is devoted to an expository survey of some basic ideas, wherein the useful terms "system", "model", and "process" are introduced. In Chapters 2 and 3 we turn our attention to discussion of basic concepts in psychotherapy, with particular reference to the nature of an initial psychotherapy interview. In these two chapters the groundwork is laid for an understanding of the models of the initial interview constructed in Chapter 6.

In Chapter 4 we present a brief taxonomy, or rather a prologue to a taxonomy, of systems. This discussion provides us with an opportunity to review some of the important ideas basic to the classical applications of the scientific method to the study of physical phenomena. Here, we define in some detail what we mean by the terms "system", "process", and "model", restricting our attention, however, solely to descriptive aspects.

Once various models have been obtained which provide some degree of predictability for the behavior of a system, they can be used for various purposes. In particular, we can consider designing, modifying and influencing systems so as to have them operate in various desirable ways. This brings us to the fields of control theory and decision processes. Chapter 5 is devoted to an expository account of some important contemporary ideas in these domains. This requires a brief excursion into uncertainty and thus into stochastic and adaptive decision processes.

In Chapter 6 we discuss the construction of some mathematical models of the initial interview. This material is basic to the consideration of computers and simulation processes presented in Chapter 7. We will discuss carefully some of the difficulties encountered in this type of study of apparently simple processes. In Chapter 8 we shall investigate in more detail questions arising in the simulation of an initial interview in the practice of psychotherapy. Chapter 9 is devoted to conceptual and operational aspects of the short simulation processes we have constructed and dubbed "Computer Vignettes".

Chapter 10 contains a brief exposition of some of the problems of evaluation of our methodology. In this chapter some directions for further research will be indicated.

Notes and references are furnished at the end of each chapter to provide more detailed and deeper discussions of both theory and practice. These are broken down by section numbers referring to topics within the chapter. These notes will be of particular interest to students of psychotherapy and to other readers concerned with human interactions and how they fit into a consistent scientific philosophy.

These efforts, begun about ten years ago, have been carried out in close conjunction with a number of practicing psychiatrists. The original work was begun with Merrill Friend and Leonard Kurland of Los Angeles while they were consultants to the RAND Corporation. Over the last two years we have collaborated with Winthrop Hopgood, in private practice in Los Angeles. In addition we have had the good fortune to be able to discuss these questions at intervals with Kenneth Colby at Stanford. We also wish to thank Joseph Krofcheck and H. J. Delchamps, both of Los Angeles, for numerous illuminating discussions on the nature and practice of psychotherapy.

Kirstie Bellman worked with devoted care in the preparation of the bibliography. Kenneth L. Cooke of Pomona read through the manuscript and made a number of helpful comments. Rebecca Karush patiently typed innumerable drafts. We are grateful for their help.

R. Bellman
C. Smith
Los Angeles, California

CONTENTS

Prologue

Chapter 1

AIMS AND OBJECTIVES

1. Introduction   3
2. The Scientific Method   3
3. Structure   4
4. A System is a System is a System   5
5. The Human Sciences   5
6. Challenge to Rationality   6
7. Particularization   6
8. Operational Pressure and the Practice of Psychotherapy   7
9. The Initial Interview   7
10. Mathematical Tools   7
11. Decision Processes   7
12. Computers   8
13. Simulation   8
14. Theory and Reality   9
15. Use of Mathematical Models   9
    Notes and References   11

Chapter 2

PSYCHOTHERAPY, AN ADAPTIVE DECISION PROCESS

1. Introduction   16
2. Operational View   17
3. Leading Systems of Psychotherapy   18
4. Theory   19

5.   Theory in Psychotherapy   20
6.   Patient and Therapist   21
7.   Problem-Solving   21
8.   Recognition of Ill-Health   21
9.   Classification   22
10. Degree of Ill-Health   22
11. Communication   22
12. Nonverbal Communication   23
13. On-Line Process   24
14. Treatment   24
15. The Initial Interview   25
16. Underlying Conceptual Structure   25
     Notes and References   26

Chapter 3

THE INITIAL INTERVIEW

1.   Introduction   41
2.   Goals of the Initial Interview   41
3.   Establishing a Therapeutic Relationship   42
4.   Basic Decisions   43
5.   Dyadic Nature of Interview   43
6.   Attitudes   44
7.   Classification of Attitudes and Responses   44
8.   Patient Attitudes and Responses   45
9.   Therapist Attitudes and Responses   45
10. Discussion   45
     Notes and References   46

Chapter 4

THE BEHAVIOR OF SYSTEMS

1.   Introduction   54
2.   Description of a System   55
3.   State of a System   55
4.   Objectives   56
5.   Discussion   56
6.   Observables   57
7.   Influence-Response Analysis   57
8.   Influence-State Analysis   58

9. State-Dependent Influence Response Analysis   59
10. Process   59
11. Interactions between Systems   60
12. Multistage Processes—I   61
13. Multistage Processes—II   61
14. Theory   62
15. Internal Structure   62
16. Understanding Versus Model-Making   63
17. Cause and Effect   64
18. Quantitative Questions   65
19. Experimental Method   65
20. Accumulation of Data   66
21. The Mathematical Method   66
22. Extrapolation and Discovery   67
23. Discussion   68
24. Digital Computers   68
25. Does the Method Really Work?   69
26. Idealized Systems   70
27. Directions of Research   71
28. An Example of Useful Simplicity   71
29. Networks and Hierarchies of Systems   73
30. Hidden Variables   73
31. Indeterminism   74
32. Discussion   74
33. Complexity Replaced by Uncertainty   75
34. Stochastic System   75
35. Influence-Response Model of a Stochastic System   76
36. Example   76
37. Average Behavior   76
38. Coin-Tossing   77
39. Discussion   77
40. Probabilities of Occurrence   78
41. Multistage Stochastic Process   79
42. Conclusion   79
Notes and References   79

Chapter 5

DECISION PROCESSES

1. Introduction   82
2. The Operation of Systems   82

3.	Allergic Reactions	83
4.	Discussion	84
5.	Control Process	85
6.	Decision Process	85
7.	Basic Structure of a Decision Process	86
8.	Operational Aspects	86
9.	Policy	87
10.	Illustration	89
11.	Optimal Policy	87
12.	Discussion	88
13.	Determination by Enumeration	88
14.	Reduction of Possibilities by Theory	88
15.	Feasibility Versus Optimality	89
16.	Absence of Criterion	90
17.	Rational Behavior	90
18.	Multi-Stage Decision Process	90
19.	Uncertainty	91
20.	Stochastic Decision Process	92
21.	Decision-Making Under Uncertainty	92
22.	Average Behavior	93
23.	Rational Behavior Under Uncertainty	93
24.	Multistage Decision Process of Stochastic Type	94
25.	Deeper Uncertainties	94
26.	Learning	95
27.	Adaptive Decision Process	95
28.	Information Pattern	95
	Notes and References	96

Chapter 6

MATHEMATICAL MODEL OF THE INITIAL INTERVIEW

1.	Introduction	99
2.	The Patient as a System	99
3.	The Therapist as a System	100
4.	Interaction Process	100
5.	Verbal and Nonverbal Responses	101
6.	Information Pattern	101
7.	States	102
8.	Multistage Decision Processes	102
9.	Objectives of an Initial Interview	102

10.	Policy	103
11.	Discussion	104
12.	Feasibility	104
13.	Description of Adaptive Decision Process	105
14.	Spectrum of Adaptive Decision Processes	105
15.	On-Line Decision Process	106
16.	Categories of Models	107
17.	Discussion	107
18.	Cause and Effect	107
19.	Operational Difficulty of Dimensionality	108
20.	Complexity Replaced by Probability	108
21.	Reduced Response Space	109
22.	Discussion	109
23.	Local Simplicity versus Global Complexity	111
24.	Simplified Quadruples	111
25.	Patient's State of Mind	112
26.	Description of New Process	112
27.	Initial Information Pattern	113
28.	Operational Difficulties	114
29.	Library of Processes	114
30.	More Complex Models	115
	Notes and References	116

Chapter 7

COMPUTERS AND SIMULATION

1.	Introduction	119
2.	Uncertainty Due to Complexity	119
3.	Experimental Approach	120
4.	Advantages	121
5.	Disadvantages	121
6.	Destructive Testing	122
7.	Identification	122
8.	Identification Using Experts	122
9.	Motivation	123
10.	Mathematical Simulation of Complexity	123
11.	Deterministic Process	124
12.	Illustration: Stochastic Process	124
13.	Sampling	125
14.	Incorrect, Illogical, Irrational	126

15. Feasibility of Mathematical Simulation   127
16. Portrait of the Digital Computer as a Glorified File Clerk   127
17. Scientific Computing   128
18. Operational Aspects   128
19. Storage Facilities   129
20. Memory   129
21. Desirability of Slowness   130
22. Terminals   130
23. Size of Influence-Response Tables   130
24. Use of Theory   132
25. Procrustean Fits   132
26. Decision Processes and Feasibility   132
27. Game-Playing   133
28. Blackjack Explicated   133
29. Testing a Simple Policy   134
30. Learning to Play   136
31. How Does a Computer Deal Cards?   136
32. Generation of Random Numbers   137
33. Evaluation of a Stochastic Decision Process   139
34. What Constitutes Optimal Play?   140
35. Rules for Optimal Play   141
36. Lack of Codified Rules   142
37. Experts   142
38. Caveat Simulator!   143
    Notes and References   144

Chapter 8

A COMPUTER SIMULATION OF THE INITIAL PSYCHOTHERAPY INTERVIEW

1. Introduction   149
2. Description of Simulation Process   149
3. Example   151
4. Termination   152
5. Discussion   152
6. Construction of Responses   153
7. Interpretation Dependent Upon Theory   153
8. Use of an Actual Interview   154
9. Use of Experience and Theory   156

10. Use of Theory Alone   156
11. Looping   156
12. Cycling   158
13. Increase in Response Possibilities   158
14. Avoidance of the Appearance of Cycling   159
15. Cumulative Response Probabilities   160
     Notes and References   160

Chapter 9

COMPUTER VIGNETTES

1.   Introduction   163
2.   Simulations   163
3.   Convergence and Divergence   164
4.   Computer Vignette I—The Young Psychotherapist   164
5.   Policy for Construction of Responses   165
6.   Computer Vignette II—The Silent Patient   166
7.   Policy for Construction of Responses   167
8.   Computer Vignette III—The Telephone Interview   169
9.   Policy for Construction of Responses   170
10. Some Sample Dialogues   171
     Notes and References   179

Chapter 10

TEACHING, TRAINING, AND RESEARCH

1.   Introduction   181
2.   Understanding   181
3.   Teaching   182
4.   On-Line Decision-Making   183
5.   Limitations of Simulation   184
6.   Realism and Referees   184
7.   Nonverbal Aspects   185
8.   Aims of the Simulation Process   186
9.   Further Research and Testing   186
10. Purpose of the Simulations   187
11. Training Possibilities   188

12. Criterion of Success of the Simulation   189
13. Hypothesis Testing   189
14. Statistical Evaluation   190
15. Simulations and Transfer of Learning   190
     Notes and References   191

Author Index   197

Subject Index   202

Prologue

A COMPUTER
GENERATED SIMULATION

The following computer vignette simulates a decision process in a psycho-therapy interaction. The dialogue was generated by one of our models of initial psychotherapy interviews. In this dialogue the therapist is proceed-ing effectively according to our standards. He is interacting with a patient who initially makes communication difficult. The remainder of the book is devoted to explaining what we mean by a number of the foregoing terms (for example, computer vignettes, model, simulations, initial psychotherapy interview) and using the vignettes themselves to illustrate some concepts of significance in our simulations.

CASE 1. The Young Psychiatrist

Patient: 50% Convergent

Therapist: 100% Convergent

Th: Mrs. Jones? I'm Dr. Brown. What can I do for you?

Pt: I expected to see an older person.

Th: I'd like to help you. Let's talk and see if we can work together.

Pt: I really wanted an older man with lots of experience to treat me. I've had this problem for so long . . .

Th: Can you tell me about your problem?

Pt: Well, it goes back a long way. Where shall I begin?

Th: Wherever you wish.

Pt: Well, it's a pretty serious problem. And I'm not so sure I want to discuss it with someone as young as you.

1

Th: It's natural for you to want the best kind of help for your problem, and to feel that an older person could understand you better. I would like to help you. Let's talk and see if we can work together.

Pt: But that's the point. I'm not sure I want to talk about my problem with you. You just seem so young.

Th: You feel that an older person might understand you better. That seems natural to me. Yet I would like to help you. Let's see if we can talk together about your problem.

Pt: But this problem that I have has been bothering me for much too long already and I want the best help I can get. You don't look old enough to have had enough experience for that.

Th: I'd like to help you with your problem if you could tell me about it.

Pt: I wish you could help me figure out where to start. I've had the problem for so long now.

Th: Why don't you start with whatever is bothering you right now.

Pt: For about the last ten years I've been having terrible spells whenever I'm in a large crowd. When I go to a movie I have to sit on the aisle. It's so embarrassing. (Patient goes on discussing her problems.)

END

Chapter 1

AIMS AND OBJECTIVES

1. INTRODUCTION

In the chapters that follow we wish to explore a number of ideas basic to two quite diverse domains, mathematics and psychotherapy. There is, however, a connecting link, a common interest in various aspects of the art of decision-making. We are particularly interested in this volume in various features of decision-making applied to psychotherapy.

We shall begin with a brief exposition of our aims and purposes. Since we are concerned with those readers previously untrained in sophisticated mathematical concepts who may wish to learn and apply some of the methods we shall use, we shall attempt to keep the presentation both elementary and complete.

Our major objective is to explore the possibility of studying some of the basic process of psychotherapy using certain of the fundamental and powerful mathematical concepts and methods developed during the last 25 years. As we shall see, some novel and interesting types of mathematical problems are posed by this research, and some new and significant directions in the study of human communication are indicated.

2. THE SCIENTIFIC METHOD

The scientific method is one of the most important manifestations of an adherence to rationality. As an approach to problem-solving it has proved astonishingly successful in explaining large classes of physical phenomena. This scientific understanding, in turn, has provided a firm grasp on the fundamental chemical, electrical, mechanical, and optical phenomena which constitute the vortices of the engineering revolution that has shaped our times, economically, culturally, psychologically, and politically.

Mathematics, as a further manifestation of this rationality, is currently the most important tool used by the scientist to interpret physical phenomena and to explore the far-reaching consequences of simple physical ideas. In addition, it is the basic language of science, used extensively for the communication of both concepts and results.

As a language, it has several purposes. One of these is to communicate succinctly and without ambiguity. Oddly, however, this very lack of ambiguity makes mathematics a difficult tool to employ in the study of human problems since these are characteristically vague, amorphous, or, as currently described, "soft". A further reason for the difficulty in employing mathematical reasoning, of course, lies in the complexity of the questions encountered. They are both of far greater magnitude and of quite different type than those treated in the physical sciences.

3. STRUCTURE

The emphasis on the use of mathematics in the physical sciences to direct and interpret measurements has helped to create the widely held impression that mathematics is solely concerned with quantitative methods and results. It was an easy step to conclude from this that mathematical reasoning is useful only where extensive numerical data exist or are obtainable. This is, fortunately, not at all the case.

Mathematics can be defined as the study of classes of structures, interactions, and relations according to certain rules. Frequently, these studies involve numbers; often they do not. It follows, then, that any intellectual area possessing structure can profit from the use of appropriate mathematical ideas. It is reasonable to surmise that all intellectual areas necessarily possess structure. The challenging problems, however, are to discern it, to impose it, and to use it.

Let us give some examples. A major part of modern mathematics is group theory, a study of symmetries. It plays a basic role in the field of pattern recognition. The study of interactions in human systems is an essential part of anthropology and sociology. This study can be fruitfully carried out using graph theory. This field in turn is a part of topology, a theory devoted in part to non-quantitative aspects of space. Here, an attempt is made to make a number of intuitive concepts precise, such as right-handedness and left-handedness and why we can't readily wear a left glove on the right hand, "outside" and "inside", shape, dimension, and so forth.

This clarification process is one of the fundamental contributions of mathematics with a systematic methodology which can be taught and learned. For example, probability theory is one attempt to understand what is meant by uncertainty, a topic of fundamental importance to Medicare. Much remains to be done here.

4. A SYSTEM IS A SYSTEM IS A SYSTEM

We state as an axiom that the level of understanding, and thus the usefulness, of any intellectual system can be increased by employing some of the many sophisticated theories developed over the past 20 years for the design and operation of biomedical, economic, industrial, engineering, and physical systems. We have seen repeatedly that mathematical theories developed in response to problems in celestial mechanics have had unexpected applications in economics; similarly that theories developed for engineering purposes have been adapted and widely applied in the biomedical area. We wish to demonstrate equally that theories developed originally for decision-making in the economic and engineering sciences can play a significant role in psychotherapy.

5. THE HUMAN SCIENCES

The mathematical method in the physical sciences relies almost exclusively upon the use of numbers. It is essential for the success of this approach not only that the system of interest be at any one time described numerically, but that, in addition, we possess techniques for predicting the way a particular numerical description changes over time. Furthermore, we insist upon having the ability to observe certain properties of the system, either by direct or indirect examination. This is essential for the experimental test of various theories.

In the human sciences we begin almost at the other extreme, with the basic assumption that the most essential of human attributes cannot be defined meaningfully in terms of numbers alone. Useful numbers are occasionally available, but far more than numbers are needed.

Furthermore, even if in some magic fashion we came into possession of a numerical description of a particular human system, we would not necessarily know what to do with it. This is because we possess no set of precise cause-and-effect relations enabling us to predict the future behavior of this system on the basis of its current state with even a small part of the accuracy to which we have become accustomed in the physical sciences.

Actually, we face serious obstacles in the very observation of human systems. Not only can reproducibility seldom be obtained, but, far worse, basic human interactions most often cannot even be observed without introducing serious disturbing influences. The effect of the observer is often critical. This point, incidentally, is particularly important in connection with training in therapeutic interviewing.

What we wish to emphasize is that most classical scientific theories specifically constructed to deal with the inanimate cannot be applied routinely to the study of the animate, and certainly not to human beings or their social systems. Often, they cannot be used at all.

6. CHALLENGE TO RATIONALITY

The foregoing remarks, if accepted, pose serious challenges to a rational mode of existence. On the one hand, we note that decisions are constantly being made and that actions are constantly being carried out. We observe all about us the translation of qualitative values into quantitative units; allocations of specific amounts of time, effort, and money to a variety of human activities. On the other hand, we must ask ourselves: Is there some way to ensure that these decisions, allocations, and actions are made in a rational fashion? In particular, how do we even go about defining what we mean by this question?

A first goal then is to analyze the rational method as carefully as possible. We wish to examine the process of recognition of different categories of questions and the construction and use of different sets of methods for problem-solving. This discussion, which we believe possesses many features of independent interest, will be found in Chapters 4 and 5.

7. PARTICULARIZATION

A famous mathematician once commented, "It is far more difficult to particularize than to generalize". To construct general theories is, of course, essential. Indeed, the formulation of a few unifying theories embracing large classes of apparently divergent phenomena is the principal goal of every discipline. Without theories of this nature, a field does not exist as a coherent unit. In turn, the value of a theory is demonstrated by its usefulness in treating particular problems.

This does not mean, however, that we rigidly require a *single* theory capable of resolving all problems encountered in a field. While we would certainly prefer to have one, we do not expect a philosopher's stone. It must be possible, nonetheless, to use any proposed theory for the examination of some significant class of questions. Conversely, a carefully chosen problem illuminates, and often extends, a theory. It has been pointed out by many scientists that a good question is in many ways more important for the development of a field than its answer.

8. OPERATIONAL PRESSURE AND THE PRACTICE OF PSYCHOTHERAPY

For operational reasons we have directed our attention to a study of psychological disturbances within the far larger domain of mental activity. We will focus on psychotherapy, the therapeutic interaction between a psychotherapist and his patients. We set ourselves the following problem: Can we provide some theoretical structures of psychotherapeutic processes which can be used for pedagogical purposes, for research purposes, and as an aid to clinical training?

9. THE INITIAL INTERVIEW

The total set of interactions between patient and therapist is both too vast and too complex for the existing level of scientific and mathematical analysis. If, however, we restrict our attention to the early stages in an initial psychotherapy interview, the first crucial meeting between patient and therapist, it appears that we can combine existing theory and mathematical methods to construct some meaningful models. In Chapters 2 and 3 we discuss the approaches we employ to psychotherapy and the initial interview to provide a conceptual basis for our subsequent work.

10. MATHEMATICAL TOOLS

Why can we contemplate undertaking these studies now as opposed to 50 years ago? There are two principal reasons. On the one hand, certain mainstreams of contemporary research, decision processes and simulation, have supplied us with some powerful theoretical tools. On the other hand, technology, responding to the pressures of the engineer, mathematician, and scientist, has provided us with the digital computer.

In subsequent chapters these matters will be discussed in finer detail. In what follows let us briefly note the nature of the contributions.

11. DECISION PROCESSES

Starting with the "Operations Research" carried out in Great Britain and the United States during World War II, there has been a tremendous effort over the last 25 years devoted to a scientific and mathematical analysis of various economic, industrial, biomedical, and military systems. The focus has been on *decision-making,* since it turns out that much of what is involved in the feasible operation of a system can be meaningfully interpreted in terms of decision processes.

A number of the important decision processes encountered in these areas can be handled in a satisfactory fashion without taking into account any elements of uncertainty. Most, however, require an explicit recognition of this aspect of reality. Of the various mathematical theories designed to handle uncertainty, the most important at the present time is the theory of probability. We shall discuss some of the basic ideas of this theory in Chapter 4.

12. COMPUTERS

Processes of importance in any scientific field characteristically possess two types of complexities: conceptual and arithmetic. Even after we have overcome formidable conceptual obstacles in the construction of a mathematical model of a particular process, we frequently find ourselves frustrated by an inability to use this model to obtain the numerical results required for a definitive answer to a specific question. In many cases we believe that we understand the logical nature of the basic interactions. Yet, because of the very large number of interactions involved we are often unable to achieve some desired numerical conclusion to check hypotheses.

The digital computer has greatly altered this state of affairs. The computer possesses the specific ability to perform vast amounts of arithmetic and, more generally, to perform many kinds of symbol manipulation. It is, therefore, an appropriate challenge at an appropriate time to determine whether or not the computer can be used, in conjunction with various guiding mathematical theories and knowledge of a specific field, to study decision-making techniques in particular situations.

Just as the use of mathematics is never routine, so the use of a digital computer is never routine. Almost always, its application raises some novel and unexpected theoretical questions.

13. SIMULATION

As the formidable obstacles to the use of traditional mathematical methods for treating problems arising in military, economic, industrial, and political spheres became more and more evident, considerable attention began to be devoted to the development and application of a variety of new mathematical techniques. Of these, the most important is that of simulation, or "gaming", as it was originally called.*

---

* The reason for the change in nomenclature was that the processes being studied were hardly "games" in the usual sense and that the word "game" had an inappropriate semantic meaning for serious research.

The theory of simulation was first applied to the study of military processes, "war games". Starting in 1957, the methods were extensively applied to the art of decision-making in the area of commercial processes, "business games". We shall apply the same general methodology to study decision-making in psychotherapy. As we shall see, simulation can be used for both theoretical and training purposes.

It is important to recognize that it is impossible to construct a simulation process which does not reflect both conscious and unconscious ideas of the modelmakers. There are no impartial mathematical analyses even in the physical domain—much less in connection with sociopsychological phenomena. All reflect a theoretical bias. With this in mind, one of the major purposes of a simulation process is to convert unformulated, often unrecognized, or unconscious, policies into precise, analyzable procedures, to make explicit assumptions heretofore implicit, and thus to emphasize a rational approach to decision-making. The useful word, "rational", however, conceals many subtleties. As we shall discuss subsequently, there are many situations where to be coldly rational is to rely heavily on intuition.

14. THEORY AND REALITY

As we repeatedly note, it is the operational approach which is perhaps most important. How do we actually use a theoretical structure to help us handle real problems involving real people in real time? How do we train a therapist to help real patients? Questions of this nature force a careful analysis of the underlying philosophy of the objectives of an initial psychotherapy interview and the roles of the therapist and patient.

15. USE OF MATHEMATICAL MODELS

Let us say a few words at this point about the possible uses and values of mathematical models. There are a number of quite different reasons for this type of activity.

In the first place, we know from considerable experience in various fields of science, in engineering, and in economics that the construction of any mathematical model of a real process, no matter how simplified initially, forces us to make precise a number of aspects of the real process that had never been previously analyzed. Mathematicization is a powerful method for forcing implicit understanding into the realm of the conscious and precise. Furthermore, operational difficulties encountered in mathematical analysis often force significant conceptual and theoretical advances. For example, in the study of the initial psychotherapy interview we must face the problem of describing in quantitative and qualitative terms what we mean by such familiar and intuitive ideas as the patient's "state", "obtaining information of value", the "response of the patient", the "response of the therapist ", and so on. Furthermore, we must analyze the nature of the set of "possible interviewing policies", the "purposes of the interview", and examine possible evaluation techniques. Frequently, the major contribution of a particular model is the unblinking spotlight it focuses on specific difficulties. Progress depends to a great extent upon a recognition of roadblocks, an analysis of their origin, and a study of their removal or circumvention.

A conceptual model of a process of the type we have been discussing provides some basis for a systematic choice of interviewing policies and the evaluation of psychotherapy interviews.

The very fact that so many different kinds of models, founded on quite different concepts, are possible promotes the overall ideas of flexibility and eclecticism. Over time, it has been established in many disciplines that it is fruitful to become adaptive in the choice of theories as well as in the choice of models within the framework of a particular theory.

A model provides additional motivation for an interpretation of experiment and observation. It focuses research, for better or for worse, on attempts to validate various features of a model. Since a large number of recorded initial interviews presently exist, it is useful to examine these observed interviews in accord with various simplified theories and to delineate the most discordant or unexplained features, as well as the happy agreements. Accepting the fact that we do not understand the true nature of the compound system of interest, the human body and mind, it is important to know when we can say with some confidence that it is behaving "as if" it were a system of a certain type. These analogies can guide our thinking.

The therapist in many cases may not be able to make his interviewing policy completely explicit. Nevertheless, it is interesting and valuable to be able to show that he too is acting "as if" he were using a specific policy. This is the traditional use of mathematics in the sciences, providing the "as if" structures.

Another traditional activity is the task of explaining observed phenomena. It is recognized that there are both competent and superior therapists. These individuals perform so well so repeatedly that it is apparent that various systematic successful techniques exist. The situation is similar to that prevailing in many other areas where the brain performs remarkable feats which, although easily observed, remain inadequately described. The intellectual pressure to understand the ideas and methods of expert therapists is great. The problems of mental health are real; the patients are real and suffer; and the treatment that is given, or not given, is real. Rational methods should be employed to provide guidance in this situation, guidance to the practitioner, guidance to the teacher. In any case, *some* methods, rational or irrational, will be employed by people, consciously or unconciously.

As one of the languages of rationality, mathematics is a powerful tool for dealing with the problems of human existence. The task that confronts us is that of using this tool effectively in the study of the initial psychotherapy interview.

NOTES AND REFERENCES

(Numbered sections in all pages of Notes and References relate to the numbered topics within the preceding chapters.)

1. A careful analysis of interactions between mathematics and science is contained in
S. Bochner, *The Role of Mathematics in the Rise of Science,* Princeton, Princeton University Press, 1966.

   For mathematical aspects of decision-making, see
R. Bellman, *Adaptive Control Processes: A Guided Tour,* Princeton, Princeton University Press, 1961.

   "For Chein, science is the human enterprise of constructing a sort of map which will help us in negotiating a passage through the world in which we find ourselves. Our scientific 'truths' are not truths in the sense that they can ever be proved or disproved but, rather, are that we take to be verities (realities) which we believe in because they parsimoniously enable us to find our way about."
from J. de Rivera, "A New Systematic Psychology", *Psychotherapy and Social Science Review,* Vol. 6 (12), 1972, p. 27.

2. For a detailed discussion of these ideas within the context of psychiatry, see:
K. Colby, *An Introduction to Psychoanalytic Research,* New York, Basic Books, 1960.
K. Colby, *A Primer for Psychotherapists,* New York, Ronald Press, 1951.

   For a brief, elementary discussion of the scientific method, including at which point in the problem-solving process to cross your fingers, see:
J. K. and J. R. Rice, *Introduction to Computer Science,* New York, Holt, Rinehart and Winston, 1969.

"... the scientific method is the best yet devised for arriving at truth ...
to date it has not succeeded in encompassing all of truth and there is
considerable doubt that it ever will." See:
J. Frank, "Psychotherapists Need Theories" in J. Aronson, Ed., *International Journal of Psychiatry*, Vol. 9, New York, Science House, 1970.

Scientific analysis involves "disembedding" a group of variables from
within a larger context and describing their interrelationships by a formal
system.
S. Koch, "Psychology Cannot Be a Coherent Science", *Psychology Today*,
September 14, 1969, pp. 64–68.

4. For an interesting discussion of the amazing success of the mathematical
method, see
F. Wigner, "The Unreasonable Effectiveness of Mathematics in the
Natural Sciences", *Comm. Pure and Applied Math.*, Vol. XIII, 1960, pp.
1–14.

5. Accounts of interactions between mathematics and society are given in
M. Kline, *Mathematics, A Cultural Approach*, Redding, Mass., Addison-
Wesley, 1962.
M. Kline, *Mathematics in Western Culture*, New York, Oxford University
Press, 1953.
C. B. Boyer, *A History of Mathematics*, New York, J. Wiley and Sons,
1968.

Joseph Schillinger, *Schillinger System of Musical Composition*, New York,
Carl Fischer, Inc., 1946. Not in Print.
Joseph Schillinger, *The Mathematical Basis of the Arts*, New York, John-
son Reprint Corp., 1948.
A. Rapoport, *Fights, Games and Debates*, Ann Arbor, Univ. of Michigan
Press, 1960.
Joseph Weizenbaum, "On the Impact of the Computer on Society", *Science*, Vol. 176, May, 1972, pp. 609–614.

6. It is perhaps not entirely redundant to emphasize this belief in rationality.
See
T. Meeham, "The Flight from Reason", *Horizon*, Vol. XII, 1970, pp. 4–19.

Clara Thompson has written that psychoanalytic approaches are similar
to other psychotherapies in using reason "as a method for meeting and
resolving situations and problems".
C. Thompson, *Psychoanalysis: Evolution and Development*, New York,
Grove Press, 1957.

7. The dictum is due to A. Hurwitz.
Defining the problem to be solved is the first major hurdle which is very
difficult even in the "supposedly well-determined, formalized scientific and
engineering areas". See
J. K. and J. R. Rice, 1969, *op. cit.*

R. Bellman and P. Brock, "On the Concepts of a Problem and Problem Solving", *Amer. Math. Monthly,* Vol. 67, 1960, pp. 119–134.

8. A major problem in the field of psychiatry was pointed out by Dr. Sem-Jacobsen when he commented that comparative studies in psychiatry cannot be made because common terminology based on common theory is not in widespread use by psychiatrists.
   C. Sem-Jacobsen, Talk on "Depth-Electrographic Stimulation of the Human Brain and Behavior", University of Southern California, Department of Mathematical Biosciences, October 20, 1969.

9. An attitude typical of many psychotherapists is expressed by Harold Kelman: "For me the initial interview is crucial . . . How an initial interview is conducted, and how the patient responds to it, can significantly determine the future of that therapy for a long time to come, and even to its completion."
   A. Burton, *Modern Psychotherapeutic Practice: Innovations in Techniques,* Palo Alto, California, Science and Behavior Books, 1965.

   A similar sentiment is expressed by Gill et al. They believe that the initial interview has an important effect on the later therapist-patient relationship since patients often refer late in therapy to an event which occurred at the start. Apparently, an occurrence in the initial interview will frequently make such a strong impression that it will operate all along to influence treatment.
   M. Gill, R. Newman, F. Redlich and M. Sommers, *The Initial Interview in Psychiatric Practice,* New York, International Universities Press, 1954.

   "What happens in the first five minutes sets the tone for the entire interview, perhaps for the entire interaction between the doctor and patient. The patient projects some of the major conflicts and themes which will later be more clearly revealed—as the overture summarizes in advance the themes in the body of the musical work." The initial interview thus consists of encapsulations of basic conflicts, attitudes toward other people and the patient's view of himself.
   E. Pfeiffer, *Disordered Behavior: Basic Concepts in Clinical Psychiatry,* New York, Oxford University Press, 1968.

10. "The source of scientific problems is the real world. These problems come from our efforts to understand and to forecast the phenomena of the real world. The formulation of the problems is based on idealized models of reality. There is always the difficulty of choosing a mathematical model neither too complex yet accurate enough to give useful results."
    J. K. and J. R. Rice, 1969, *op. cit.*

    For a discussion of some of the difficulties in human communication disclosed by contemporary linguistic research, as well as many other important ideas, see

G. Birkhoff, "Mathematics and Psychology", *SIAM Review*, Vol. 11, 1969, pp. 429–469.

11. According to A. Rapoport, mathematical decision theory is concerned with the problem of arriving at a decision after all the available, relevant facts are known.
A. Rapoport, "Psychoanalysis as Science", Communication #208 (Paper presented at Menninger School of Psychiatry, Faculty and Fellows Evening Lecture Forum, April 17, 1967, Topeka, Kansas).

There is, however, much more to it, as we shall discuss subsequently.

12. A discussion of "hard" and "soft" data is found in
N. Kline and E. Laska, *Computers and Electronic Devices in Psychiatry*, New York, Grune and Stratton, 1968, p. 2.

13. A detailed discussion of the many problems encountered in the use of simulation is contained in
R. Bellman et al., "On the Construction of a Multi-Person, Multi-Stage Business Game", *Operations Research*, Vol. V(4), 1957, pp. 469–503.

In an unpublished paper entitled "Principles of Transactional Analysis" written while *Games People Play* was in press, Eric Berne states that "transactional games are similar to the 'games' of mathematical game theory in that they involve moves, choices, and strategies".

"For the sake of simplicity, exactness, conciseness", a simulation is constructed to simplify a complex problem in communication and to control variables. See:
K. Colby and D. Smith, *Dialogues Between a Human and an Artificial Belief System*, Stanford Artificial Intelligence Project, Memo A1-97, August 1969.

In science, the principle of "operationism" "holds that the position and interventions of the scientists cannot be divorced from ideas about his data".
R. Liefer, "The Medical Model as Ideology" in J. Aronson, Ed., *International Journal of Psychiatry*, Vol. 9, New York, Science House, 1970.

14. On the operational value of theory: "Theories are essentially a set of speculations which seem to explain empirical facts. A sound and accurate psychological theory should give a practitioner confidence in what he is doing and why he is doing it. A good theory of human behavior should generate more effective methods of treatment."
A. Lazarus, "Behavior Therapy" in J. Aronson, Ed., 1970, *op. cit.*

"A practitioner is a practical man and he requires theories closely connectible to the operational terms he uses in thinking about and applying skills. Progress in the field of psychotherapy will involve improvements in

methods and techniques but most of all it will require better explanatory theories at what is going on in the clinical dialogue."
K. Colby, "Computer Simulations of Neurotic Processes", in R. Stacy and B. Waxman, Eds., *Computers in Biomedical Research*, Vol. I, New York, Academic Press, 1965.

"Good theories are often utilitarian and occasionally powerful", says William Reese in his discussion of models and principles relevant to administrative psychiatry.
W. Reese, "An Essay on Administration," *The American Journal of Psychiatry*, Vol. 128 (10), April 1972, p. 74.

15. The method of simulation forces assumptions into the open and requires that implicit ideas be made explicit. See:
J. Starkweather, M. Kamp, A. Monte, "Psychiatric Interview Simulation by Computer", *Math. Inform. Med.*, Vol. 6, 1967, pp. 15–23.

Chapter 2

PSYCHOTHERAPY, AN ADAPTIVE DECISION PROCESS

1. INTRODUCTION

In this chapter we turn to an examination of some of the complexities of psychotherapy. Our objective is to show subsequently that a number of important features of both theory and practice in this field can be described by the mathematical ideas discussed in Chapters 4 and 5.

The process itself, the practice of psychotherapy, is extraordinarily complex. Yet the structure of the process is neither complex, nor necessarily different abstractly from other two-person interaction processes which have been explored in business games and other simulations using mathematical theory. This difference between complexity of structure and complexity of operation is well illustrated by the Oriental game, *Go,* a game simultaneously of extraordinarily simple format and of formidably difficult play.

We view *psychiatry* in today's world as the study, identification, prevention, treatment and cure of mental ill-health by medical practitioners. In addition, the domain of psychiatry includes the management and care by society of the psychiatrically disturbed. We view *psychotherapy* as a set of operational techniques developed according to combinations of theory and practice to treat various types of psychological and behavioral disturbances which are believed to be of emotional nature. We also use the term, psychotherapy, to refer to the interaction between a patient or client and the professional helper who will work with him. The interaction, of course, is intended to benefit the patient.

A widely accepted definition is that of Karl Menninger: "For practical purposes let us define psychological therapy as comprising efforts made by one or more individuals to further a beneficial change in a particular indi-

16

vidual by modalities not physical or chemical, but depending upon an interchange of communication."

We thus conceive of no sharply defining lines in the psychotherapy practiced with voluntary patients for example by a psychiatrist, psychologist, counselor, psychiatric resident, or psychiatric social worker.

While we address ourselves to psychotherapists and their patients, we do not adhere closely to any model of sickness or health. Nonetheless, we repeatedly use the terms "mental health" and "patient" to avoid the introduction of new terminology and various circumlocutions. Following current practice, we view the individual in terms of his problems, maladjustments and strengths. Our loosely defined medical model is used for illustrative purposes, for the convenience of employing a model which is both widely taught in schools, and, more importantly, universally understood. Our model may be adapted to a broad spectrum of theories. The psychotherapist is then a professional who has expertise in using psychological means to educate and benefit the patient.

2. OPERATIONAL VIEW

We begin with the observation that the psychotherapist is committed to relieving the symptoms and suffering of people who either voluntarily seek his aid or are required to do so by social pressures. From the beginning we take a problem-oriented stand; people who exhibit symptoms of mental ill-health under certain circumstances exist in large numbers and they need to be helped. What can be done to meet these needs?

Mental ill health is here defined negatively as an absence or loss of mental health. This condition is recognized objectively, or intuitively, by some impairment of physical, mental or social functioning which could benefit from psychological intervention. The general goal of the psychotherapist is to restore mental health or to promote its growth if at all possible. Specifically, he attempts to relieve or ameliorate symptoms, to help a patient achieve insight into his emotions, motives and characteristic ways of behaving, and to help free the patient from inhibiting fears and habits in order that maladaptive behavior and crippling emotional responses can be replaced.

An individual's mental health may be recognized by such variable characteristics as an ability to use knowledge and experience freely, past and present, for effective decision making; the willingness to take risks and to tolerate a certain amount of ambiguity; and to accept responsibility.

The Psychiatric Dictionary quotes K. E. Appel in the Journal of the American Medical Association* and defines mental health as "psychologic

* *JAMA*, **172**, 1343–46, (1960).

well-being or adequate adjustment, particularly as such adjustment conforms to the community accepted standards of what human relations should be". The definition continues with some of the characteristics of mental health ". . . reasonable independence, self-reliance, self-direction, ability to do a job . . ." and other such traits which are difficult to evaluate.

The psychotherapist, then, uses ill-defined criteria to determine that a would-be patient needs his professional help. Based on his highly individual qualifications, experience, training and judgment, he will use a treatment plan which may include and range from physiologically inclusive methods, such as electroconvulsive therapy and chemotherapy, to behavior modification based on muscular or other physical manipulations, or ego strengthening or directive-supportive techniques.

3. LEADING SYSTEMS OF PSYCHOTHERAPY

There are many modifications of these approaches to psychotherapy, and others as well. What are the common denominators?

All will use the influence of the therapist to the benefit of the patient. Most use rationality to understand and treat emotional responses. Those who do not use rationality in specific interactions with the patient nevertheless employ it to understand the interaction in terms of their own empathetic and other responses, and to direct the course of therapy.

The nature of the relationship between the patient and therapist, the quality of the feeling between them, is considered to have a strong effect on the outcome of therapy. What is particularly interesting is that it has been found in a number of studies that the practice of psychotherapy by experts with different theoretical orientations is more alike in many respects than that of expert and non-expert from the same school, or than that of non-experts from different schools. The differences among experts is in consequence seen by some as essentially semantic, referring to the names they apply to themselves and to the different theoretical languages they speak. What they have strongly in common is the ability to establish a relationship in which a patient and therapist have a degree of confidence that somehow the therapist will be able to help the patient. In addition, the patient will feel that he may share and examine his feelings and experiences in an atmosphere of respect, trust, and empathy. Experts of all theoretical positions exhibit a common concern for human qualities, understanding and growth. Some references are found in Section 3 at the end of the chapter to this frequently noted idea that although practices among both novice and expert of different schools may appear to vary greatly, there are perhaps subtle similarities in the therapeutic bond and situation established by experts. It may be these similarities which may account for the thera-peutic movement in the interview. These references are to the works by Frank, Wolff and Scheflen. Additional references to related ideas may be found in Chapter 10, Section 3.

4. THEORY

Since we have adopted an operational view as primary throughout, we begin from the classical position of Helmholtz that there is nothing as practical as a good theory. Therapists have various philosophies, methods and goals. The theories they use provide systematic technique for the inter-pretation, synopsis and utilization of experience in the treatment of patients. Further, the consistency in the recognition and treatment of mental illness which comes from theory is essential for teaching purposes, for comparative studies, and for the communication of experiences among psychiatrists.

A well-constructed theory furnishes a language for the transmission of fundamental principles and the fruits of years of experience. In addition, it provides a set of guidelines for research as well as techniques for primary training and education.

Theories also provide the framework within which to identify an indi-vidual who needs therapy, for the acceptance or referral of a patient for treatment, for decision about the techniques to be used, for setting the goals for treatment and for assessing progress in reaching them. Finally, theory provides a means for steadfastly continuing a treatment during periods of no observable progress.

Theory thus functions as a basic bulwark against doubt. An occasional loss of self-confidence is apt to affect any practitioner of any art. But it may be of critical importance in psychotherapy where the favorable expectancy of both patient and therapist plays so large a role in the therapeutic result. In any case, confidence on the part of a therapist is a vitally important feature of any patient-therapist relationship, and is thus essential to instill. How a novice may become more confident is of central importance to the applied value of our work.

Let us observe that time imposes vital constraints such as the length of individual sessions or number of patient-therapist interactions. The thera-pist must always ask himself how best he can help his patient, suffering now in real time, with his problems. Perhaps his problems will never be completely understood; perhaps treatment under some widely accepted therapeutic plan may take longer than it seems reasonable for the patient to continue to suffer. A careful, self-conscious analysis based on theory may well be the only short cut to an understanding and basis for change which alleviates pain. The more powerful the theory, the easier to translate it into practice. The greater the gap between theory and practice, the more the need for further research to obtain an improved theory.

The tentative nature, however, of any theory in a complex field, particularly one such as psychotherapy, must be explicitly recognized. There is always danger that theory will lead to dogmatism and thus close off further inquiry, or that it will lead to a refusal to recognize new or apparently contradictory information. The risks of premature closure, or that a theory becomes a self-fulfilling prophecy, is ever-present. It follows that the construction of an effective theory comes from regarding the process of theory-construction as an adaptive one. As we learn more from experience and further research, each testing the substance of a theory, we modify existing methods and concepts. In the traditional view, no theory in science springs fullbloom into final form. Each requires careful nursing and pruning over time. A principal goal, then, of any theory is to pave the path for a better theory. As there are no human problems invariant in time, no eternal scientific truth in this sense, so there are no absolute theories, only successively more accurate approximations to a temporal truth.

We shall be concerned with some aspects of the foregoing in the study of the initial interview. Although we shall be somewhat guided in our efforts by a particular theory, see Section 15 below, we are very much more interested in a theory of psychotherapeutic theories. Our aim is to construct a common language and methodology which can be employed for research and training purposes by adherents of widely differing views and theories.

5. THEORY IN PSYCHOTHERAPY

Where theory is difficult and sketchy, there is strong motivation and, often, irresistible temptation to bypass it. In many fields of engineering, for example, experience is still more essential than broad scientific training. In the medical arena, we know that broken arms can often be set expertly without any detailed understanding of anatomy and that a midwife may be more expert at the delivery of a child than a university-trained M.D. There are a large number of important, highly specialized tasks that can be learned and performed without a broad theoretical background in that field.

The psychotherapist, however, is in a different position. From the very beginning, his focus of attention is the set of thoughts and emotions of the patient. Dealing as he does with both fact and fantasy (and where does one start and the other end?) he requires, from the outset, theory and philosophy for both understanding and choice of action.

It is doubly important, then, in the practice of psychotherapy to delineate the theories that are employed consciously and unconsciously, explicitly and implicitly. What follows is a start in this direction.

6. PATIENT AND THERAPIST

The two protagonists in the psychodrama of therapy are the patient and the therapist. The patient is a person with psychological problems and the therapist is a person with theories about such problems and techniques for teaching the patient how to deal with them.

Our aim in this chapter is to examine some of the processes involved in the patient-therapist interaction and to identify these processes as far as possible as various types of multistage decision processes.

7. PROBLEM-SOLVING

Prior to a discussion of specific aspects of psychotherapy, let us examine some of the stages in problem-solving. To begin with, there must be recognition, perhaps only in very general terms, that a problem requiring some decision or action exists. Secondly, we need some means of formulating the problem which usually require more precise terms, and then of specifying the nature of possible decisions or actions. Thirdly, we try to construct more or less detailed classificatory schemes.

Following this effort, or often times parallel with it, there is the question of determining appropriate treatment of the problems. What decision should be made, which actions taken? Subsequent to this is the task of evaluating progress. It is essential to know when the problem is resolved, or when more of the same treatment or a different treatment is required.

Observe then that problem-solving is a multistage process. We also note that each of the individual stages, in addition, contains within it further multistage decision processes. Let us examine them in connection with psychotherapy.

8. RECOGNITION OF ILL-HEALTH

The same types of stages are involved in the treatment of either physical or psychological disturbances. To begin with, a broad determination of whether or not an individual is ill or not is required. Swellings, fever, and unconsciousness are some of the immediate physiological indicators which alert the layman, no less than the professional, to the need for expert attention.

In the field of mental health there are comparable varieties of grossly aberrant behavior which signal the existence of disturbances. Some of these are independent of the manners and mores of the external society: severe depression, catatonic states or verbal confusion, for example. Some behavior, however, which may be considered deviant in a particular society may not attract attention in a sub-culture or in a different society: for example, alcoholism, drug addiction, sexual promiscuity, obesity, hysteria or sadism.

A conclusion we can draw from this, which we wish to emphasize, is that in the field of mental health one is strongly dependent upon theory, and the interpretation of theory, for the very recognition of illness, and, consequently, for the recognition of cure.

9. CLASSIFICATION

Much time and effort has been devoted to the construction of detailed taxonomies of abnormal behavior by psychologists and psychiatrists, by the churches, the courts, and others.

For our purposes, a study of some early phases of the interactions in an initial interview, we have devised a relatively simple classification of behavior to describe both patient and therapist. It is based on the responses they make which either further the aims of the therapy interaction, or which do not. The scheme is operational, designed to be used in connection with specific objectives within the framework of a particular theory.

10. DEGREE OF ILL-HEALTH

There are two parameters of obvious immediate importance: whether the erratic thought or behavior processes are: (1) acute, episodic or chronic; and, (2) mild, moderate or severe.

A problem that any physician faces, in physical or psychological areas, is that of determining as quickly as possible how critical is the need for immediate action and what the appropriate steps are if immediate action is required. One of the computer simulations in a later chapter is devoted to this theme.

11. COMMUNICATION

A basic assumption in psychotherapy is that there is enormous potency in the communication, both verbal and non-verbal, between patient and therapist. Treatment relies essentially on this interchange which reflects an interaction between their personalities. The belief that disturbed communication between the patient and the surrounding society is at the heart of psychiatric disturbances has long been a popular one. It is probably a truism that an individual must participate successfully in acts of communication with other humans in order to survive as a human. We shall discuss these vital interactions in much more detail in the next chapter.

The problem of establishing a link with the patient is a fundamental one that requires great skill. The cable of communication is woven of many fragile threads which may easily be warped, or snapped and cut off at the very start of the interview. The simulation processes occurring later are all devoted to variations on this theme.

One basic difficulty in communication between the patient and therapist lies in the fact that different languages are often used by each. It is further the case that each often holds widely varying theories about the significance of problems in which they are mutually interested. How to establish a common basis for understanding and transmission of ideas in a situation of this nature is part of the larger problem of communication between cultures and perhaps involves the very nature of human learning as well. Except for the views supported by the Rogerians notably, therapists of most schools believe that the changes in behavior and thinking which occur to benefit a patient are the result of the learning and unlearning experiences of the therapeutic interactions. Learning in this case is broadly defined as by Hilgard* to be those changes in an individual which are not solely the result of physical maturation.

Let us note finally that the patient-therapist interaction takes place in real time. The therapist opens the session, the patient makes a response; the therapist responds to the patient, and so forth. Thus by its basic time-involved nature, the structure of an interview is a multistage process.

The therapist guides the interview by his responses. He continually makes conscious or unconscious decisions concerning the nature of his communication. His responses are based on factors of his own personality and on his goals for the interview, as well as on the responses of the patient. They are determined both by the previous response of the patient, and by the character of the previous exchanges between them, as well as by the therapist's training and experience. To a lesser extent, the patient also makes decisions concerning the nature of his responses to the therapist based on his motives and goals—lesser, because typically the patient learns that he is expected both to express his feelings spontaneously and not to monitor his words. From the standpoint, then, of both patient and therapist, the interview is a multistage decision process of adaptive type.

12. NONVERBAL COMMUNICATION

Verbal communication is substantially increased and improved by all of these elements which are lost when speech is written down. These include

* See the reference in Notes (No. 11) at the end of the chapter.

such vocal factors as voice volume, the length and frequency of pauses, rate of speech, sighs, pitch, accents, ease or difficulty of enunciation, and so forth. Words may sometimes be denied by the attendant vocalization; for example, a technique of sarcasm is to use a tone of voice and emphasis which give opposite meaning to words that are spoken.

Although occasionally distracting, appearance, mannerisms, gestures, facial and eye expressions, body movements and postures all contribute to fuller and more accurate communication. The amount of increase in what is communicated is, however, open to question. It is sometimes held that the major amount of patient information may be gained from verbal and other vocal factors.

13. ON-LINE PROCESS

The therapist in an interview is engaged in an interaction process with a feeling and self-conscious person. This means that his responses, including his delays or the rapidity with which he reacts are of extreme significance in the relationship. A long delay between the patient response and his response, for example, tends to create feelings of anxiety in the patient. The therapist thus faces the formidable task of carrying on a number of complex intellectual activities simultaneously. He must interact in the relationship, and observe and appraise various aspects of the patient and himself in the light of the patient history, what has already transpired in the session, and his self-knowledge. He then uses his observations and appraisals in this ongoing, continuously changing relationship before he responds again. There is no better example of an on-line adaptive decision process. We shall discuss processes of this nature in a later chapter.

14. TREATMENT

Once a person's psychological disturbance has been recognized, the question of specific treatment arises. Treatment is also an adaptive decision process in several respects. In the first place identification and treatment often go hand-in-hand. This means that a great deal of learning about the patient by the therapist is required while he is simultaneously making treatment decisions based on that learning. In the second place, the therapist may have to try different types of treatment in the course of therapy and to discard those of lesser value.

The types of treatment employed by the therapist depend, as is to be expected, upon the objectives of the treatment. The goals themselves will be tentative and subject to change during the process of treatment as the therapist understands more about the patient and the nature of his problems.

If a major change in the behavior and ideas of the patient is not possible or feasible, there must be some evaluation of the advantages and disadvantages of various alternative treatment procedures. Thus, for instance, the time and costs for different treatments must be considered.

15. THE INITIAL INTERVIEW

The therapy process as practiced with voluntary patients can reasonably be divided into four phases: preliminary screening often carried out by the patient himself; the initial interview in which the patient is introduced to therapy; continuing therapy; and the termination interview. These divisions are rarely found clearly separated. There are, nonetheless, times in therapy when the process may be described by tasks more characteristic of one of these phases than another. We shall focus here solely on the opening phases of the initial interview. There are a number of valid reasons for this decision. There is a reasonable homogeneity about the aims and objectives of the initial interview which does not appear to exist for the therapy which follows until we come to the termination interview. It is thus easier to gather ideas and data from therapists and journals which can be used to construct models of the initial interview than it is to obtain equivalent data concerning the details of subsequent therapy.

Secondly, the initial interview is the first contact that the therapist has with the patient. This is perhaps the most important interview of all, if for no other reason than its outcome will determine whether the therapist will keep or lose contact with the patient. There are other widely accepted important reasons as well for devoting a great deal of attention to this interaction, both theoretically and pedagogically. As a result it occupies a relatively prominent position in clinical training.

16. UNDERLYING CONCEPTUAL STRUCTURE

We have stated that one of our principal objectives is to construct a theory for the analysis of the structure of psychotherapy theories. It is inevitable, however, that our own theoretical underpinnings will consciously, or unconsciously, influence the exposition of matters apparently far removed.

Let us then briefly sketch our major view of psychotherapy. We will regard the patient, for the moment, as a complex, malfunctioning system. We conceive of this malfunctioning in the following manner:

1. The patient does not base his ideas, decisions, and actions upon the appropriate data.

2. He may have access to the appropriate data, but misinterprets or misuses it; i.e., his decision processes are faulty.

3. He may analyze the appropriate data in a satisfactory fashion, come to the appropriate conclusions, and yet be incapable of communicating his decision, or taking appropriate action.

It is to be expected that in general various combinations of these phenomena will be observed. Different psychological theories look at these malfunctions in different ways depending on the model of psychological activity chosen. We carefully eschew any discussions of this nature and will adhere only to the foregoing model.

We subscribe to the view that the patient needs to become aware of the above distortions to increase his self-understanding and freedom. Underlying causes are to be identified and eliminated if at all possible. At the very least, the malfunctioning is to be kept from destructiveness, with the aid of re-education in the three areas cited. On the basis of his training and experience the therapist can guide and encourage the patient in this education process and help him understand and use new models of behavior. He will help the patient free himself from those habit patterns which prevent him from experiencing himself and his environment fully and to help him substitute effective and satisfying behaviors. These are the principal tasks of the therapist.

A subsidiary and vital task is to relieve as much pain and distress as possible in the course of this process. To guide without controlling, to educate without indoctrinating, to help without weakening self-reliance, these are some of the important objectives in the practice of psychotherapy.

NOTES AND REFERENCES

1. The literature in this area is vast. See:
F. Alexander, "The Dynamics of Psychotherapy in the Light of Learning Theory", *Amer. J. Psychiatry*, Vol. 120, 1963, pp. 440–448.
F. Alexander, *Fundamentals of Psychoanalysis*, New York, Norton, 1963.
F. Alexander, *Psychoanalysis and Psychotherapy*, New York, Norton, 1956.
M. and E. Balint, *Psychotherapeutic Techniques in Medicine*, London, J. B. Lippincott, 1961.
G. Caplan, *Principles of Preventive Psychiatry*, New York, Basic Books, 1964.
K. Colby, 1951, *op. cit.*
J. Frank, *Persuasion and Healing*, New York, Schocken Books, 1963.
F. Fromm-Reichmann, *Principles of Intensive Psychotherapy*, Chicago, University of Chicago Press, 1950.

F. Fromm-Reichmann, "Psychoanalytic and General Dynamic Conceptions of Theory and Therapy", *J. Amer. Psychoanalytic Assn.*, Vol. 2, 1954, pp. 711–721.

M. Gelder, I. Marks, H. Woolff, "Desensitization and Psychotherapy in the Treatment of Phobic States: A Controlled Inquiry", *Brit. J. Psychiat.*, Vol. 113, 1967, pp. 53–73.

Gill, et al., 1954, *op. cit.*

E. Glover, "The Indications for Psychoanalysis", *J. Ment. Sc.*, Vol. 100, 1954, pp. 393–401.

Group for the Advancement of Psychiatry, *Clinical Psychiatry*, Part I, New York, Science House, 1967.

J. Haley, *Strategies of Psychotherapy*, New York, Grune and Stratton, 1963.

S. Harrison and D. Carek, *A Guide to Psychotherapy*, London, J. and A. Churchill, 1966.

H. Kelman, et al., "Goals in Therapy", *Amer. J. Psychoanal.*, Vol. 16, 1956, pp. 3–23.

L. Kolb, *Noyes' Modern Clinical Psychiatry*, 7th Ed., Philadelphia, W. B. Saunders, 1968.

L. Krasner, Ed., *Research in Behavior Modification: New Developments and Implications*, New York, Holt, Rinehart and Winston, 1965.

M. Levine, "Principles of Psychiatric Treatment", in F. Alexander, and H. Ross, Eds., *Dynamic Psychiatry*, Chicago, University of Chicago Press, 1952.

J. Marmor, *Modern Psychoanalysis: New Directions and Perspectives*, New York, Basic Books, 1968.

J. Matarazzo, "Psychotherapeutic Processes", *Amer. J. Psychotherapy*, Vol. 20, 1966, pp. 439–461.

K. Menninger, *A Manual for Psychiatric Case Study*, 2nd Ed., New York, Grune and Stratton, 1962.

K. Menninger, M. Mayman, P. Pruyser, *The Vital Balance: The Life Process in Mental Health and Illness*, New York, Viking, 1963.

C. Patterson, *Theories of Counseling and Psychotherapy*, New York, Harper, 1966.

M. Pearson, *Strecker's Fundamentals of Psychiatry*, 6th Ed., Philadelphia, J. B. Lippincott, 1963.

P. Polatin, *A Guide to Treatment in Psychiatry*, Philadelphia, J. B. Lippincott, 1966.

F. Redlich and D. Freedman, *The Theory and Practice of Psychiatry*, New York, Basic Books, 1966.

H. Sullivan, "The Psychiatric Interview, II", *Psychiatry*, Vol. 15, 1952, pp. 127–141.

H. Sullivan, *The Interpersonal Theory of Psychiatry*, New York, Norton, 1953.

J. Watkins, "Psychotherapy, An Overview" in I. Berg and L. Pennington,

Eds., *An Introduction to Clinical Psychology,* 3rd Ed., New York, Ronald Press, 1966.

D. Whitaker and M. Lieberman, *Psychotherapy Through the Group Process,* New York, Atherton Press, 1964.

D. Wiener, *A Practical Guide to Psychotherapy,* New York, Harper and Row, 1969.

L. Wolberg, *The Technique of Psychotherapy,* 2nd Ed., New York, Grune and Stratton, 1967.

J. Wolpe and A. Lazarus, *Behavior Therapy Techniques: A Guide to the Treatment of Neuroses,* New York, Pergamon Press, 1966.

More complete definitions are found in

L. Hinsie and R. Campbell, *Psychiatric Dictionary,* 4th Ed., London, Oxford University Press, 1970.

And more concise ones in:

A Psychiatric Glossary, 3rd Ed., Washington, D. C., American Psychiatric Association, 1969.

Diagnostic and Statistical Manual of Mental Disorders, 2nd Ed., Washington, D. C., American Psychiatric Association, 1968.

A. Lazarus says that the dichotomy is false which suggests that "clinicians must either choose between the 'disease model' of psychoanalysis . . . or adhere to the 'learning model' of behavior therapy" or between the approach which stresses insight and the one concerned with ameliorating the present behavior. Dr. Lazarus believes there is common ground expressed for example in a functional model which examines the effects of the patient's behavior on his life situation and deals with both the patient's understanding and his behavior.

A. Lazarus, "Behavior Therapy" in J. Aronson, Ed., 1970, *op. cit.*

The ultimate goal is to cause a change in the patient's living not just to induce insight. See:

L. Salzman, *The Obsessive Personality, Origins, Dynamics and Therapy,* New York, Science House, 1968.

Dr. Polatin defines psychotherapy as "a form of treatment in psychiatry relying essentially on the verbal communication between therapist and patient and on the interaction between the personalities of therapist and patient in a dynamic interpersonal relationship, whereby maladaptive behavior is altered toward a more effective adaptation, relief of symptoms occurs, and insights are developed."

P. Polatin, 1966, *op. cit.*

Colby views psychotherapy as repair work. "The goal is to relieve the patient of distressing neurotic symptoms or discordant personality characteristics which interfere with his satisfactory adaptation to a world of people and events."

K. Colby, 1951, *op. cit.*

Phillips and Wiener see psychotherapy as a means of solving current problems and teaching problem solving techniques. The purpose is to produce concrete behavior change.
E. Phillips and D. Wiener, *Short-Term Psychotherapy and Structured Behavior Change,* New York, McGraw Hill, 1966.

From the medical point of view, or is it behavioral? "that branch of medicine concerned with abnormal human behavior". See:
E. Gildea, "Teaching of Psychiatry to Residents" in S. Arieti, Ed., *American Handbook of Psychiatry,* v. 2, New York, Basic Books, 1959.

On the definition of psychotherapy from the standpoint of the patient: ". . . the patient comes to be treated and everything that is done for him, so far as he is concerned, is treatment, whatever the doctor may call it". K. Menninger, 1962, *op. cit.*

Harrison and Carek support this view with their observation, "The general structure is that of the sufferer approaching the healer for relief of distress". See:
S. Harrison and D. Carek, 1966, *op. cit.*

Sullivan wrote of psychopathology, "It does not deal with disease in the sense of medical entities like scarlet fever, but instead with processes of living that are unusually inefficient, productive of strain and unhappiness, and contributory to failures of the individual as a self-respecting unit." H. Sullivan, *Personal Psychopathology,* New York, W. W. Norton, 1972.

"Despite his wishes, perhaps, treatment of a patient does not await the therapist's formulation of a diagnosis but begins concurrently with the history taking and examination."
Gill et al., 1954, *op. cit.*

A little discussed view of psychotherapy sees it as a means of social control which fosters acceptance of prevalent cultural patterns and which sometimes may protect law breakers from the legal consequences of their behavior. See
R. Leifer, *In the Name of Mental Health: The Social Functions of Psychiatry,* New York, Science House, 1969.

"Today, in mental health care delivery, the similarities are much greater than the differences in the work done by psychiatrists, psychologists, social workers and nurses, not to mention psychiatric aides and pastoral counselors. Only differences in ability, education and supervised experience should determine the degree of responsibility assumed by each individual as well as his position in the professional hierarchy."
S. Sharfstein and H. Grunebaum, "The Physician as Professional: Obligations and Commitments," *Medical Dimensions,* November, 1972, pp. 44.

2. Speaking of the operational pressure, Dr. Lawrence Kubie has said: "The highly charged psychotherapeutic relationship is one of the most important

relationships in the world, but also one of the most subtle and difficult. It puts demands on us as psychotherapists for which the human race is hardly ready. We have not reached a degree of maturity or a quality of wisdom and generosity that justifies our attempting to apply this role at all. Yet the pressing needs of sick patients force us to attempt it."
L. Kubie, "The Destructive Potential of Humor in Psychotherapy", *The American J. of Psychiatry,* Vol. 127(7), January 1971, pp. 861–866.

On defining mental health: Jack R. Ewalt, Director of the Joint Commission on Mental Illness and Health, writes: "One value in American Culture compatible with most approaches to a definition of mental health appears to be this: An individual should be able to stand on his own two feet without making undue demands or impositions on others." In
M. Jahoda, *Current Concepts of Positive Mental Health,* New York, Basic Books, 1958.

L. C. Kolb says: "Since all behavior is but a reaction to personality and life factors, it is not always easy to define criteria of mental illness. An unbroken line of continuity exists from normal behavior through neurotic to psychotic behavior. Definitions of mental health, or absence of illness, though more general are useful in assessing the presence or extent of illness." He considers healthy behavior to be "behavior which confirms an awareness of self with personal identity coupled with a life purpose, a sense of personal autonomy . . ."
L. Kolb, 1968, *op. cit.*

Emphasizing different facets of normality, McLean talks about the "capacity to learn from experience, the ability to endure in consciousness the wish and the reality, the ability to work and love without excessive guilt and anxiety . . ."
P. McLean, "Psychiatry and Philosophy" in S. Arieti, 1959, *op. cit.*

A book which describes the healthy personality in positive terms is
E. Pfeiffer, 1968, *op. cit.*

Dr. Guntrip sees therapy as a process of liberation from inhibiting fears and freeing the individual for self realization which occurs in a reliable, good relationship.
H. Guntrip, "The Obsessive Personality", *Psychiatry and Social Science Review,* Vol. 3(4), April 1969, pp. 10–12.

See also:
H. Strupp, *Psychotherapists in Action: Explorations of the Therapist's Contribution to the Treatment Process,* New York, Grune and Stratton, 1960.

Harry Stack Sullivan has defined psychiatry as the science of human relations.
H. Sullivan, *The Psychiatric Interview,* New York, Norton, 1954.

Karl Menninger believes that all mental illness is the same qualitatively

but differs quantitatively and in external appearance. While he accepts the concept of mental illness he does not accept categories. See:
K. Menninger, *The Vital Balance*, New York, Viking, 1961.

Thomas Szasz goes several steps farther and takes the position that not only all diagnostic categories but the entire concept of mental illness must be discarded. See:
T. Szasz, *The Myth of Mental Illness*, New York, Harper and Row, 1964.

"It is a tribute to the enduring qualities of the institution of medicine that doctors can advocate and even proselytize anti-medical views among patients without destroying the basic doctor-patient relationship between them."
M. Siegler, H. Osmond and H. Mann, "Laing's Models of Madness", repr. from *The British Journal of Psychiatry, Psychiatry and Social Science Review*, Vol. 4 (1), 1970, pp. 3–18.

Ruesch and Bateson take the position that treatment can be more concrete and constructive if diagnostic categories are not used but instead a description of how the patient handles his problems and what are his strengths and weaknesses.
T. Ruesch and G. Bateson, *Communication: The Social Matrix of Society*, New York, Norton, 1951.

From the general medical viewpoint: "The concept of disease provides a set of operational models that allow the physician to generalize about the defect and imbalances that arise from time to time in the individual."
L. Chesler, A. Hershdorfer and T. Lincoln, "The Use of Information in Clinical Problems Solving: A Framework for Analysis", *Mathematical Biosciences*, Vol. 8, 1970, pp. 83–108.

Another pragmatic approach to a definition of mental ill-health: ". . . we may describe mental sickness as those disorders in which the patient has his intellectual activities or his emotions disturbed . . ."
P. Moran, "Statistical Methods in Psychiatric Research", *J. Royal Stat. Soc.*, Vol. 132, 1969, pp. 484–525.

More on the medical model: "Psychiatry is the medical specialty concerned with the study, diagnosis, treatment and prevention of behavior disorders."
F. Redlich and D. Freedman, 1966, *op. cit.*

And on the anti-medical model: "Psychotherapy restores wholeness, purpose and creativity to the patient—who looks for disease? The difference between a patient and non-patient may be selective facts of culture, opportunity or social coercion."
A. Burton, 1965, *op. cit.*

The limitations of the disease model in psychotherapy are discussed by
H. Eysenck, "Learning Theory and Behavior Therapy" in

H. Eysenck, Ed., *Behavior Therapy and the Neurosis,* New York, Pergamon Press, 1960.

"... many psychotherapists do not wish to be thought of as curing anything. The word 'cure' is not liked because it implies elimination of disease and the problems which bring people to psychotherapists are not of this order."
B. Steinzor, *The Healing Partnership,* New York, Harper and Row, 1967.

The "biological concept of adaptation ... (is) ... framework for interpretation of healthy and disordered behavior".
S. Rado, *Adaptational Psychodynamics: Motivation and Control,* New York, Science House, 1969.

3. For a descriptive presentation of the major theories in psychotherapy brought together in one book, see:
C. Patterson, 1966, *op. cit.*

A briefer, evaluative discussion is found in
F. Redlich and D. Freedman, 1966, *op. cit.*

Theories in the practice of psychotherapy closely tied to direct, observable behavior, to efficient, pragmatic resolution of problems and to the techniques of problem solving are found in
E. Phillips and D. Wiener, 1966, *op. cit.*

See also:
M. Stein, Ed., *Contemporary Psychotherapies,* New York, Free Press of Glencoe, 1961.

Frank discusses the common denominator in approaches to psychotherapy in terms of the patient's favorable expectancy. He goes further to say in talking about the different schools of thought, "Since the leading conceptual systems of psychotherapy are not logically incompatible but represent primarily differences in emphasis on alternative formulations of the same ideas, adherents of each school should feel comfortable about holding to own positions while being tolerant of alternative views."
J. Frank, "The Dynamics of the Therapeutic Relationship, Determinants and Effects of the Therapist's Influence", *Psychiatry,* Vol. 22, 1959, pp. 17–39.

W. Wolff makes the point that therapists "seem to do well or poorly because of subtle personality factors rather than because of their particular orientation".
W. Wolff, *Contemporary Psychotherapists Examine Themselves,* Springfield, Illinois, Charles C. Thomas, 1956.

A. Scheflen says that all psychotherapy is similar in practice despite the training or theory espoused by the therapist. "Rather than finding differences in what happens between a patient and therapist, there are found differences in conceptions about what happens."

A. Scheflen, "The Significance of Posture in Communication Systems", *Psychiatry*, Vol. 27(4), Nov. 1964, pp. 316–331.

A. Stone discusses the self "limited intellectual horizons of the various 'schools of psychotherapy'" and states his position thusly: "...I am committed to the belief that the protean nature of our subject matter allows for, indeed requires, an informed eclecticism which encompasses a variety of models or systems".
A. Stone, "Play: The 'Now' Therapy", *Psychiatry and Social Science Review*, Vol. 5(2), Feb., 1971, pp. 12–16.

An excellent discussion of interview methods according to various theories of personality is found in
J. Matarazzo, "The Interview", in B. Wolman, Ed., *Handbook of Clinical Psychology*, New York, McGraw-Hill, 1965.

4. Novalis has said "Theories are nets: Only he who casts will catch". See Chapter III, "Theories" in
K. Popper, *The Logic of Scientific Discovery*, New York, Basic Books, 1959.

A danger of scientific classification is that it tends to become dogmatic and close off further inquiry. A good clinician always thinks hypothetically and is careful of premature or rigid closure of inferences.
S. Applebaum, "The Accidental Eminence of George Kelly", *Psychiatry and Social Science Review*, Vol. 3(12), January 6, 1970, pp. 20–25.

5. See F. Alexander, 1963, paper and book cited in Section 1 and
A. Enelow and M. Wexler, *Psychiatry in the Practice of Medicine*, New York, Oxford University Press, 1966.
P. Nathan, *Cues, Decisions and Diagnosis: A System Analytic Approach to the Diagnosis of Psychopathology*, New York, Academic Press, 1967.

"...warm human interest in alleviating the patient's symptoms is not enough...It is characteristic of the work of the physician that he has... not only a therapeutic attitude of human helpfulness but also a concomitant attitude of looking beyond the symptoms to an understanding of diagnosis and etiology which can then be used for a more effective therapy."
M. Levine, "Principles of Psychiatric Treatment", in F. Alexander and H. Ross, Eds., 1952, *op. cit.*

The therapist's hypotheses form the frame of reference for patient and therapist and help to set the goal of treatment as well as helping to maintain treatment in the face of setbacks.
Wilbur in Burton, 1965, *op. cit.*

See also
C. Aldrich, "Brief Psychotherapy: A Reappraisal of Some Theoretical Assumptions", *American Journal of Psychiatry*, Vol. 125, 1968, pp. 585–592.

On prediction as a tool to test theory:
R. Wallerstein, "The Role of Prediction in Theory Building in Psycho-analysis", paper read in abbreviated form at a panel on "Some Aspects of Psychoanalytic Methodology", Chas. Brenner, Chairman, Midwinter Meeting of the American Psychoanalytic Assn., December 6, 1963, New York.

7. See
R. Bellman and P. Brock, 1960, *op. cit.*

9. The number and variety of taxonomies which exist attest to the differences of opinion regarding both definitions and the value of any one of them for practical use. Yet, there are traditional, well-known taxonomies:
L. Hinsie and R. Campbell, 1970, *op. cit.*
Diagnostic and Statistical Manual of Mental Disorders, 2nd Ed., Prepared by the Committee on Nomenclature and Statistics of the American Psychiatric Association, Washington, D. C., American Psychiatric Association, 1968.
N. Fodor and F. Gaynor, Eds., *Freud: Dictionary of Psychoanalysis*, New York, Philosophical Library, 1958.
A Psychiatric Glossary, Washington, D. C., American Psychiatric Association, 1969.

A systems approach based on traditional diagnostic models is found in
P. Nathan, 1967, *op. cit.*

Another new and interesting approach to classification is
R. Spitzer and J. Endicott, *Current and Past Psychopathology Scales,* Evaluation Unit, Biometrics Research, New York State Department of Mental Hygiene, New York State Psychiatric Institute, Department of Psychiatry, Columbia University, New York, November 1968.

For additional discussion of this matter, see:
H. Brill, "The Role of Classifications in Hospital Psychiatry", in M. Katz, J. O. Cole and W. Barton, Eds., *The Role and Methodology of Classification in Psychiatry and Psychopathology,* U. S. Dept., H. E. W., P. H. Service Pub. No. 1584, NIMH, Chevy Chase, Maryland, 1965.
E. Gardner, "The Role of the Classification System in Outpatient Psychiatry", *ibid.*
K. Kramer, "Classification of Mental Disorders for Epidemiologic and Medical Care Purposes: Current Status, Problems and Needs", *ibid.*
F. Kanfer and G. Saslow, "Behavioral Analysis—An Alternative to Diagnostic Classification", *Arch. General Psychiat.,* Vol. 12, 1965, pp. 529–538.
L. Rockland and W. Pollin, "Quantification of Psychiatric Mental Status —For Use with Psychotic Patients", *Arch. Gen. Psychiat.,* Vol. 12, 1965, pp. 23–28.
C. Ward, A. Beck, M. Mendelson, J. Mock and J. Erbaugh, "The Psychiatric Nomenclature: Reasons for Diagnostic Disagreement", *Arch. Gen. Psychiat.,* 1962, Vol. 7, pp. 198–205.

H. Weinstock, II., "The Role of Classification in Psychoanalytic Practice", in M. Katz, et al., 1965, *op. cit.*
J. Zubin, "Cross-National Study of Diagnosis of the Mental Disorders: Methodology and Planning", *American J. Psychia.*, Vol. 125, 1969, pp. 12–20.

10. See
Sir Aubrey Lewis, *Inquiries in Psychiatry: Clinical and Social Investigations,* New York, Science House, 1967.

11. A pragmatic approach to normal vs abnormal behavior discusses patient concepts in terms of operations—by what is done or omitted in order to acquire information. See:
P. Bridgman, *The Way Things Are,* Cambridge, Harvard University Press, 1959.

Psychotherapy viewed as a specialized variant of communication systems is discussed by
A. Scheflen, "Communication Systems Such as Psychotherapy", in *Current Psychiatric Therapies,* Vol. V., Grune and Stratton, 1965.

W. Percy discusses his opposition to forcing communication into a S-R model in
"The Symbolic Structure of Interpersonal Process", *Psychiatry,* Vol. 24, 1961, pp. 39.

"Psychotherapy is a communication process involving mutual interchange between patient and therapist. This interchange involves non-verbal behavior and verbal or symbolized communication."
H. Teitelbaum, "Defensive Verbal Communication Processes", in P. Hoch and J. Zubin, *Psychopathology of Communication,* New York, Grune and Stratton, 1958.

The founder of "general semantics" believes that neurotic behavior results from lack of clear understanding in the use and meanings of words.
A. Korzybski, *Science and Sanity,* 3rd Ed., Lakeville, Conn., International Non-Aristotelian Library Pub. Co., 1948.

For a discussion of some of the difficulties in human communication turned up by contemporary linguistic research, as well as many other important ideas, see:
G. Birkhoff, 1969, *op. cit.*

Communication is defined by Cameron as those signals made by an individual to another or detected in each other, conscious or unconscious. For a report of interesting experimentation, see:
D. E. Cameron, "Ultraconceptual Communication", in P. Hoch and J. Zubin, 1958, *op. cit.*

"The communication act is at the very heart of psychopathology."
J. Zubin in P. Hoch and J. Zubin, *ibid.*

Communication, in terms of language, content, emotion is discussed by
J. Ruesch, "The Tangential Response", in P. Hoch and J. Zubin, *ibid.*

"The driving force inherent in any form of psychotherapy is related to the
patient's experience of pleasure when a message has been acknowledged.
Successful communication is gratifying; it brings about a feeling of inclu-
sion and security and leads to constructive action." Conversely, "Disturbed communication is frustrating; it brings about a feeling of loneliness
and despair and leads to destructive action."
J. Ruesch, "Psychotherapy and Communication", in F. Fromm-Reichmann
and J. Moreno, *Progress in Psychotherapy*, New York, Grune and Stratton,
1956.

A report on the communication aspect of health care.
B. Korsch and V. Negrete, "Doctor-Patient Communication" *Scientific
American*, August 1972, pp. 66–74.

An interesting experiment in communication between therapist and patient
is reported by
A. Siegman and B. Pope, "Effect of Interviewer Specificity and Topical
Focus on the Predictability of Interviewee's Responses", *Proceedings of
the 74th Annual Convention of the American Psychological Association*,
1966, pp. 195–196.

On "learning" in psychotherapy: "Therapy is a learning process which
requires the active interest and participation of the patient."
L. Salzman, 1968, *op. cit.*

Psychotherapy is considered to be a learning process in which the coun-
selor tries to provide optimum conditions for quick learning by insight.
The goal of this re-education is to replace emotional behavior with behav-
ior which is rational and adaptive.
F. Thorne, "Principles of Personality Counseling", Brandon, Vermont:
Journal of Clinical Psychology, 1950, p. xii.

"The therapeutic process thus recapitulates the process of emotional
maturation, the child learns from the parents, incorporates their attitudes
and eventually will no longer need them for guidance."
F. Alexander, 1963, *op. cit.*

The counselor's effort according to Rogers is healing as he demonstrates
to his client that he is ". . . with him in his suffering". Emphasis on self-
revelation rather than imparting of knowledge is the primary contribution
the therapist makes to therapy. A major goal is that the patient learns to
know himself.
B. Steinzor, 1967, *op. cit.*

Steinzor states for himself that a therapist is expected to teach a patient
how to relate to others by increasing his self-knowledge, to understand
his own motives and strategies.
B. Steinzor, *ibid.*

According to Norman Cameron, therapy is for the patient an active learning situation which takes place in a setting provided by the therapist.
N. Cameron, *The Psychology of Behavior Disorders,* New York, Houghton Mifflin, 1947.

Hilgard's broad definition of learning may be found in
E. Hilgard, *Theories of Learning,* (Rev. Ed.) New York, Appleton-Century-Crofts, 1956.

A similar definition states that a change in behavior as a result of experience is due to learning. See
J. Wilson, M. Robeck and W. Michael, *Psychological Foundations of Learning and Teaching,* New York, McGraw-Hill, 1969.

Both cognitive and affective types of learning are discussed in the light of the following theories: Freud, Guthrie, Hull, Pavlov, Skinner and Tolman.
E. Hilgard and G. Bower, *Theories of Learning,* New York, Appleton-Century-Crofts, 1966.

Theories are discussed which range from a psychoanalytically influenced approach related to reinforcement learning theory to more manipulative approaches in
C. Patterson, 1966, *op. cit.*

How learning is defined is crucial to therapeutic procedures. A behavioral skill such as playing the piano consists of combined motor and cognitive changes. Only cognitive and sometimes affective changes are considered in the acquisition of knowledge about one's motives. On the other hand, the learned responses may not result in any observed change. Visceral habits may be formed in response to pain, for example. A major dispute between the Freudian and behaviorists is unresolved: do feelings cause action, or do actions cause feelings?
E. Porter, Jr., *An Introduction to Therapeutic Counseling,* Boston, Houghton Mifflin, 1950.

Learning, according to Wilson et al., is a by-product of the process of making choices.
Wilson, et al., 1969, *op. cit.*

Psychotherapy rests on the assumption that human behavior is modifiable through psychological procedures. "If psychotherapy is considered a learning process then methods of treatment should be derived from knowledge of learning and motivation."
A. Bandura, "Psychotherapy as a Learning Process", *Psychological Bulletin,* Vol. 58(2), 1961, pp. 143–159.

Thomas Szasz expresses the oft-quoted view that the disturbances of a patient are due to faulty learning, that the therapist is a teacher, and that psychotherapy is a form of corrective relearning.
T. Szasz, *"The Myth of Mental Illness",* American Psychologist, Vol. 15, 1960, pp. 113–118.

The feelings therapist and patient have for each other "provide an environment for the learning experience which psychotherapy must be if it is to be successful".
A. Scheflen, "Quasi-Courtship Behavior in Psychotherapy", *Psychiatry*, Vol. 28(3), Aug. 1965, pp. 245–257.

The therapist's personal attributes make it possible for him to establish the therapeutic climate in which constructive personality change can occur. His technical knowledge permits him to engage in the learning and unlearning experiences necessary to free the patient from neurotic behavior.
H. Strupp, "The Psychotherapist's Contribution to the Treatment Process: An Experimental Investigation", *Behav. Sc.*, Vol. 3, 1958, pp. 34–67.
See also
J. Wolpe, "Psychotherapy Based on the Principle of Reciprocal Inhibition", in A. Burton, Ed., *Case Studies in Counseling and Psychotherapy*, Englewood Cliffs, New Jersey, Prentice-Hall, 1959.
and Part Two on Learning and Communication in
A. Bachrach, *Experimental Foundations of Clinical Psychology*, New York, Basic Books, 1962.

Roger A. MacKinnon and Robert Michels, "The Psychiatric Interview in Clinical Practice", *Psychotherapy and Social Science Review*, Vol. 6(8), 1972, pp. 2–5.

12. In addition to other non-verbal information such as postural changes or facial expression, vocal communications may reveal emotionally charged areas the patient is unable to put into speech. Some of these have to do with inflections, intonations, accents, emphasis, pauses and slurring of speech.
Wolberg, 1967, *op. cit.*

"Behavior is a major form of communication." Information not contained in words is often expressed by other behavior.
A. Mehrabian, "Communication Without Words", *Psychology Today*, Vol. 2(4), Sept. 1968, pp. 53–55.

"Although we seek to communicate in the abstract symbols of speech, in doing so we should observe that much—perhaps the greater and more significant portion—of what goes on in the therapeutic exchange is non-verbal."
Wilbur in A. Burton, 1965, *op. cit.*

Harry Stack Sullivan believed that vocal communication such as intonation, rate of speech and ease or difficulty of enunciation can serve as guides to vital areas of difficulties. He believed that most non-verbal clues come via our ears and that facial expression, posture, etc., are not especially revealing.
H. Sullivan, "The Psychiatric Interview", *Psychiatry*, Vol. 14, 1951, pp. 361–373.

H. Sullivan, 1952, *op. cit.*

"While not all the communication in an interview is at the verbal level, most of it is."
I. Berg and L. Pennington, Eds., *An Introduction to Clinical Psychology,* 3rd Ed., New York, Ronald Press, 1966.

The therapist should check his own behavior to see if he is conveying disapproval, boredom, irritation. Ideally, facial expression should be pleasant, relaxed, non-critical.
Wolberg, 1967, *op. cit.*

There is promise for measuring depressive symptoms from power spectrum of voices.
W. Hargreaves, J. Starkweather, K. Blacher, "Voice Quality in Depression", *Journal of Abnormal Psychology,* Vol. 70(3), 1965, pp. 218–220.

Rate, time of pauses, range and rate of change in pitch are related to meanings expressed.
G. Fairbanks and L. Hoaglin, "An Experimental Study of the Durational Characteristics of the Voice During Expression of Emotion", *Speech Monogr.,* Vol. 8, 1941, pp. 85–90.

Scheflen discusses non-verbal communication as an interacting system.
A. Scheflen, 1964, *op. cit.*

See also:
M. Berger, "Nonverbal Communications in Group Psychotherapy", *International Journal of Group Psychotherapy,* Vol. VIII(2), April 1958, pp. 161–177.
C. Winick and H. Holt, "Seating Position as Nonverbal Communication in Group Analysis", *Psychiatry,* Vol. 24(2), May 1961, pp. 171–182.
A. Scheflen, 1965, *op. cit.*
J. Ruesch and A. Prestwood, "Anxiety: Its Initiation, Communication and Interpersonal Management", *Arch. Neurol. and Psychiat.,* Vol. 62, 1949, pp. 527–550.
J. Davitz, et al., *The Communication of Emotional Meaning,* New York, McGraw-Hill, 1964.
A. Enelow and M. Wexler, 1966, *op. cit.*

15. See, in addition, the notes at the end of Chapter 1 for Section 9.

    Every therapy starts off with an initial diagnostic interview and a good technique is the heart of psychological diagnosis. The form of the technique is neither routine nor objective however. The doctor must enter into a personal relationship with the patient and his diagnosis will strongly depend on his own subjective experience in the relationship.
    M. and E. Balint, 1961, *op. cit.*

16. According to Sullivan, the psychiatrist is a professional expert whose strategy is affected by systematic considerations. See

Sullivan's various writings, *op. cit.*

A new model for practice is proposed by Carkhuff and Berenson in which the essence lies in establishing a genuine, open relationship between the patient and therapist. The dominant technique is confrontation with the therapist considering himself an enemy of those defenses which are self-destructive and prevent a patient from experiencing himself fully. See: R. B. Carkhuff and B. G. Berenson, *Beyond Counseling and Therapy,* New York, Holt, Rinehart and Winston, 1967.

In his book, Porter, who espouses a non-directive therapy, discusses how the therapist may direct the course of the initial interview by what he chooses to clarify to the patient and when. Like others, he considers the therapist an expert who knows more on a conscious, utilizable level about the patient than he knows about himself. Because he sees a wider context and is free of the patient's emotional distortions he is more aware of meaning. See: E. Porter, Jr., 1950, *op. cit.*

"Every interpretation . . . aims at making the patient aware of something he has kept away from himself. The aim of the interpretation remains the same, to extend the patient's consciousness—which, in principle, is therapy." M. and E. Balint, 1961, *op. cit.*

Chapter 3

THE INITIAL INTERVIEW

1. INTRODUCTION

Some general features of psychotherapy were examined in the foregoing chapter. In this chapter, we narrow our focus considerably and discuss various aspects of an initial interview. Our objective is to provide some background material for the discussions in Chapters 4 and 5 and for the mathematical models of Chapter 6.

As previously noted, in this volume we are eschewing any study of the extraordinarily complex processes involved in continuing therapy. We concentrate solely upon the first session in which a patient is introduced to therapy, which is to say the first set of interactions between the patient and therapist. Since the goals for this interview can be reasonably identified, to a considerable extent we can measure our progress in achieving them.

Furthermore, let us emphasize that the discussion which follows is limited to practice with patients who voluntarily seek the help of a professional therapist.

What occurs in this interview is important for a number of reasons. To begin with, the patient's experience here will often determine whether or not he continues in treatment. In addition, a number of therapists believe that the manner in which the initial interview is conducted, as well as the patient's responses in this interaction, can significantly influence the course of therapy.

2. GOALS OF THE INITIAL INTERVIEW

We consider a successful initial interview to center about these principal tasks:

1. Establishing a therapeutic relationship;
2. Gathering information concerning the nature and severity of the patient's problems and his characteristic ways of handling them;

41

3. Assessing the patient's motivation, need, and capacity for therapy; and if appropriate, reinforcing his desire to continue;

4. Establishing a tentative clinical diagnosis, treatment plan or appropriate referral;

5. Making the patient feel better, if possible.

A major constraint on the therapist is that he does not add to the patient's present burden of pain. He must do no further injury to a person already suffering. Specifically, this means that the therapist does not engage in random probing for "sore spots". This imposes a serious constraint on the ways in which the therapist can gather information.

The elements or objectives of the interview presented here in neatly linear fashion are crude approximations to their counterparts in real life since it is not easy to disentangle the complex pattern of the actual interview and identify individual elements. To enter into the personal relationship with his patient that is necessary to treatment, the therapist must be flexible, spontaneous, and intuitive. In the actual interview, a fluid interplay between the information given by the patient and the personalities of the two participants dominates the clinical picture. One or another of the objectives may be prominent in any one interaction, or any number of them may be inextricably bound together. For example, making the patient feel better may result from efforts to establish a link for communication, and this, too, may reinforce the patient's desire for continuing therapy.

3. ESTABLISHING A THERAPEUTIC RELATIONSHIP

We have indicated above that the therapist strives to estabish various types of communication links with the patient. He wishes also to ascertain as far as possible the nature and severity of the patient's problems, as well as his present emotional state and some pertinent background history. Further, he wishes to determine the patient's motivation, capacity, and need for therapy, to reinforce his desire for continued treatment, and to formulate a tentative therapeutic plan or decide on a referral. From the beginning, the therapist's principal aim is to create a cooperative working relationship which makes possible these specific goals and the general goals of psychotherapy described in Chapter 2. It requires of the therapist a clear focus on his goals and a high degree of adaptability to create such a relationship with many different individuals, each of whom brings with him strongly personal attitudes, and habits of thinking and behaving.

This relationship is frequently characterized as being "in rapport" or "establishing a therapeutic alliance or climate". What is precisely meant by these phrases, however, is not at all clear, nor is it evident by what concrete signs this relationship, or its absence, is to be recognized. The identification of the presence or absence of this therapeutic climate is one of our principal tasks.

4. BASIC DECISIONS

Let us cite some basic decisions that must be made at the very outset. To begin with, there is the problem of determining whether the patient is in need of psychotherapy. Are the difficulties primarily emotional, primarily physical, or some combination of both? If the patient can be helped by psychotherapy, how urgent are his needs in terms of time and immediacy of attention?

A fundamental problem which we shall explore in some depth is that of establishing communication. Until the therapist knows something about the patient, it is not clear what lines to pursue. A certain amount of information is clearly necessary to formulate even tentative short-term objectives.

No single prescribed routine can be guaranteed to provide this information. Rather, a flexible relation with the patient must be developed and maintained, one that allows free use of training and intuition for the evaluation of the verbal and nonverbal responses of the patient, and for the understanding of the nature of the interaction between therapist and patient. These evaluations form the basis for the choice of both objectives and procedures.

5. DYADIC NATURE OF INTERVIEW

There is substantial agreement concerning many of the ingredients of the patient-therapist interaction. Nonetheless, this apparently makes it no easier to describe them in clear, unambiguous terms. For example, in describing an ideal patient-therapist relation we find such ideas as that there is found a mutual liking and respect for each other as human beings; that there must be a willingness on the part of the therapist to help the patient although he may find some or many of his characteristics personally displeasing; and that the therapist must use techniques and policies which will enable the patient to behave in such a way that the therapist will be able to help him.

We wish to propose some reasonably precise means of analyzing this imprecise therapeutic relationship. Specifically, one of our principal objectives is to provide a method for identifying, recognizing, and evaluating desirable and undesirable responses and trends in an interview.

An additional goal is to provide some theoretical and operational bases for the training of novice therapists. They must learn the difficult task of developing highly personal and professional relationships with patients they see for the first time.

6. ATTITUDES

How do we describe the effects of the therapist and patient on each other and indicate changes in the character of the responses from stage to stage?

To begin with, we regard the interview as a series of couplets, response-response pairs. The therapist's response is usually a question or observation with nonverbal components, while that of the patient is an answer or response which may be totally verbal, nonverbal, or some combination of both. The quality and ultimate value of the interview are largely determined by the effectiveness of the therapist's techniques as they are indicated by his responses.

We shall describe responses in terms of *attitudes* rooted in the individual's personal and cultural background. In the terminology of a later chapter where these ideas are explored more fully the attitude is the basic state variable and the response is a manifestation of the attitude, an "observable". We classify these attitudes *convergent* and *divergent*. Let us explain what we mean by these terms.

7. CLASSIFICATION OF ATTITUDES AND RESPONSES

We distinguish two principal attitudes from an analysis of patient and therapist responses, convergent and divergent. In general, a convergent response is one which tends to facilitate communication, enlarge the information pool, and achieve the goals of the interview. Briefly, paraphrasing what has been previously discussed, these are primarily to establish a therapeutic relationship and begin treatment, and, without adding to the patient's burden of pain, to obtain the necessary information to assess the present functioning of the patient and, tentatively, to formulate a plan for treatment.

A divergent response is defined in terms of convergence. It is simply a response which lacks those elements which would make it a convergent response. It is important to emphasize that these terms are relative rather than absolute. They are dependent at all times on the state of the interview and on the patient.

The above dichotomy, a restriction to two principal categories at each stage, is less confining than appears at first reading because of the multistage nature of the interview. This will be discussed in some detail in a later chapter.

8. PATIENT ATTITUDES AND RESPONSES

In broad terms, we may describe patient behavior in the following way: when convergent, the patient approaches the therapy situation positively. In particular, he admits to having problems and gives information about them. His responses indicate willingness to continue with the therapeutic interaction.

A patient's divergence on the other hand is expressed by hostility to the therapist personally or to the therapy situation. He may deny problems or any need for help or, again, he may be argumentative. He gives too little information about his feelings; he is either too brief or deals in generalities; he may often be silent or, if talkative, irrelevant and tangential.

9. THERAPIST ATTITUDES AND RESPONSES

The therapist may be described in rather similar fashion.

In general, a convergent therapist is concerned for the patient and interested in him. He is calm and accepting, and offers to help the patient with his problems, persistently if necessary. He accepts the patient's feelings, including negative ones, while remaining nonjudgmental and matter-of-fact. He forms questions which encourage narrative replies, rather than simple agreement or disagreement, and he does not suggest either answers or modes of answering.

A divergent therapist may tend to over-intellectualize and be more concerned with his own role than he is with the helping relationship. He concentrates on the patient's accounts of events rather than feelings about them, or dwells on a problem not yet adequately established. He takes an overactive or underactive role in the therapy situation, and may be ingratiating, judgmental, argumentative, threatening, or even punitive. His behavior may be perceived as threatening and tends to be anxiety-producing, or he frames responses which don't furnish leads for exposition or which may be confusing, by asking for more than one kind of information in one request. He may abruptly change the subject or he may suggest answers or modes of answering.

10. DISCUSSION

It is not to be expected that it will be easy to apply these criteria of convergence and divergence. In the first place there is the problem of accounting for nonverbal aspects. The same written statement can be spoken in many different ways; in other words, the affective tone can easily change the message. More importantly, the foregoing terms represent degrees of attitudes and responses on scales which are not necessarily linear, and may not readily be made quantitative. We would like to point out, however, that at any single stage of the interview, differences in opinion and evaluation concerning the character of a response are not too significant if the process has been constructed carefully. When we average over the total number of responses in an interview, given a particular theoretical position, there should be found general agreement as to what constitutes a set of convergent or divergent responses.

We believe that one of the chief values of the distinction between convergent and divergent lies in a discussion or analysis of what, in a particular interaction, constitutes one or the other. Since the terms convergent and divergent depend crucially on the basic assumptions of the therapist for interpretation, theorists of different philosophical orientations may designate any single response by the therapist or patient more or less desirable, acceptable, or perhaps destructive of the goals of the interview. Different policies and principles for the analysis of convergent and divergent responses would inevitably follow.

It remains to demonstrate that we can nonetheless use the foregoing conceptual structure to construct some precise mathematical models.

NOTES AND REFERENCES

1. For a traditional approach to the problems of initial interviewing, see:
   F. Deutsch and W. Murphy, *The Clinical Interview*, 2 vols., New York, International Universities Press, 1955.
   L. Kolb, 1968, *op. cit.*
   L. Wolberg, 1967, *op. cit.*

   The importance of the initial interview is discussed in valuable detail in Gill et al., 1954, *op. cit.*

   A typical view of the importance of the initial interview is: "Psychotherapy commences with the initial evaluative interviews ... We contend that the patterns and attitudes established during these first meetings are likely to have a substantial and abiding influence on the relations between physician and patient."
   Group for the Advancement of Psychiatry, 1967, *op. cit.*

   Wolberg considers the initial interview to be the most critical of all. He heads a list of eight important tasks to be accomplished at this time with these: 1) establish rapport, 2) get pertinent information, and 3) establish a tentative clinical diagnosis.
   L. Wolberg, 1967, *op. cit.*

A not uncommon phenomenon is observed by P. Giovacchini when he notes that in the space of the initial interview some patients "anticipate the future course of the therapeutic interaction". He hypothesizes that it is necessary for some patients to replicate the future therapeutic contact at the beginning or they might not continue with treatment.

P. Giovacchini, "Modern Psychoanalysis and Modern Psychoanalysts", *Psychiatry and Social Science Review*, Vol. 4(3), March 10, 1970, pp. 3–15.

More than representing a potential therapeutic alliance, the initial interview may usefully be looked at as a paradigm of all human encounters.
H. A. Wilmer, "The Role of the Psychiatrist in Consultation and Some Observations on Video Tape Learning", *Psychosomatics*, Vol. 8(4), July-August 1967, pp. 193–195.

See also:
F. Alexander, and H. Ross, 1952, *op. cit.*
Balint, 1961, *op. cit.*
I. Berg and L. Pennington, 1966, *op. cit.*
K. Colby, 1951, *op. cit.*
J. Davitz, *The Communication of Emotional Meaning*, New York, McGraw-Hill, 1964.
A. Enelow and M. Wexler, 1966, *op. cit.*
H. Kelman, in A. Burton, 1965, *op. cit.*
G. Caplan, 1964, *op. cit.*
M. Pearson, 1963, *op. cit.*
D. Stafford-Clark, *Psychiatry for Students*, New York, Grune and Stratton, 1964.
H. Wilmer, 1967, *op. cit.*
H. Witmer, Ed., *Teaching Psychotherapeutic Medicine*, New York, The Commonwealth Fund, 1947.
See also notes in Section 9, Chapter 1.

2. The goals of the psychiatrist are "to discover who the patient is and what is troubling him at the moment, to discover the patient's characteristic patterns of behavior and how these relate to his present difficulties, to establish a meaningful relationship with the patient which can then facilitate further personality exploration and provide a basis for eventual behavioral change".
The goals of the patient are "to obtain relief from his suffering, to make a good impression on the psychiatrist and to be liked by him, to be told what (outside of himself) is causing his present difficulties, to learn something about himself that might explain his present troubles and prevent future ones".
E. Pfeiffer, 1968, *op. cit.*

"... the first aim is to create an atmosphere in which the patient can reveal ... enough of himself to be confident that his assessment of the

patient's state and his potentialities for developing human relationships, arrived at on the basis of this observation, will be fairly reliable. The second aim is to form an opinion whether anything, and if so what, should be done in the case."
Balint, 1961, *op. cit.*

"One basic function of existential therapy is to provide a setting in which as little as possible will impede the patient's capacity to discover his true self."
R. Laing, *The Self and Others,* Chicago, Quadrangle Books, 1962.

Wolberg sees the principal objective as the establishment of an adequate working relationship with the patient. Subsidiary tasks are to clarify the patient's misconceptions about therapy, to motivate him to accept treatment, to tentatively define the objectives in therapy and to allow the patient to know that the therapist understands and can help him.
L. Wolberg, 1967, *op. cit.*

According to Gill et al, the initial interview has three aims. The first is to establish rapport, the second is to appraise the patient's psychological status, the third is to reinforce the patient's wish to continue with therapy and to plan the next step in accomplishing this with the patient.
Gill, et al, 1954, *op. cit.*

The traditional approach to the introductory interview are these, as formulated by Polatin: The therapist uses the patient's descriptions of his symptoms and personal history "to gain a general impression of the psychopathology, ego strength, the nature of his defenses, motivations in seeking treatment, the capacity for introspection, the reality factors impinging on the patient. The therapist will formulate psychodynamic factors, prognostic possibilities and therapeutic goals".
P. Polatin, 1966, *op. cit.*

And according to Deutsch: The major purpose of this interview is to establish contact and for the preparation of the transference situation, for collecting and selecting key words, for testing the patient's reactions to various word stimuli.
F. Deutsch and W. Murphy, 1955, *op. cit.*

The multiple aims of the initial psychiatric interview are to establish a type of relationship which will make a diagnosis possible, to evaluate possibilities for therapy, to formulate tentative goals for treatment, to recommend a program, and to prepare the client to accept such a program.
Group for the Advancement of Psychiatry, 1967, *op. cit.*

Foulkes believes the interview is important to get some tentative answers to the questions: Can the patient change? How far? By what means? The purpose is to formulate treatment aims which are consistent with the reality of the therapy situation.
S. Foulkes, "Psychotherapy and Group Psychotherapy", in A. Kadis,

J. Krasner, C. Winick, S. Foulkes, *A Practicum of Group Psychotherapy*, New York, Harper & Row, 1965.

"... the findings about the patient's potentiality to form and maintain relationships are the basis for or against recommending psychotherapy." Balint, 1961, *op. cit.*

The objectives in the initial interview are the development of rapport, learning about the patient in order to understand him and his problems and to outline some reasonable treatment plans, and being helpful to the patient.
S. Harrison and D. Carek, 1966, *op. cit.*

The Group for Advancement of Psychiatry (1967, op. cit.) expresses it thus: "The most important of these aims is to establish a special kind of relationship with the patient which will permit sufficient understanding to make a diagnosis, to evaluate therapeutic possibilities, to formulate tentative goals of treatment, to recommend a therapeutic program and to prepare the patient, and his family when necessary, to accept such a program."
Enelow and Wexler express the purpose of the initial interview succinctly. They say the aim of the interview is to get information to help the doctor treat the patient more effectively. They consider the subject of information to be both interview content and process. They wish to obtain a subjective verbal account of behavior and a sample of the patient's behavior as he interacts with the therapist.
Enelow and Wexler, 1966, *op. cit.*

On diagnosis: "A psychiatric diagnosis is a complex set of conclusions which describe an individual, his environment, and interactions with it but is continuous since it describes a process which is ever changing and only accurate as of the date it is recorded."
K. Menninger, 1962, *op. cit.*

See also:
K. Menninger, "The Psychiatric Diagnosis", *Bull. Menninger Clinic*, Vols. 23–24, 1960, pp. 226–239.

Diagnosis, traditionally thought to be a necessary precursor to successful treatment, involves description and differentiation. See:
P. Nathan, 1967, *op. cit.*

"... the therapist has two aims: (a) to formulate from the facts gathered a working clinical and dynamic diagnosis and (b) to acclimatize the patient to the interview methods and procedure of psychotherapeutic work."
K. Colby, 1951, *op. cit.*

The function of the clinician is to diagnose and then excite change in any patient seeking help.
E. Shostrom, *Man the Manipulator*, Nashville, Tenn., Abingdon Press, 1967.

According to Dr. Steinzor, the prevailing opinion of psychotherapists today emphasizes such traditional medically originated models as diagnosis and prognosis. The patient has however made the first diagnosis when he decided that his life could be improved with psychotherapeutic help.
B. Steinzor, 1967, *op. cit.*

Nevertheless, although it has fallen into disrepute among many therapists: "Beginning with Freud, the prevailing opinion of psychotherapists today still places more or less heavy emphasis on accurate diagnosis, prognosis and other traditional medically originated models. The notable exception of course for nearly twenty years has been Carl Rogers ... who has stood virtually alone in his opposition."
Enelow and Wexler, 1966, *op. cit.*

In discussing the questioned value of diagnosis: The purpose of medical diagnosis is not to label someone "to discriminate against him but to bring the knowledge of medicine to bear upon him. It is an essential step which precedes and determines treatment. It may save his life."
It is frequently considered a useless diversion in the psychoanalytic model since "treatment is the same in any case, and every relationship between patient and therapist is unique".
M. Siegler, et al., 1967, *op. cit.*

"... neither academic psychiatry nor psychoanalysis has been able to devise a real classification of mental illness amounting to a kind of natural system; hence, attaching a diagnostic label to the patient as a result of our interview is only of very limited value."
Balint, 1961, *op. cit.*

This vagueness accentuates the importance of the new theory of "fuzzy sets" created by L. Zadeh to treat types of uncertainty not readily handled by the theory of probability. See
L. A. Zadeh, "Fuzzy Languages and Their Relation to Human and Machine Intelligence", *Proc. Conference on Man and the Computer,* Bordeaux, France, 1970, organized by Institut de la Vie, Paris,
where many other references may be found.

"In psychiatry, routine procedures have little value" and treatment therefore must be individualized, however ... "there remains some value in a partial preservation of attempts at clinical diagnosis" since there is value in reliable or partly reliable generalizations that are based in the long experience of many.
M. Levine, in F. Alexander and H. Ross, 1952, *op. cit.*

3. The importance of establishing a therapeutic relationship is expressed in part as follows: "... rapport between the psychiatrist and patient is a vital and primary consideration, whether a continuing therapeutic relationship develops from the initial interview, or whether its sole purpose is limited to obtaining information for a diagnosis."

Group for the Advancement of Psychiatry, 1967, *op. cit.*

"The relationship between the patient and physician influences to a large extent his motivation to reveal the nature of his problems and their sources in his past experiences."
Kolb, 1968, *op. cit.*

Basic to the establishment of the relationship is the therapist's attitude communicated to the patient: "The essential thing is to convey to the patient that you are seriously interested in him, desirous of helping him, prepared to listen attentively and uninterruptedly, and capable of understanding and responding."
K. Menninger, 1962, *op. cit.*

". . . the first task is to establish an emotional bridge, a line of communication."
S. Harrison and D. Carek, 1966, *op. cit.*

"If the doctor is not able to make a good enough rapport with his patient, the result of his examination will be unsatisfactory, patchy or even misleading."
Balint, 1961, *op. cit.*

The immediate goal of treatment according to Dr. Norman Cameron is to establish a biosocial interrelationship, the therapeutic situation in which both patient and therapist participate.
N. Cameron, 1947, *op. cit.*

According to Wolberg, the essential data needed to fulfill the purpose of the initial interview must be obtained in an atmosphere of understanding and sympathy.
L. Wolberg, 1967, *op. cit.*

Another good discussion of the importance of the therapeutic alliance in treatment is found in
R. Greenson, *The Technique and Practice of Psychoanalysis*, New York, International Universities Press, 1969.

"Something in the analyst's attitude creates a setting in which the patient is not overwhelmed by anxiety. The analyst's attitude communicates feelings of security and calm and a devotion to understand the patient's thoughts and feelings."
P. Giovacchini, "Modern Psychoanalysis and Modern Psychoanalysts—II", *Psychiatry and Social Science Review*, Vol. 4 (4), March 31, 1970, pp. 11–19.

"The only real differences that seem to exist among experienced therapists as a group are semantic. They differ only insofar as the name they apply to themselves and the theoretical language they speak."
E. Dreyfus, "Humanness: A Therapeutic Variable", *Personnel and Guidance Journal*, February 1967, pp. 573–578.

Frank has found that the patient's "favorable expectation is a key to understanding and success in psychotherapy, and that this is derived from such factors as the therapist's attitude of confidence that he can help the patient, that he cares about him as a person and is somehow able to communicate this concern."
J. Frank, "The Dynamics of the Psychotherapeutic Relationship; Determinants and Effects of the Therapist's Influence", *Psychiatry*, Vol. 22, 1959, pp. 17–39.

There has been reported some evidence of concordance between the physiologies of therapist and patient—that heart rate patterns are similar when therapist and patient are in rapport but not when the therapist is annoyed or impatient.
R. Coleman, M. Greenblatt, and H. Solomon, "Physiological Evidence of Rapport During Psychotherapeutic Interviews", *Diseases of the Nervous System*, Vol. 17 (3), 1956, pp. 71–77.
and
A. De Mascio, R. Boyd, M. Greenblatt, and H. Solomon, "The Psychiatric Interview: A Socio-physiological Study", *Diseases of the Nervous System*, Vol. 16 (1), 1955, pp. 4–9.

5. Dr. Polatin says that the therapist communicates his acceptance of the patient as an individual who has value, a feeling of warmth, understanding, protection, and unfailing interest. In addition, the therapist must believe that the patient has the capacity to be helped.
P. Polatin, 1966, *op. cit.*

Interviewer warmth tends to increase verbal productivity and thus aid the information-gathering objective of the initial interview.
B. Pope and A. Siegman, "Interviewer Warmth and Verbal Communication in the Initial Interview", *Proceedings, 75th Annual Convention, A.P.A.*, 1967, pp. 245–246.

"... the psychiatric interview is the sum total of the patient's reactions to a particular doctor, at a particular moment, in a particular setting; and as nothing of this can be left out from the interview, what in fact is examined is exactly this interaction. It is essentially a two person relationship built up from the contributions of both participants."
Balint, 1961, *op. cit.*

In describing an ideal patient-therapist relation, this statement is found: "The therapist regardless of the type of therapy he employs ... should have a liking for people, possess a warm capacity for projecting himself into the situations and feelings of others, and be able to understand human motivation. Both therapist and patient must relate meaningfully to the other."
L. Kolb, 1968, *op. cit.*

Sullivan, in his definition of psychiatry, states: "... an expanding science

concerned with the kinds of events or processes in which the psychiatrist participates while being an observant psychiatrist."
H. Sullivan, 1953, *op. cit.*

Bernard Steinzor comments on the unevenness of the patient-therapist relationship. He says that while the therapist must be warm, attentive, responsive, the "patient is supposed to let go of his feelings spontaneously" and since patients often equate anger with rejection, his words must be "understanding, calm, measured . . ."
B. Steinzor, 1967, *op. cit.*

In considering the success of the interview, E. Pfeiffer says that the goals of patient and psychiatrist may differ and that the interview can't be successful for either unless some of the goals for both are attained.
E. Pfeiffer, 1968, *op. cit.*

For a different view of the therapeutic dyad, see
A. Rapoport, "Experiments in Dyadic Conflict", *Bull. of the Menninger Clinic,* 1966, Vol. 30, pp. 284–291.

"If the therapist assumes a superior attitude and the patient endows him with superior power, the self-concept emerging through the revelations will be of a different order from what it would be if the two meet in mutuality and equality."
B. Steinzor, 1967, *op. cit.*

In the first interview, the patient is made to feel that the therapist genuinely wants to help him, that he can and will help him, and that he is himself expected to contribute to the treatment situation.
I. Berg and L. Pennington, 1966, *op. cit.*

The content of the interview is determined by the personalities of the participants, how they view their own and each other's roles, the conscious and unconscious purposes each is pursuing, and the technique used by the interviewer.
M. Gill et al, 1954, *op. cit.*

Redlich discusses the elements of a successful initial interview from the standpoints of both therapist and patient.
F. Redlich and M. Pines, "How to Choose a Psychiatrist", *Harpers,* Vol. 220 (1318), March 1960, pp. 33–41.

Chapter 4

THE BEHAVIOR
OF SYSTEMS

1. INTRODUCTION

In this chapter we wish to discuss in some detail some fundamental aspects of the concept of *system,* one of the most useful words in the lexicon of the contemporary scientist. This term, system, was used in a rather free and intuitive fashion in the previous chapters. In the discussion that follows we will carefully explore this concept and describe some of the conventional uses of scientific and mathematical methods in the treatment of systems. After we have considered both the wide scope and the severe limitations of traditional techniques, we will turn in subsequent chapters to a careful blend of old and new methods to treat the questions of interest to us.

We begin with the primary observation that science is concerned with the behavior of systems—mechanical, electrical, biological, chemical—a veritable tintinnabulation of systems. This conceptual framework is utilized in a variety of ways to explain the processses of the real world, and ultimately, to cope with them. We deliberately speak of a variety of explanations since any single explanation may either be too general to be of value in a particular application, too difficult to use, or, it may not be applicable at all. Although a unified theory is certainly desirable, as we have previously noted we don't necessarily expect to develop one in a field of any complexity. To a great extent, we believe that what qualifies as an explanation will depend critically upon why we want an explanation, which is to say the context of the explanation. This is the operational point of view once again.

We shall restrict our attention to those types of systems occurring naturally in the context of psychotherapy, thus preparing the ground for certain specific applications we have in mind.

2. DESCRIPTION OF A SYSTEM

One way to begin making precise the use of the term "system" is to consider the task of providing some means of describing a particular system. By *description* we mean a specification of properties in quantitative or qualitative terms.

Thus, in a hospital system we may wish to provide such data as the number of beds, the average number of patients per week, the number of resident physicians, and so forth. An analysis of an educational system may provide such data as the number of students in each class per semester; the number of faculty members with advanced degrees; and, perhaps, the number and intensity of student disturbances, together with their causes. A physical system, such as a gas in a container, might be described in terms of pressure, volume, and density. A satellite can be characterized at any time in terms of its position in the sky and its velocity. In an ecological system, we may want to note the age and distribution of animals of different species in any season.

To avoid ambiguity, we attempt wherever reasonable to describe properties in terms of numbers. Attributes important in human or psychological systems, such as "redness", "heaviness", "hardness", "illness", and "pain", are initially ambiguous, which is to say that no precise information is communicated by use of these terms. In an attempt to resolve this ambiguity, we construct scales of different types. This has been carried out successfully as far as "redness" and "heaviness" are concerned. We may, now, as a result of scientific effort over the past 300 years, specify "redness" in terms of a particular frequency or wavelength, and "heaviness" by means of pounds or grams. Attempts have been made, with varying degrees of success, to construct analogous scales for "hardness" and "pain". Although attempts at classifying mental illness in both nature and degree have been tried, all retain some major degrees of ambiguity. Some of this vagueness seems to be intrinsic; some the result of insufficient study. Until a great deal of effort has been expended, it is not clear what the situation is. But it seems probable that we shall have to live without precise descriptions in the psychological domain for some time to come, and learn to deal with this phenomenon rationally.

3. STATE OF A SYSTEM

For the moment, let us assume that the quantitative labeling we desire can be carried out. The set of numbers we can then use to describe that system will be called the *state* of the system. By this means we are able to transform a complex entity such as a physical system into a set of numbers, x_1, x_2,

. . . , x_N, as illustrated below. This set of numbers is called a *vector* and
the state is occasionally called the state vector (see Figure 1).

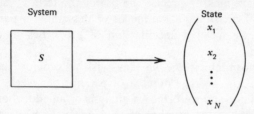

Figure 4.1

This transformation can be carried out in many ways. Which particular
set of numbers we use at a particular time depends on what we want to
do, and what we can do. Any particular set of numbers contains, then,
only a part of the information available concerning a system. Thus, there
is a great deal of flexibility and opportunity for individual ingenuity. In
return, there is always a certain amount of subjectivity, and an acknowl-
edgment of some characteristic features and rejection of others.

A state of a system is in consequence not an intrinsic property of a
system. The system itself is real; any description is superimposed. For two
people to discuss a system, they must agree upon the conventions employed
to describe it.

4. OBJECTIVES

A principal objective of the scientific investigation of systems is to be able
to predict the future. Specifically, we wish to determine various ways of
establishing the state at some particular time in the future on the basis of
the current state. Prediction is required for planning, and planning is
essential for orderly development and control.

Alternatively, we may wish to reconstruct the past history of the system,
or to deduce properties of one part of a system on the basis of the characteristics of another part. Generally, we are interested in how certain
properties of a system vary in time, and from one part of a system to
another, and how one system affects another.

5. DISCUSSION

Our goals automatically restrict the allowable ways of describing systems.
If we use too few numbers to specify the state, we may find that accurate
prediction is not possible on the basis of the available data. If we introduce

too many numbers, the description may become unmanageable in terms of time and effort required to gather and use these numbers and, thus, again is useless for predictive purposes. A narrow path, then, must be followed between oversimplification and overcomplication. It is a path, unfortunately, much more visible to hindsight than foresight. The point we wish to emphasize is that the history of science shows that it is not at all easy to provide meaningful, useful quantitative descriptions of systems. Qualitative descriptions are equally difficult to provide. If this is true of inanimate systems, it holds even more forcefully for animate and human systems.

6. OBSERVABLES

The study of a particular system begins with the observation of the system and an attendant quantitative or qualitative appraisal of individual properties of the system. Thus, for example, we can measure the temperature of a gas, the position of a satellite, the output per week of an automobile factory. We can also note the external responses of a patient to various questions, of both verbal and nonverbal type. Properties of this nature we call *observable*. Ideally, we would like to base a theory explaining the behavior of a system solely on observables. In general, we cannot.

It is usually necessary to introduce certain properties of the system which cannot be directly observed or measured. For example, we can think in terms of the internal temperature of the earth, the acceleration of a satellite, the efficiency of the labor force at a factory, or the frame of mind of a patient. Some of the foregoing are "real" but unobservable at our present level of ability to measure; some are merely useful intellectual constructs. On the whole, we attempt to "think loose", and not make a fetish out of a particular philosophy. As Lewis Carroll's Humpty Dumpty pointed out to Alice, "The question is, which is to be master—that's all."

In any case, it is not generally easy to define precisely what is meant by a "real property". Often we become so familiar with a concept that it assumes a reality independent of any tangible physical basis.*

7. INFLUENCE-RESPONSE ANALYSIS

In some cases the internal structure of the system is so complex that we renounce for the moment the possibility of any description of the state of the system or any use for this description if we possessed one. From the beginning we accept the idea that we will describe the system solely in terms of its observed behavior, the set of its responses to a prescribed set of influences (see Figure 2).

_____
* Consider, for example, gravity. See Section 37.

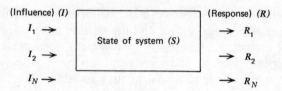

Figure 4.2
Description of a System

In the foregoing we wish to indicate that the input I_1 yields the response R_1, the input I_2 yields the response R_2, and so forth.

Let us note that the entire set of influences and responses need not be expressed in terms of numbers. One set may be expressed numerically and the other not, or some influences and some responses may be expressed qualitatively and the others quantitatively.

This conception of a system views it as defined by a set of couples $[I_1, R_1]$, $[I_2, R_2], \ldots, [I_N, R_N]$. In the fields of econometrics and engineering, this is called "input-output" analysis. As recognition of the fact that we possess no understanding of the internal structure and mechanisms of the system, we occasionally call a system of this nature a "black box".

In many important cases the inputs and responses are not individual quantities, but vectors. Sometimes many inputs will yield a single response; sometimes a single input will yield a multiple response.

A basic and continuing scientific problem is that of ascertaining possible structures and mechanisms that will account for the observed influence-response pairs. This is the "as if" property mentioned earlier. We will return to this interesting occupation below. Ultimately, of course, we would like to obtain a more satisfying description. But it usually turns out that quite simplified descriptions serve useful ends in carefully chosen situations.

8. INFLUENCE-STATE ANALYSIS

In a number of important cases, there is no immediate response, or output, when the system is subjected to an influence, or input. The effect of the influence is solely to change the state of the system.

The system may in this case be described by the sets of pairs $[I_1, S_1]$, $\ldots, [I_N, S_N]$. By this we mean that we observe that the effect of the influence I_1 is to convert the system into state s_1, that of I_2 to convert it into S_2, and so forth (see Figure 3).

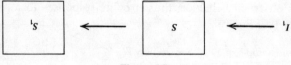

Figure 4.3

9. STATE-DEPENDENT INFLUENCE RESPONSE ANALYSIS

In general, the foregoing descriptions are not adequate. We soon observe that most often the response of a system to a particular influence depends crucially upon the current state of the system, as well as upon the influence. For example, the response of a patient to a question, or action, of the therapist can hinge to a large extent upon the frame of mind of the patient, the length of time he has been in therapy, and other factors of current influence.

Hence we enlarge the previous influence-response pair, $[I, R]$, to a triple $[I, S, R]$. This contains the information that when the system is in state S, its response is R to the influence I (see Figure 4).

Figure 4.4

We must now go one step further. The effect of the influence upon the system is to produce a response, R, and in addition to alter the original state, S (see Figure 5). The triple $[I, S, R]$ is thus replaced by a quadruple $[I, S; R, S_1]$ which provides us with the desired information that a system in state S, subject to an influence (input) I, produces a response (output) R, and is transformed into a new state S_1.

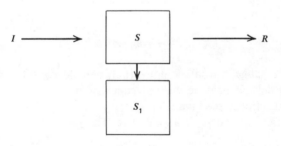

Figure 4.5

This formulation includes all of the previous cases, which we can retrieve by ignoring either the state or the response.

10. PROCESS

The foregoing enables us to provide a precise definition of another important term used in the previous chapters. We say that the quadruple

$[I, S; R, S_1]$ defines a *process*. In any particular case, the task is to identify the set of allowable states, the set of external influences, and the set of responses, and finally the correlations.

There are many processes associated with any system, determined by the specific properties under examination and the particular mathematical description employed. We can consider then that a *system* is the set of all its associated processes.

11. INTERACTIONS BETWEEN SYSTEMS

We have hinted by use of some of the illustrative examples that it may be useful in a study of psychotherapy to regard the patient as a system.

Observe carefully that we are not saying that he *is* a system of conventional, or even unconventional, scientific type, but that it may be useful in certain contexts to regard some of the influence-response behavior *as if* he were. This "as if" attitude is a key to the application of the mathematical method.

There are, however, two people present in a psychotherapeutic session, the patient and the therapist. In order to provide a fuller explanation of some aspects of the psychiatric process, we must introduce the further concept of two interacting systems, that of the therapist and that of the patient (see Figure 6).

Figure 4.6

Each interchange, verbal or nonverbal, can be considered to result in responses which change the current states of both systems, as well as to cause some reactions (see Figure 7).

The situation, of course, is asymmetric. The patient's effect on the thera-

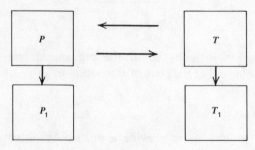

Figure 4.7

pist is different in some important ways from the effect of the therapist on the patient. This interaction process basic to our further work will be discussed in some detail in Chapter 6. We have already discussed various aspects in Chapter 3.

12. MULTISTAGE PROCESSES—I

In most significant situations, we are interested in processes in which a system undergoes changes over time. The structures we have already constructed enable us to study the behavior of a system subject to a succession of influences $I_1, I_2, \ldots, I_N$ (see Figure 8).

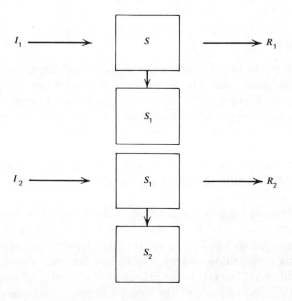

Figure 4.8

Given the sequence of influences $I_1, I_2, \ldots, I_N$, where the order is the order of the events in time, the initial state S, and the set of quadruples $[I, S; R, S_1]$, we can predict the sequence of responses $R_1, R_2, \ldots, R_N$ and the final state of the system.

This is the classical approach to the study of systems. As usual in science, the guiding idea is simple, but its implementation need not be.

13. MULTISTAGE PROCESSES—II

Sometimes we are engaged in an examination of what happens when a particular input is sent through a succession of systems shown in Figure 9.

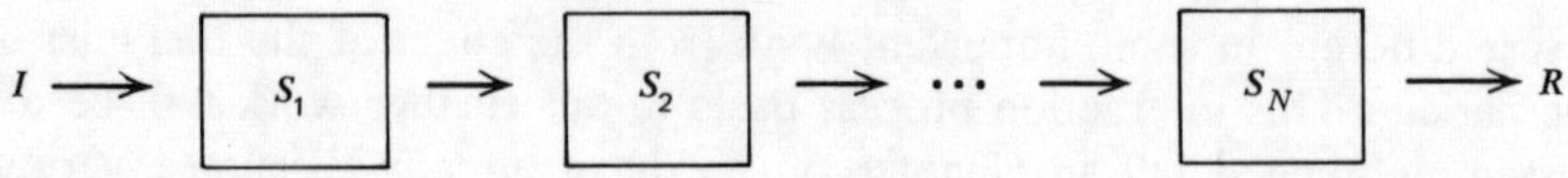

$$I \longrightarrow \boxed{S_1} \longrightarrow \boxed{S_2} \longrightarrow \cdots \longrightarrow \boxed{S_N} \longrightarrow R$$

Figure 4.9

For example, a patient in a hospital or community clinic, the "input" in this case, may be subjected to a series of medical examinations, one after the other. The final result R is a diagnosis followed by treatment. We mention this second type of process in passing since we focus on what follows only on multistage processes over time of the type described in the previous section.

14. THEORY

As a large number of influence-response pairs, and more generally quadruples, are gathered, results of continuing observation and planned experiment, questions begin to arise concerning the internal mechanisms of the system, S. This is not solely a matter of scientific curiosity. If the set of $I - R$ pairs begins to expand enormously in number, it becomes increasingly awkward first to store these data, and then to retrieve and display them, much less to interpret them. We need some economical ways of presenting the accumulated data if we want to make effective applications of our study of the system.

This intellectual frugality is accomplished by use of a theory. Theory, however, turns out to be much more than a local mnemonic device. A theory constructed to handle one system can often be extended to handle many systems with analogous features. Theory becomes a tool for the discovery of additional facts. It is the existence of a number of global theories of this nature which represents the signal triumph of science over nature.

Thus, for example, we can expect theories of human behavior which will allow the uniform treatment of patients with problems linked by common characteristics.

15. INTERNAL STRUCTURE

If we can endow the system with a suitable internal structure, we should be able to predict in advance the response resulting from a certain influence, as well as the change in state, on the basis of certain well-defined interactions occurring in simpler component systems. Our ambition then is to decompose S into subsystems of known behavior as indicated in Figure 10.

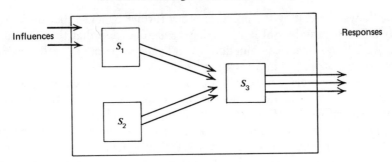

Figure 4.10

Having obtained this first level of decomposition, we can pose the same problem for the individual systems S_1, S_2, and S_3. We attempt to continue in this fashion until we encounter subsystems which do not permit further decomposition in terms of the theoretical concepts and experimental techniques we presently possess, or until the complexity of internal structure poses problems beyond our current intellectual or computational capacities. These are three quite different kinds of complexity.

This means that we must operate on a phenomenological level as far as certain subsystems are concerned. In every scientific study of a system there is a point in which all that can be said is that a subsystem operates in a certain fashion as far as the influence-response pairs is concerned. We naturally try to delay this admission as long as possible. But the point must be made that logical reasoning, based essentially upon accumulated experience, can be used only up to a certain point. Past that point all we can assert is that this is the way things are.

16. UNDERSTANDING VERSUS MODEL-MAKING

We have stated in the foregoing sections that one aspect of understanding the behavior of a system is that of being able to ascertain how it will change over time and how it will react to specified stimuli or external influences. If, however, we do possess a simple mechanism for accomplishing these objectives, can we assert that we understand the true nature of the system?

One hundred years ago, perhaps even as recently as 60 years ago, a number of scientists would have unhesitatingly given an affirmative answer. As a consequence of a number of simple concepts (such as the inverse-square law of gravitational attraction due to Newton and the equations of Maxwell in electromagnetic theory) that had proved remarkably successful in unifying complex sets of phenomena, many felt that these generalizations were "laws" regulating the universe. They further believed that there were only a few such universal laws, perhaps even one, and that these could be discovered by some combination of diligent experiment and brilliant research and expressed in precise mathematical terms.

The contemporary scientist is far more cautious. Increasingly, experiment and observation reveal a seemingly capricious side to the character of the natural world. He is willing to accept on faith the proposition that he can find reasonably simple mechanisms for the prediction of any particular set of phenomena—granted a sufficient amount of time and effort. He is reasonably confident that he can construct models of reality that behave in all current observable ways as if each were the actual physical system.

But he is now philosophically and psychologically prepared to discard any existing hypothetical structure whenever additional experimental data exhibit sharp enough disagreement between theory and observation. In general, these "incorrect" models are not discarded totally but are used in a selective fashion with various corrections for the known inaccuracies.

Increasingly, science shies away from the words "true" and "real". Nonetheless, scientists continue their dogged search for regularity in nature. There is both tangible reward and emotional comfort in superimposing simplicity upon complexity and order upon chaos. One can construct a plausible argument tracing the gradual development of science from primitive magic and religion in terms of this continued effort. That a great deal of order exists is obvious; that reality, whatever it is, is always understandable on the basis of existing concepts is a different matter. Furthermore, it is not clear that certain aspects of reality will ever be more understandable.

The new significant feature in science is that of accepting the concept of levels of understanding. We must face some of these matters squarely if we wish to treat complex processes.

17. CAUSE AND EFFECT

In what has preceded, we have considered systems with the property that a specific input produced a specific output. They were further characterized by the fact that the future history of the system was completely determined by the present state and the nature of the external influences. We call a system of this type *deterministic*. Equivalently, we say that the property of cause and effect holds.

Subsequently, we shall discuss some of the questions connected with systems in which this property does not hold. These are by far the most important types of systems in studies of the nature we are pursuing.

18. QUANTITATIVE QUESTIONS

We began with the modest objective of accumulating influence-response pairs for various systems. With each success we naturally become bolder and a bit more ambitious. Eventually, we find ourselves asking quite detailed questions and obtaining equally intricate answers. How then do we avoid being inundated by $[I, S:S_1, R]$ quadruples? How does science withstand success?

Let us give two examples of facts we might gather. It has long been clear that putting a pot full of water over a fire would result in the water becoming hotter, and that taking it away from the flame would result in a gradual cooling. It was also clear that the heating and cooling proceeded in a steady fashion, with increasing and decreasing temperatures, respectively. Another fact also readily noted was that a stone thrown into the sky would initially rise, reach a maximum height, and then fall back to earth. Having this level of theoretical sophistication in the fields of thermodynamics and mechanics, we could ask more searching questions such as:

1. How long after the water has come to a boil, and then been removed from the flame, must we wait before placing a hand in the water to remove an egg?
2. If we throw a stone straight up, at what point should we remember to step aside?

Observe that the original qualitative observations have been superseded by questions of a quantitative nature.

19. EXPERIMENTAL METHOD

Questions of this nature can be answered partially or completely on the basis of experimentation. Why then bother with a theory?

There are some immediate answers. The first question introduces certain subjective elements such as tolerance of heat and pain. As previously pointed out, a certain amount of quantitative research on pain has been carried out. Nevertheless, no satisfying scale currently exists. It may then be better to compartmentalize the research into an investigation of the dependence of the temperature of the water on time and the size and heat of the flame, and a separate investigation of the ability to remove objects from hot water by hand.

The point we are getting to is that an experiment need not be an easy process to carry out, and we may wish to consider different parts of a question in different ways. Without careful planning, it is not always clear what is being measured and to what degree of accuracy. Perhaps the simplest statement is that there can be no measurement without an underlying theory, no experiment without some conceptual basis. Any accumulation of data presupposes a theoretical foundation, unfortunately often implicit rather than explicit.

20. ACCUMULATION OF DATA

Let us consider the second question, where the experimentation seems easier to carry out. It appears reasonable to suppose that the time required for the stone to return to earth will depend upon the velocity with which the stone is thrown upward. Let us suppose that careful experimentation has provided the table of values shown in Table 1.

Table 1

Upward Velocity, ft/sec	Time to Return, sec
10	0.625
20	1.250
30	1.875
40	2.500
50	3.125
60	3.750

Presumably we can also determine the return time when the launching velocity is 37.6 ft/sec, 53.4 ft/sec, and so on. But what do we do with all the data we accumulate in this fashion? It is clear that continued experimentation will inundate us with data. This deluge of numbers will make it impossible to store, retrieve, and use individual facts in any convenient fashion. We continue our stern operational attitude: only data that can be used, in a meaningful sense, exist.

21. THE MATHEMATICAL METHOD

It is at this point that mathematics begins to assume its major role in science. By means of mathematical formulae we can express succinctly the content of many scientific concepts and observations. The essence of countless experiments and complex analyses can thus be stored in capsulated form; mathematics in this role may thus be considered an intellectual shorthand. A formula may be considered to be a form of dehydrated experience, a means of conveniently recording, storing, and retrieving significant data and ideas.

The reader, for example, may have noticed that the time of return to earth in Table 1 is obtained in each case from the upward velocity by dividing by 16. This simple rule eliminates the necessity for extensive, rarely used, hard-to-remember numerical tables such as Table 1.

Similarly, the tremendous mass of astronomical data accumulated by Tycho Brahe was condensed by Kepler into the famous three laws of motion. The existence of these simple rules in turn stimulated Newton to find a still simpler rule, and then a methodology, from which they could all be deduced.

22. EXTRAPOLATION AND DISCOVERY

This brings us to one of the most important applications of the mathematical method: the extrapolation from the known to the unknown. So far we have traced the following path:

a. Problem recognition
b. Scientific formulation
c. Scientific description
d. Accumulation of observations
e. Scientific rules
f. Mathematical rules

Once we have attained the last stage, we can often predict behavior which is not easily observed experimentally, or even obtainable at all. For example, once we see the way the numbers in Table 1 are related, we can readily predict the time for a projectile with an upward velocity of 1000 ft/sec to return to earth.* This could have been accomplished long before any method capable of achieving a velocity of this magnitude was available. Furthermore, long before powerful rockets were built, there was no difficulty in calculating the velocity required to escape from the earth's gravitational field.

By means of manipulation with mathematical formulae, which is to say by exploring the logical consequences of these formulae, according to established mathematical rules, we can gain insight into many recondite physical processes. This mathematical experimentation leads to physical experimentation, which produces new data for more extensive mathematical theories, which suggest new experiments, and so on. Mathematics thus provides vicarious experience, an experience which need not unfold in real time, in real space—or with real people. Naturally, any such experience must be carefully and closely examined to make sure that it furnishes help in treating actual problems. We have pointed out above that there is nothing simple about the use of theory and we shall return to this theme.

---

* An idealized projectile, of course.

23. DISCUSSION

We wish to pursue a similar, if far more modest, path in the field of psycho-therapy, constructing certain mathematical models of human interaction which will enable us to test, modify, and, hopefully, improve various existing concepts and techniques. If the history of scientific exploration in other areas is any guide, we can anticipate that something of value will emerge.

Particularly important is the idea that we may be able to carry out experimentation in this area without the risk of using untried techniques on actual patients.

24. DIGITAL COMPUTERS

It turns out that the mathematical descriptions of physical systems we currently possess require both ingenuity and vast amounts of tedious arithmetic if we wish to use them to derive numerical results. These results are necessary both for application and investigation of the validity of existing concepts. A tremendous amount of effort has been expended by some of the most distinguished mathematicians and scientists of the last 300 years to replace and augment arithmetic ability using various mathematical artifices, devices, stratagems, and tours de force. Some impressive victories have been recorded, but the fact remains: large-scale arithmetic is hard to do.

Consequently, up until about 20 years ago, the type of mathematical experimentation described in the foregoing section could not readily be carried out in any extensive fashion. Since a realistic description of a physical process required a complicated mathematical formulation which could not, in general, be handled either by the aid of an explicit solution or by means of a reasonable algorithm for a computational solution, the scientist was forced either to use simplified descriptions which very often made no allowance for essential features of the physical system under study, or to condemn himself to the penance of prolonged arithmetical calculation.

It was thus both frustrating and time-consuming. Astronomers would spend years calculating, rather than thinking. The great Euler went blind in the course of some detailed astronomical computations. The equally great Gauss spent three months on the calculations of an orbit that would today require a few hours of preliminary effort and a few minutes, at most, on a contemporary computer.

The computer has revolutionized man's capacity to do arithmetic and, in consequence, revolutionized the scientific world. It has freed mankind from the tyranny of arithmetic. This means that for the first time in history we are truly in a position to explore the universe of the mind.

A digital computer may be characterized as a device with the following characteristics:

1. It can store large quantities of numbers to be used at assigned times in predetermined calculations.

2. It can carry out certain types of logical operations according to stored instructions.

3. It can perform the elementary operations of arithmetic, addition, subtraction, multiplication, and division rapidly and accurately. It can compare two numbers, and tell which is greater.

4. It can follow instructions to perform unbounded sequences of these operations in any specified order, and stop according to preassigned instructions.

How these tasks are carried out using electrical, mechanical, or pneumatic components is an interesting story in itself. Let us merely accept the fact that devices exist that can operate in the fashion described. Subsequently, we shall return to some analysis of these statements which barely portray the remarkable abilities of the digital computer. We will then examine far more sophisticated uses for computers connected with decision-making and learning which enable us to probe deeply into the mysteries of human intelligence.

In a subsequent chapter, we shall say a few more words about the basic properties of the digital computer. Although we shall not do any arithmetic, we shall do a great deal of manipulation of non-numerical data, an area in which the computer is equally outstanding.

25. DOES THE METHOD REALLY WORK?

It all sounds too good to be true. We began with cautionary comments concerning the complexity of the cosmos, and we conclude with a cornucopia of kudos for the mathematical method superimposed upon the scientific method. Surely there are some inconsistencies, some unpleasant realities being swept under the ubiquitous rug.

Is it actually possible to use simple, or even complicated, mathematical formulae to predict physical occurrences? As might be expected, it all depends critically upon the particular phenomena we choose to analyze. It cannot be overemphasized that the successes of science, as in engineering and technology, depend crucially upon the objectives. Enormous, overwhelming success in some areas such as astronomy and spectroscopy contrasts with results far less striking to date in other areas: for example, weather prediction and the analyses of biological systems.

Let us return to the stone-throwing experiment to illustrate these remarks. If we were to step outside with a stopwatch with access to some mechanism for hurling stones into the air, say a ballista, and actually time the descent of the stone, we would in all probability find serious disagreements with the numbers of Table 1.

What are some reasons for this?

26. IDEALIZED SYSTEMS

In order to appreciate some of the causes of the easily noted disagreement between theory and experiment in this case, it is necessary to examine carefully the origins of the theoretical results cited in Section 19. If our objective, for example, is to find the time at which a stone hurled into the air with a given velocity returns to earth, we begin by constructing an *idealized system*, some approximate picture of the actual situation.

We assume, among other things, that:

a. The stone is a point particle.
b. The atmosphere is a vacuum.
c. The earth is flat.
d. Newtonian mechanics can be used in the description of motion.

An important consequence of the first assumption is that the shape of the stone is ignored, as well as any possible spin that it possesses as a consequence of the way it was hurled into the air. We know, however, that no two stones possess the same shape, unless we have carefully ensured this in advance. This automatically means a lack of complete reproducibility of any particular experiment with actual stones in their native habitat.

Let us note parenthetically that this lack of reproducibility is one of the bugaboos of the social sciences. All human beings are individuals, complex systems with varying characteristics which change over time. What then can we deduce about one individual from observation of others? What can we deduce about his behavior at one time in terms of his behavior at other times? We shall return to this essential point in Section 37. Meanwhile, let us continue to examine some difficulties in dealing with the inanimate.

The assumption that the atmosphere is a vacuum means that there is no atmosphere and no wind. The third and fourth assumptions combined with the first two permit us to deduce the results of Table 1.

It is clear from this discussion that it would be surprising, and very suspicious indeed, if any experiment involving real falling bodies yielded agreement with the numbers obtained from such crude assumptions. Generally speaking, we should distrust theories that predict too much, or agree too well with observation. We don't know that much about real systems to enjoy that much success. We can usually conclude that a simplified system is being examined, or that the theory has been constructed specifically to fit the particular set of facts.

27. DIRECTIONS OF RESEARCH

Stimulated by the foregoing, we can contemplate two major directions of research. The first is an exploration of ways of creating artificial laboratory conditions under which idealized systems can be examined and studied in detail. This will enable us to test various concepts in preparation for a study of more realistic systems. The second is an exploration of different ways of modifying the original idealized systems to achieve behavior which will coincide more closely with observed behavior.

We shall describe in later chapters techniques for accomplishing both types of tasks in connection with the mathematical models we construct of psychotherapy interactions.

The question we wish to raise here is that of the value, if any, of the investigation of simplified processes, particularly if our goals are to be operational. Is this study of simplified systems and approximate theories meaningful? All too often, we encounter an attitude which is best described by the following story.

It seems that a man walking along the street one evening saw another man on his hands and knees looking for something under a lamppost. "Can I help you?" he inquired.

"Oh, yes," said the other, "I lost a ring down the street."

"Why, then, are you looking here?"

"It's lighter here," was the reply.

28. AN EXAMPLE OF USEFUL SIMPLICITY

Before any further discussion of the cogent question posed above, which must be honestly acknowledged, let us give an example of a simple description which has proved extremely useful. It is important to provide illustrations of this nature to counter a uniform pattern of objection that occurs whenever it is proposed to use mathematical methods in a field in which mathematical methods are not traditional.

Since any real system is clearly so much more complex than any proposed idealized system, is it not true that any effort expended on analysis of an idealized system is a waste of time? The first part of the question concerning the complexity of reality is certainly valid; the interpretation of the question is not.

Take the problem of predicting an eclipse of the sun by the moon. We may begin by drawing a diagram showing the location of the sun, earth, and moon, with the moon blocking the sun—a simple representation of an eclipse (see Figure 11).

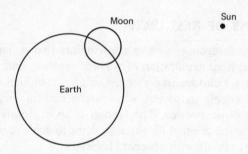

Figure 4.11

Next with the aid of straightforward Newtonian mechanics, regarding the earth, moon, and sun as point particles, we can calculate how long it will take the earth and moon to achieve this configuration, given their present positions in space. In this way, it turns out that we can quite accurately predict the date of the next eclipse.

Yet the sun is clearly not a point fixed in space, nor is the earth a point particle moving in a plane in an elliptical orbit with the sun as one focus, nor the moon a point particle moving in an eclipse about the earth. All three bodies are huge inhomogeneous masses of material with small irregular motions superimposed on much more regular motions. The earth and moon are reasonably solid, while the sun is completely gaseous. Furthermore, we make extensive use of the intellectually absurd idea of action at a distance* in considering a gravitational force, a hypothesis of such strange nature that it quite sensibly prevented the acceptance of Newtonian mechanics for many years after Newton's death. As a matter of fact, it seriously disturbed Newton himself, despite its obvious operational success. Nonetheless, for the purposes of explaining an eclipse, insofar as being able to predict its occurrence, and for many other objectives, the foregoing idealized system is remarkably effective.

On the other hand, explanations of many other celestial phenomena require far more complicated models of the planetary system. It is the same

---

* This is a well known myth which is an example of the limitation of rationality in science.

in every field; there are levels of complexity of phenomena, levels of complexity of model systems, and levels of scientific success. We learn by experience how to use specific models and theories for specific purposes.

29. NETWORKS AND HIERARCHIES OF SYSTEMS

The essential point of all of this, a point we have previously emphasized, is that a contemporary scientist does not try at all costs to construct a single global model of reality. He assumes on the basis of experience that such a model cannot be used to provide answers to all possible questions concerning the behavior of all physical systems. He has learned over time that it may be preferable to construct a network of local models, perhaps of comparable complexity, but almost certainly of entirely different structure. Each local model may then be located in a hierarchy of a family of models of increasing complexity.

As an example of the vast difference in structure that can occur, let us note in the field of physics that the theories of quantum mechanics and relativity are based upon fundamentally different ideas of space and time. Yet, each works remarkably well in carefully chosen areas, with a certain natural confusion occurring where there is overlap and concurrent use is required. Nonetheless, the physicist has learned to live with this logical ambiguity.

It is conceivable that it is possible to construct a single mathematical edifice, a "unified theory", which can be used, at least theoretically, to answer all scientific questions. Practically, operationally, it turns out to be impossible. The complexity of nature requires a different type of simplicity of thought.

How then does the scientist know which model of reality to use for which purpose? How, for example, does he know whether different conceptual and mathematical models are logically and philosophically consistent, and what does he do when they are not, which is often the case? These are interesting and important questions to which we shall devote a little time and space below, but with no pretense to a detailed discussion.

30. HIDDEN VARIABLES

So far we have assumed that a specific influence produces a definite response or, equivalently, that the state of a system at some time in the future is completely determined by its current state and external influences. A system of this type we have dubbed *deterministic*. It is reasonable to begin with systems of this nature in the study of physical processes.

On the other hand, we observe all about us systems which produce sometimes one response and sometimes another response when apparently subjected to the same influence in the same state. There are several ways of treating phenomena of this nature conceptually.

To begin with, we can suppose that there are hidden variables. By this we mean that a system which appeared to be in the same state at the times when exposed to these two influences actually differed in certain of its fundamental properties. Secondly, we can suppose that the influences which appeared to be the same actually weren't. These properties which we cannot discern at the moment are called *hidden variables* or unobservables. It is clearly not very satisfactory philosophically to base a theory on properties of this type, yet we must face experimental facts.

31. INDETERMINISM

To avoid this philosophical objection, we can make an assumption which is equally objectionable, but on other philosophical grounds. We renounce determinism and assert that the nature of the system is such that the response is *not* uniquely determined by the influence of the state (see Figure 12).

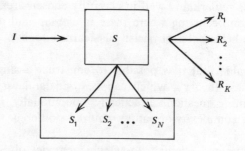

Figure 4.12

What the foregoing figure indicates is that when a system in state S is subject to an influence I, sometimes its response is R_1, sometimes R_2, . . . , sometimes R_K, and that sometimes its transforms into state S_1, sometimes into S_2, . . . , sometimes into S_N.

The task that confronts us is that of providing some type of precise mathematical structure to handle the word "sometimes".

32. DISCUSSION

As might be expected, there are serious difficulties associated with the rejection of cause and effect. Indeed, this abdication strikes at the very heart of the notion of a well-ordered universe and represents a serious blow to the idea of control over our environment. Needless to add, the surrender of the basic concept of cause and effect is made neither lightly, nor totally, not forever.

We have emphasized the serious difficulties associated with the application of the scientific method in the real world. Some approaches face difficulties of one type, some of another type. This means that we may have to make costly ideological concessions of various types in order to accomplish certain tasks. We have already made one in renouncing any immediate plans for a single unified theory.

Progress consists of a careful analysis of the failures of existing theories. Carried out properly, this is a process leading to the construction of more effective theories. We never lose faith, however, in the rational approach, even if we are led to nonintuitive theories. Indeed, these new theories alter our view of what the terms "rational" and "intuition" mean.

33. COMPLEXITY REPLACED BY UNCERTAINTY

An example commonly used to demonstrate uncertainty, the tossing of a coin, illustrates a conceptual device of fundamental scientific import, one that is frequently used in many scientific investigations. If we think about it for a moment, the tossing of a coin is a fine example of a deterministic process. On the basis of the laws of mechanics, we should be able to predict the ultimate position of a coin given sufficient information concerning its initial position, the way in which it was thrown into the air, and the composition of the floor which determines how it bounces.

Abstractly, this prediction is possible in the sense that it is conceivable. In actuality, it is far too difficult a problem for contemporary science. As a matter of fact, a detailed examination on the basis of current scientific ideas (i.e., those of quantum mechanics) makes it plausible that the problem cannot be solved. We cannot determine the outcome of a single toss of a coin in any way short of carrying out the actual experiment.

We cut this Gordian knot of complexity by introducing the concept of uncertainty, and changing some of our objectives. We renounce cause and effect in any single toss of the coin and settle for a different type of physical law.

34. STOCHASTIC SYSTEM

In place of the original model of reality, a deterministic system of quite complicated structure, we consider a system with partial determinism of much simpler structure. A system in which some aspects of determinism are restored by means of the regularity of probability theory is called *stochastic*.

35. INFLUENCE-RESPONSE MODEL OF
A STOCHASTIC SYSTEM

Let us now describe precisely the type of stochastic process of primary interest to us. We consider as before the quadruple $[I, S; R, S_1]$ with the difference that there are now a set of possible responses, $R_1, R_2, \ldots, R_K$, and a set of possible new states $S_1, S_2, \ldots, S_L$, associated with each influence. The situation is represented schematically in Figure 13.

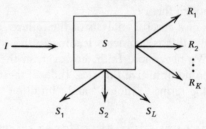

Figure 4.13

As a result of the influence I, when the system is in state S, we observe one of the allowable responses, $R_1, R_2, \ldots, R_K$ and one of the new states, $S_1, S_2, \ldots, S_L$.

36. EXAMPLE

To illustrate the foregoing, let us anticipate a bit and consider the patient as a system where S denotes his state of mind, and I (the influence) a question, or other response, of the therapist. We allow two consequences of this, a reaction of some type on the part of the patient P_R and a change in his state of mind.

It is certainly reasonable to expect that the new state of mind can be the same as before; that is to say, no change is a possible result. Furthermore, the patient's response need not be observable. Consistent with this is the idea that no action on the part of the therapist is a perfectly allowable influence from our point of view. As a matter of fact, it can produce significant effects. We shall examine this crucial point again in the next chapter, which is devoted to decision-making.

In general, responses by the therapist will produce responses by the patient. However, we do not insist that these be uniquely determined in the mathematical model we construct.

37. AVERAGE BEHAVIOR

One way to overcome the frustration of uncertainty is to introduce the concept of *average behavior*. Instead of concentrating on an individual event, we examine a set of events. If a system behaves in some satisfactory fashion in some overall sense, we may then be willing to accept its performance despite occasional lapses.

For example, we may describe an individual in terms of his average behavior over time, or a social system at any time in terms of the average behavior of its members. Once we accept the idea of average behavior as a basis for description, we see that processes involving uncertainty over a long period of time, or involving many different individual systems, may be far easier to treat both conceptually and analytically than those involving a small number of interactions.

To make the idea of average behavior precise, let us introduce some elementary notions of probability.

38. COIN-TOSSING

To illustrate some important ideas simply, let us again consider the tossing of a coin. As previously pointed out, we possess no theoretical approach at present capable of handling the accurate prediction of a coin landing heads or tails when tossed.

Nonetheless, we do have confidence in our ability to predict a certain regularity in the behavior of the coin when a large number of tosses is made. If the coin is a fair coin (one with no particular predilection for heads or tails on a given toss), and if a large number of tosses are made, the number of heads observed will approximately equal the number of tails.

This counting, or frequency, approach enables us to introduce the concept of probability. We say in the foregoing case that the probability that heads will occur is one-half. Clearly, we are evaluating the probability of heads by taking the ratio of the number of heads occurring to the total number of tosses made. This is an intuitive notion of probability that is both reasonable and psychologically satisfying. It can readily be extended to far more general situations.

39. DISCUSSION

Unfortunately, despite this appeal, the foregoing approach possesses serious drawbacks which any analysis immediately discloses. As a matter of fact, we deliberately sprinkled about words like "predilection", "large", and "approximately" to alert the reader to certain ambiguities and lack of precision. For example, if we toss a coin 10,000 times and observe 6,000 heads and 4,000 tails, do we immediately conclude that the coin is not fair, or do we accept the possibility that this could be a most unusual set of tosses for a fair coin? Can we even perform experiments with complex systems which yield the data we want? For example, can one be sure that a coin tossed a second time is in the same condition as it was in the first toss? As was pointed out some time ago, one never steps into the same stream twice —the question of reproducibility again. We shall return to this point in connection with our model of the initial interview.

Faced with these, and many other perplexing questions connected with real systems, the mathematician takes refuge in axiomatics. He creates a mathematical theory of probability, abstract in the same way that geometry with its points and lines is abstract, but meaningful in the same way that its axioms, like the axioms of geometry, were carefully chosen on the basis of experience.

It now requires considerable skill on the part of the physical and social scientist to match the simplicity and elegance of the abstract system to the complexity and crudeness of reality. We repeat the point that the successful use of mathematical systems in the real world is basically an art, an art that can be considerably enhanced by knowledge and experience, but always fundamentally an art.

Some of the ideas of the theory of probability will be employed in what follows, with full awareness that it provides only partial answers to the many questions raised by uncertainty. The concepts, however, are extremely useful for the purposes we have in mind, and particularly for preliminary theories.

40. PROBABILITIES OF OCCURRENCE

To begin with, Figure 13 is replaced by Figure 14.

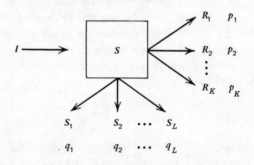

Figure 4.14

This new schematic indicates that when there is an influence I on the system in state S, response R_1 occurs with probability p_1, R_2 with probability p_2, ..., the new state is S_1 with probability q_1, S_2 with probability q_2, ..., and so on.

41. MULTISTAGE STOCHASTIC PROCESS

With the aid of the set of responses associated with a given influence and the set of resultant states, we can define what we mean by a multistage stochastic process; I_1 produces R_{1i} and state S_{1i}; I_2 produces R_{2j} and state S_{2j}; and so on, with associated probabilities. The process is now repeated. We can imagine more generally that the influence can be partially deterministic and partially stochastic.

We use the word stochastic rather than random to avoid confusion with the ordinary English meaning of the word random—i.e., subject to no rules at all. On the contrary, a stochastic process must obey strict laws of regularity on the average.

42. CONCLUSION

In the foregoing pages we have presented some of the basic ideas concerning the use of the mathematical concept of a system and have discussed some of the questions arising in the study of real systems. We were concerned not only with the concepts themselves but with some of the interactions of these idealized concepts with reality.

In the following chapter we show how these ideas can be used to study processes involving decision-making. There we will have to study deeper types of uncertainty.

NOTES AND REFERENCES

1. More detailed discussion of the topics of this chapter with many additional references will be found in
   R. Bellman, 1961, *op. cit.*
   particularly Chapters IX, XV, and XVI.

4. For a scientific inquiry into the methods of psychoanalysis, see
   R. Wallerstein, "The Role of Prediction in Theory Building in Psychoanalysis", *J. Amer. Psychoanalytic Assn.*, Vol. 12(4), October 1964, pp. 675–691.

7. Some interesting research viewing human beings as information processing and physical energy transforming systems is found in
   F. Redlich and D. Freedman, 1966, *op. cit.*
   and also in
   C. Shannon and W. Weaver, *The Mathematical Theory of Communication*, Urbana, Illinois, University of Illinois Press, 1964.

11. A particularly interesting treatment of general system theory applied to psychotherapy is:
L. von Bertalanffy, "General System Theory and Psychiatry" (unpublished paper).

General system theory and organismic biology provided the basis for Karl Menninger's theory of psychiatry in
K. Menninger, et al., 1963, *op. cit.*

A number of other investigators give some aspect of general system theory a prominent role. Some of the more interesting are the following:
G. Allport, *Pattern and Growth in Personality,* New York, Holt, Rinehart and Winston, 1961.
D. Rapoport, "The Structure of Psychoanalytic Theory", *Psychological Issues,* Vol. 2, Monograph 6, 1960.
S. Arieti, "The Microgeny of Thought and Perception", *Archives of General Psychiatry,* Vol. 6, 1962, pp. 454–468.
D. Krech, "Dynamic Systems as Open Neurological Systems", *Psychological Review,* Vol. 57, 1950, pp. 283–290.
H. Lennard and A. Bernstein, *The Anatomy of Psychotherapy,* New York, Columbia University Press, 1960.
J. Miller, "Toward a General Theory for the Behavioral Sciences", *American Psychologist,* Vol. 10, 1955, pp. 513–531.
L. von Bertalanffy, "Theoretical Models in Biology and Psychology" in D. Krech and G. Klein, eds., *Theoretical Models and Personality Theory,* Durham, Duke University Press, 1952.
A. Scheflen, "Communication and Regulation in Psychotherapy", *Psychiatry,* Vol. 26(2), May 1963, pp. 126–136.
G. Bateson, Chapter 1 in N. McQuown, ed., *The Natural History of an Interview,* New York, Grune and Stratton, 1964.
J. Butler, L. Rice, and A. Wagstaff, "On Naturalistic Definition of Variables" in H. Strupp and L. Luborsky, eds., *Research in Psychotherapy,* Washington, Psychological Association, Inc., 1962.

14. A nice comment (source unknown) is that there are geniuses in all fields. Theory is their attempt to communicate their ideas.

16. J. B. S. Haldane states that the universe is not only stranger than we imagine, but most likely stranger than we can imagine.
See also
R. Bellman, "Mathematical Models of the Mind", *Mathematical Biosciences,* Vol. 1, 1967, pp. 287–304.

22. See
R. Bellman and P. Brock, 1960, *op. cit.*

23. See
R. Dawson, "Simulation in the Social Sciences", in H. Guetzkow, ed.,

Simulation in the Social Sciences, Englewood Cliffs, New Jersey, Prentice-Hall, 1962.

24. The human mind does possess remarkable abilities for doing arithmetic, but we don't understand them. For an amusing account of calculating prodigies, see
J. Bryan III, "Who Needs Computers?" *Horizon,* Vol. XII(2), 1970, pp. 46–47.

See
A. Marshall and H. Goldhamer, "An Application of Markov Processes to the Study of the Epidemiology of Mental Disease", *J. Amer. Stat. Assoc.,* Vol. 50, 1955, pp. 99–129.

39. In the area of nonquantitative investigations, the new concept of mathematical fuzziness introduced by Lotfi Zadeh will play an important role. See
L. Zadeh, "Fuzzy Sets", *Information and Control,* Vol. 8, 1965, pp. 338–353.
and the previous reference to Zadeh.
T. Kitagawa, "The Foundations of Statistics", *International Review of Philosophy of Knowledge,* Dialectica, Vol. 8, 1954, pp. 95–111.
L. Zadeh and R. Bellman, "Decision-Making in a Fuzzy Environment", *Management Sciences,* Vol. 17(4)B, 1970, 141–164.
J. Goguen, "L-fuzzy Sets", *J. Math. Anal. Appl.,* Vol. 18, 1967, pp. 145–174.
T. Kitagawa, *Successive Process of Statistical Inferences* (1), Kyushu Univ., Series A, 5, 1960, pp. 139–180.
T. Kitagawa, "The Logical Aspects of Successive Processes of Statistical Inferences and Controls", *Bulletin International Statist. Inst.,* 32 Session, 6, Tokyo, 1960.

Chapter 5

DECISION PROCESSES

1. INTRODUCTION

In the preceding chapter we have considered a traditional scientific approach to the study of the behavior of systems covering both deterministic and stochastic aspects. From this foundation, we will discuss along more contemporary lines some of the questions that arise when we are required to operate a particular system. This often means that we will wish to alter the behavior of a system in some fashion in order to make its performance more acceptable.

Our theme will be the feasible operation of systems set within the more general area of decision-making. A number of very interesting and sometimes quite perplexing problems arise in the course of this investigation. Some of these can be treated in a reasonably satisfying fashion on the basis of existing theory, particularly those associated with processes of deterministic nature. Those, however, involving decision-making under uncertainty are, as might be expected, more complex and subtle. Some will yield to determined effort, using existing theories. Many others require new concepts and new methods and represent genuinely new kinds of mathematical problems.

Decision-making, as well as the evaluation of alternatives available for decision-making, is a major educative aim of psychotherapy. The goal is to increase the patient's freedom by expanding the number of alternatives he has available for decision-making and action.

2. THE OPERATION OF SYSTEMS

Our prototype schematic shown in Figure 1 represents a system in state S subject to an influence I, transforming into a system in state S_1, and producing a response, R. The response and the new state will, in general, depend upon the old state and the influence.

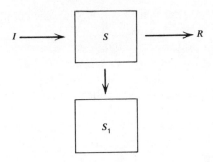

Figure 5.1

It is frequently the case that we are not as satisfied with either this new state or the response as we might be, and that we want to do something about this. We can contemplate pursuing several courses of action singly, or in tandem:

1. Eliminate, avoid, or suppress, the influences that lead to undesirable responses or states;
2. Alter the initial state of the system to produce a new state that reacts in a more desirable fashion to the prescribed set of influences;
3. Add additional influences to reinforce the desirable behavior and counteract, or neutralize, the undesirable behavior;
4. Modify the standards of behavior; in other words, redefine the criteria for desirable and undesirable behavior; i.e., compromise.

In dealing with any particular system, some combinations of all four approaches may be employed. Observe, that the four alternatives are clearly interconnected.

3. ALLERGIC REACTIONS

To illustrate the foregoing ideas let us consider the case of an individual suffering from allergies of various types.

Let us begin with the observation that it is often difficult to determine whether specific signs of distress are allergic in nature or not. This is part of the universal comment that it is seldom easy in the study of complex systems to isolate cause–and–effect or influence-response couples. After it has been accepted that allergies are to blame, it is a further problem to ascertain the principal offenders, the dust, pollen, cat-dander, and so forth, which may act as irritants. Let us assume, however, that the causes, which we can take as the influences on the human system, and the symptoms, which we may consider as the responses, have been systematically identified and isolated. The question that then arises is what should be done with this information?

To begin with, a policy of avoidance can be pursued. Certain foods can be omitted from the diet, allergy-free pillows can be used or air conditioners can be installed. Or, more drastic yet, the sufferer can leave for the seashore or the mountains whenever the pollen count in his vicinity indicates saturation.

Secondly, an immunization process can be inaugurated. By systematic injection of small amounts of the allergens over long periods of time, one can sometimes train, and thus bolster, the natural defenses of the body to the point where a seasonal onslaught of some particular substance can be withstood. The task of maintaining an appropriate threshold against irritants may be likened to that of building a dike.

We also know that there are strong links between physiological and psychological reactions, some psychosomatic and others somatopsychic. Hence, we can combine with the foregoing physiological treatment, some philosophic or psychological counseling which attempts to teach the patient to maintain a more equable temperament. It is well-known that a particular combination of allergens in the environment concomitant with a disturbed emotional state may trigger an allergic reaction such as an asthmatic seizure, for example.

Alternatively, rather than pursue the preceding paths, we can try to suppress the symptoms of allergic distress by the use of antihistamines, or, in more severe cases, steroids. In some cases, if an investigation of the causes and continuing treatment is too expensive or time-consuming to be acceptable, we may content ourselves with this sweeping under the rug technique.

A fourth approach involves education for the acceptance of a certain amount of pain and discomfort. The discomforts of asthma may be considerably allayed if the anxiety connected with a seizure is diminished, since anxiety itself tends to intensify the seizure. In addition, if an individual subscribes completely to the psychosomatic theory of allergies, he may decide to endure his afflictions while engaging in psychotherapy.

4. DISCUSSION

What we wish to indicate by the foregoing discussion is that the ways in which a control process is carried out depend critically both on the version of the process, the model, to which we subscribe and on the objectives that we have in mind. This is a characteristic feature of decision-making in the operation of systems.

Precise formulation of both the model and the objectives is essential if the result is to be meaningful.

5. CONTROL PROCESS

In place of Figure 1, let us use the diagram of Figure 2 to denote a control process. A *control process* in our terminology is thus determined by a quintuple $[I,S,C; S_1R]$. This is a brief way of saying that a system in state, S, subject to an influence, I, and a control action, C, is transformed into a state, S_1, while producing a response, R.

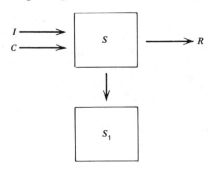

Figure 5.2

Let the set of possible control actions C_1, C_2, . . . , be specified. The problem we pose ourselves is that of choosing some appropriate control actions to ensure that the behavior of the system, subject to the influences, $I_1, I_2, . . .$, is more acceptable than it would be without the control.

As previously mentioned, we will consider only this particular type of control process here. There are many other classes of control processes as will be noted upon examining the cited references.

6. DECISION PROCESS

The choice of a control action necessarily requires a decision. We have already noted that a decision to do nothing is as meaningful, sometimes even more so, as a decision to do something.

We can consider a control process of the type described above as a particular kind of *decision process*. From our present standpoint there is no difference mathematically between a control process and a decision process. We shall, however, use the term decision process, since there are unfortunate connotations to the word control, particularly in psychotherapy.

A great operational advantage of recognizing a situation as one involv-

ing a decision process is that we can then systematically employ the existing
methods for dealing with such processes, conceptual and analytic. In particular, we must learn how to recognize the pattern of a decision process.

7. BASIC STRUCTURE OF A DECISION PROCESS

Let us identify the principal components of a decision process. They are:

1. A system with a set of allowable states;
2. A set of admissible decisions;
3. Rules for determining the result of any decisions; that is to say, a
prescription for the determination of the new state and the response of the
system, the quintuple $(I,S,D;S_1,R)$, in terms of the original state of the
system, S, the influence, I, and the decision, D;
4. A rule for evaluating the behavior of the system, i.e., a method of
evaluating the acceptability of the new state and response as compared
with the effort expended in the decision process.

8. OPERATIONAL ASPECTS

There are a number of operational aspects of a decision process, which we
shall not discuss in any detail. Nonetheless, it is worth briefly mentioning
some of these. To begin with, sensing devices are required. By this we mean
that we must possess methods of observing a system in order to ascertain
the influences, the responses and the states. Frequently, indeed, the success
of a proposed sequence of decisions hinges crucially upon the availability
of this data. We shall return to this point below.

Secondly, data processing devices are required to extract meaningful
information useful for decision-making from the larger mass of data
furnished by the signals from the sensing devices. We have already noted
in Chapter 3 that to carry out this data processing in a reasonable time is
a major obstacle to effective behavior in a number of situations. Sometimes,
there is insufficient data. Usually, the situation is the opposite; there is too
much to assimilate completely in a limited time.

Finally, control devices are necessary to carry out the decisions and thus
to influence the system in the desired fashion.

A point we wish to emphasize is that there is a considerable distance
between an abstract version of a decision process and the effective operation of an actual system. For example, if a decision must be made within
a minute, a method requiring an hour for the gathering and processing of
data is not acceptable. Consequently, a constant stimulus to the development of new theories is a close attention to the feasibility of existing
theories. It is this which dictates our constant return to "operationalism".

9. POLICY

Let us introduce a very useful term we shall employ repeatedly, *policy*. A policy is a rule for making a decision based on a knowledge of the state of the system and the external influences, which is to say, the environment. Equivalently, a policy dictates the choice of an action.

There are various types of policies a therapist might pursue: repetition of key words of the patient; repetition of the patient's last words; asking set questions; use of encouraging, nonspecific verbalizations such as "I see". Indeed, one of the purposes of developing simulation processes is to develop a tool for identification and systematic testing of different policies.

10. ILLUSTRATION

This concept is basic to all that follows. To illustrate the use of policy in a simple context, consider the procedures we follow when driving an automobile. We stop at a red light but continue if there is a green light, unless there is a pedestrian in our sights, legally or illegally, or another car making a turn or blocking our course in some other fashion. There are, in addition, emergency situations when other vehicles are given the right-of-way regardless of local signals or ordinary driving regulations; for example, ambulances, police cars and fire engines. There are also emergency situations when we might feel justified in an illegal action such as going through a red light; for example, when another driver is following too closely at a high rate of speed.

In all cases, the decision to continue or stop is dependent upon the input signals we receive, the influences to which we are subject, including perhaps the presence of a police car, i.e., the environment, and our personal criteria for acceptable behavior.

11. OPTIMAL POLICY

If a criterion for evaluating a policy exists, we can introduce the further concept of *optimal policy*. A policy which results in the most desirable behavior of the system according to the agreed upon criterion is dubbed optimal. In many economic and engineering processes we can thus think in terms of determining the best possible actions by means of a combination of sophisticated mathematical techniques and digital computers. For example, we can think of minimizing either the cost of a certain process or the time required to complete it. The mathematical procedures may be, and often are, complicated analytically and arithmetically, but the guiding ideas are conceptually simple: we are seeking either a smallest or largest number.

In general, however, we do not know enough about a particular system to make precise what we mean by best, and we are fortunate if we even know what we mean by good. In subsequent chapters we shall carefully examine this obstacle to the use of mathematics in the human sciences, with particular reference to two-person interactions. We shall then discuss some ways of circumventing this characteristic difficulty associated with basic human systems.

12. DISCUSSION

What we wish to stress here is that the major problems in the treatment of systems are far more of a conceptual nature than they are technical. It is not that we cannot solve the mathematical problems once formulated, it is rather that it is so difficult to formulate them. Any field whose problems can be posed in precise mathematical terms is well on its way to being brought under control.

13. DETERMINATION BY ENUMERATION

To choose an optimal policy we can proceed to examine the result of each particular decision, one after the other.

$$A_1 \qquad\qquad A_2 \quad \ldots$$

Figure 5.3

We call this type of behavior the *enumerative* approach. All the possibilities are listed, examined, and then evaluated using the specified criterion.

It is at this point that the digital computer plays a fundamental role in the study of decision processes. Working at micro-second speed, the computer can routinely explore literally millions of possibilities, rejecting the inferior ones and retaining the superior ones. In many cases, this straightforward approach can be effectively used to determine an optimal policy.

14. REDUCTION OF POSSIBILITIES BY THEORY

In general, however, the number of possible courses of action is so great that even the awesome powers of the digital computer are of no avail if we wish to determine the best course of action by means of a straightforward examination of all cases. At first, this may seem quite surprising in view of the much-touted ability of the computer to do rapid arithmetic. Let us, however, give a very simple example of the remarkable way the number of possibilities can accumulate.

Suppose that we are given the task of assigning ten men to ten different jobs with a prescribed measure of effectiveness available for each particular assignment. Let us attempt to obtain the most efficient arrangement by examining all possible assignments of men to jobs, one after the other, the route indicated above. How many different arrangements are there?

We can determine this number by means of the following simple argument. The first man can be assigned to any of ten different jobs, the second man to any of the remaining nine, and so on. Hence the total number of possibilities for assignment is $10 \times 9 \times 8 \times \cdots \times 2 = 10! = 3,628,800$. This is large, but not a particularly large number by contemporary standards. If, for example, in some way we could examine each arrangement in a micro-second, we would consume less than four seconds scrutinizing all the possibilities, and choosing those which are most desirable.

Suppose, however, we faced a task apparently only a little more complex, that of assigning twenty men to twenty jobs. The total number of possibilities is, proceeding as above, $20 \times 19 \times 18 \times \cdots \times 2 = 20!$, a very large number indeed. The reader can convince himself, using a table of logarithms, that at the same rate of examination it would consume over 50,000 years to examine all possibilities. A convenient fact is that a year contains about 3×10^7 seconds.

This simple example shows that quite rudimentary decision processes can readily lead to problems which cannot be solved in a routine way even with the fastest, most powerful, computers available. To treat any type of problem of significance we need sophistication, the sophistication of theory. Then, and only then, by combining the computer with a theory, can we gain a viable hold on important decision processes.

15. FEASIBILITY VERSUS OPTIMALITY

Our original objective was to operate a system in some desirable, or at least acceptable, fashion. In order to make this task precise, a substantial step towards its accomplishment, we introduced first a mathematical version of the original system, along the lines previously indicated, and then the concept of optimality. The problem of making the best decision is thus well-defined as that of choosing an optimal policy.

Sometimes, however, the price for this mathematical exactitude can be too high, particularly in the operation of complex systems. When the cost in time and effort begins to be exorbitant, we can always retreat to the original aim, the determination of *feasible policies*. It is well to remember that we rarely lose anything in the real world in accepting this less rigid approach. We shall return to the topic of feasible policies in Chapter 8.

16. ABSENCE OF CRITERION

One of the major advantages of thinking in terms of policies is that experience and intuition will usually permit the formulation of meaningful feasible policies even when the process is too complex for any precise analysis.

In particular, this may be the case when no explicit criterion exists for evaluating the outcome of a decision process. This is often the case when there are several goals which cannot be rated in terms of a common unit—the incommensurability problem. This is also a common situation when uncertainty is present since there are no unique measures of uncertainty. We shall return to this point in connection with simulation processes.

17. RATIONAL BEHAVIOR

It is easy now to define in terms of the foregoing what we mean by rational behavior in connection with a decision process of the type described in Section 7. It consists quite simply in choosing optimal or at least feasible policies. Conversely, if an individual involved in a decision process does not use at least feasible policies, we can make a number of interesting deductions. Either he is receiving different or partial data, or he is employing a criterion different from ours to interpret the data, or he is irrational, or some combination of the three.

18. MULTI-STAGE DECISION PROCESS

So far we have considered processes where a single decision sufficed. This, however, is very seldom the case in the real world. Almost all decision processes of any significance require a sequence of decisions. We proceed in the following fashion: a decision is made, the response and new state are observed; a second decision is made on this basis; the ensuing response and state are observed, and so on (see Figure 4). A process of this type is called a *multistage decision process*. Sequential processes of this nature enter into the physical and social sciences in a number of basic ways. In general, the determination of optimal polices now requires an evaluation of a large number of states, responses, and decisions. The high order of complexity of problems of this nature requires the development and use of new mathematical theories, one of which is the theory of dynamic programming. We shall make extensive use of the concepts of this theory without, however, introducing any of its analytic formalism.

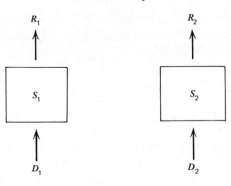

Figure 5.4

The importance of sequential decision processes for all of our subsequent work is based on viewing the initial psychotherapy interview as a multi-stage decision process.

19. UNCERTAINTY

In the foregoing pages we sketched a plausible pattern for decision-making in deterministic processes. This structure in turn can be used to provide a basis for a theory of rational behavior under determinism. That our investigations do not cease at this point is a tribute to the complexity of the real world.

What provides the spur for much further research is *uncertainty*. In almost all situations of importance, we face the problem of lacking certain basic knowledge required for applying decision-making procedures along the lines previously described. The question, then, is that of making as precise as possible what we mean by rational behavior under conditions of uncertainty and ambiguity. We have already indicated that we consider the ability to take risks one of the signs of a healthy personality.

In order to make a start on this major challenge to rationality, we turn to a study of some of the questions connected with decision processes involving uncertainty. Let us pose four different types of uncertainty associated with a process of the kind previously considered;

1. Incomplete information concerning the state of the system.
2. Incomplete information concerning the results of a decision.
3. Incomplete information concerning the set of allowable decisions.
4. Incomplete information concerning the criterion.

All of these examples of uncertainty are commonly encountered simultaneously in important applications. This is particularly the case in the practice of psychotherapy as we have discussed in Chapter 2. For the sake of simplicity, let us, at this point, consider only processes in which the second type of uncertainty arises.

20. STOCHASTIC DECISION PROCESS

A *stochastic decision process* may be considered a stochastic process with decision-making features, or a decision process with stochastic features. Some examples are stock market investment, management of a baseball or football team, and clinical diagnosis and treatment.

We consider here an important class of stochastic decision processes possessing the following, much simplified, structure: We observe both the state of the system, (S) and the influence (I) and the results of a decision (D). The consequence of that decision is that the system transforms into one of a number of possible states and produces one of a set of possible responses; see Figure 5.

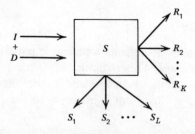

Figure 5.5

21. DECISION-MAKING UNDER UNCERTAINTY

The problem that confronts us at the moment is that of providing some mechanism for making decisions where we have incomplete *a priori* information concerning the results of a decision. With complete certainty concerning the outcome of any particular decision, we can, in principle at least, ascertain the optimal policy by examining the set of all possible decisions and their associated outcomes. We have discussed this in Section 15.

What can we do, however, when we cannot predict the result of a particular control action? It is well to emphasize that this is an eternal problem which can never be answered in any definitive fashion, for reasons we shall discuss later. There are, however, particular methods which can be used effectively in particular situations. How to recognize these situations is not a simple matter, and may well represent the crux of the problem.

A powerful mathematical theory for gaining a hold on large and important classes of decision processes involving uncertainty is the theory of probability. Let us recall some of the basic ideas considered in Chapter 4.

22. AVERAGE BEHAVIOR

As we have discussed in the preceding chapter, one way to overcome the frustration of uncertainty is to introduce the concept of *average behavior*. Instead of concentrating on an individual event, we examine a set of possible events. If a system behaves in a satisfactory fashion in some overall sense, we may then be willing to accept an occasionally unsatisfactory performance.

In the deterministic case, the concept of the value of an outcome, or, more generally, of a state-response pair, provides us with a reasonably simple way of coming to a decision. Namely, we choose the decision which furnishes the largest value.

Similarly, in the stochastic case, the decision which furnishes the largest average value provides us with an optimal policy. What is important about this is that it furnishes a systematic mechanism for taking risks.

More generally we must take into account the cost of a control action. But let us ignore this at the moment.

23. RATIONAL BEHAVIOR UNDER UNCERTAINTY

As in the deterministic case, a mechanism for decision making furnishes a criterion for rational behavior. The situation is more complex in the stochastic case since there are many methods that can be used to replace with a single number a set of possible values associated with a range of outcomes or responses, apart from the familiar average value. For example, we may decide that we wish to make that decision which makes the probability of obtaining a specified value as large as possible.

There is general agreement that it is desirable, if at all feasible, to replace a set of possible values with a fixed number. As a rule, however, this emphasis upon numbers is not a completely satisfactory procedure, particularly in human affairs, and we must combine the procedure with some additional qualitative judgments. Furthermore, it is rarely easy to determine which statistical average to employ.

We see then that a stochastic decision process contains several levels of decision-making:

1. A choice of a model of uncertainty;
2. A choice of a criterion;

3. A choice of the averaging technique to be used;
4. A choice of the decision to be made once the first three choices have been made.

Which average measure of value is employed depends upon many factors which are often not mathematical at all, such as an attitude toward risk. This is a point we have previously stressed, and which we will stress again: Both the choice of mathematical models to be employed and the interpretation of results are only partly mathematical questions.

24. MULTISTAGE DECISION PROCESS OF STOCHASTIC TYPE

A multistage decision process of stochastic type consists of a sequence of decision processes of stochastic type (see Figure 6).

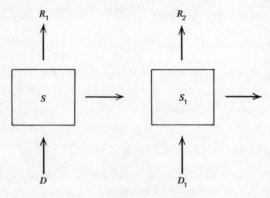

Figure 5.6

The process proceeds as follows: We observe the system in state, S, and make a decision, D; we observe the new state, S_1, and the response, R_1; and make a decision, D_1; and so on. The value of any set of decisions can be evaluated in terms of some average of the possible outcomes and states. The concept of policy is the same as for the deterministic case; a rule for making a decision in terms of the information available.

25. DEEPER UNCERTAINTIES

In the previous pages we have examined a simple example of a stochastic decision process. There are far more complex types, representing deeper levels of uncertainty. Just as one type of uncertainty forces us to use a stochastic process rather than a deterministic process, so these more complex uncertainties force us to use a different type of stochastic process.

To illustrate the sort of problem that generates these novel and more complex processes, consider the problem of calling heads or tails for the toss of a previously unknown coin. Similar in mathematical structure, but of far greater significance, is the problem faced by a physician who has to choose between a relatively new drug and one that has been used extensively in the past. The problem with which we are particularly concerned is still more complex. It is that of a therapist interviewing a patient for the first time. How is decision-making carried out in situations of this nature?

26. LEARNING

In situations of the foregoing type we use ongoing experience in the operation of the system as a guide to better understanding of the structure of the system and thus changed and improved subsequent behavior. We call this process *learning*. This quite natural approach raises a host of important and difficult questions. One of these is discussed in the following chapter: How do we learn from experience?

27. ADAPTIVE DECISION PROCESS

A multistage decision process of stochastic type involving learning will be called an *adaptive decision process*. It possesses at least five levels of uncertainty:

1. What model of uncertainty are we using?
2. What criterion do we use?
3. What type of average behavior is to be used?
4. How is experience to be used to diminish uncertainty?
5. How are optimal and feasible decisions made once the previous questions have been answered?

Observe that there are two types of decisions essentially, what to do on the basis of information already available, and what additional information to gather. These basic activities are carried on concurrently.

28. INFORMATION PATTERN

In an adaptive decision process, one needs in addition to information about the present state, a history of the process, or similar processes, in order to determine feasible and optimal policies. The complete set of data, influences, responses and states, available to the decision-maker is called the *information pattern*.

Thus, in the initial psychotherapy interview the therapist is guided at each stage by all that has occurred up to that time.

NOTES AND REFERENCES

1. "A major therapeutic intent is to expand the content of consciousness to include the many options available to the dreamer."
N. Stockhamer, "Review of *Dream and Symbols*" by L. Caligos and R. May, *Psychology Today*, Vol. 2(11), April 1969, pp. 10 and 59.

"A patient is treatable if he manifests some autonomy—if he can understand that he has some freedom to make choices at least in the therapeutic setting."
H. Spotnitz, *Modern Psychoanalysis of the Schizophrenic patient*, New York, Grune and Stratton, 1969.

See also
R. Bellman, *Adaptive Control Processes*, 1961, *op. cit.*
for more detailed discussion and many further references.
A. Rapoport and C. Orwant, "Experimental Games: A Review", *Behavioral Sciences*, Vol. 7(1), pp. 1–37.
J. M. Roberts, B. Sutton-Smith and A. Kendon, "Strategy in Games and Folk Tales", *Journal of Social Psychology*, Vol. 61, 1963, pp. 185–199.

6. For a relevant discussion of the use of the digital computer in decision processes, see
J. Starkweather, "Computer Simulation of Psychiatric Interviewing", in N. Kline and E. Laska, *Computers and Electronic Devices in Psychiatry*, New York, Grune and Stratton, 1968.
Also,
R. Abelson, "Simulation of Social Behavior", in G. Lindzey and E. Aronson, Eds., *Handbook of Social Psychology*, Rev. Ed., Redding, Mass., Addison-Wesley Pub. Co., 1966.

Another approach is exemplified by the *Psychiatric Status Schedule*, a branching interview with open ended questions. This instrument is designed to evaluate the psychopathology and role-functioning of both patients and non-patients.
R. Spitzer, J. Endicott, J. Fleiss, J. Cohen, "The Psychiatric Status Schedule", *Arch. Gen. Psychiat.*, Vol. 23, July 1970.

9. See:
L. Bellak and M. Smith, "An Experimental Exploration of Psychoanalytic Process", *Psychoanal. Quart.*, Vol. 25, 1956, pp. 385–414.
K. Colby, 1951, *op. cit.*
R. Ekstein and R. Wallerstein, *The Teaching and Learning of Psychotherapy*, New York, Basic Books, 1958.
A. Enelow and M. Wexler, 1966, *op. cit.*
J. Fleming and D. Hamburg, "Analysis of Methods of Teaching Psychotherapy with Description of a New Approach", *Arch. of Neurol. and Psychiatry*, Vol. 79, 1958, pp. 179–200.

M. Pearson, 1963, *op. cit.*

B. Pope and A. Siegman, 1967, *op. cit.*

F. Redlich and D. Freedman, 1966, *op. cit.*

J. Ruesch, "Psychotherapy and Communication", in F. Fromm-Reichmann and J. Moreno, Eds., *Progress in Psychotherapy*, 1956, *op. cit.*

A. Siegman and B. Pope, 1966, *op. cit.*

H. Strupp, "The Nature of Psychotherapist's Contribution to Treatment", *Archives of General Psychiatry*, Vol. 3, 1960, pp. 219–231.

H. Strupp, "Patient-doctor Relationships: Psychotherapist in the Therapeutic Process", in A. Bachrach, Ed., 1962, *op. cit.*

S. Tarachow, *An Introduction to Psychotherapy*, New York, International Universities Press, 1963.

H. Witmer, 1947, *op. cit.*

L. Wolberg, 1967, *op. cit.*

17. A. Rapoport describes rationality in a simulation process in terms of the best outcome a player can achieve given the rules of the game and the constraints imposed by other players striving to reach their goals.

A. Rapoport, "Formal Games as Probing Tools for Investigating Behavior Motivated by Trust and Suspicion", *Journal of Conflict Resolution*, Vol. 7(3), 1963, p. 570.

See also:

G. J. Rath, "Randomization of Humans", *American J. of Psychology*, Vol. 79, 1966, pp. 97–103.

Y. Rim, "Decisions Involving Risk in Dyads", *Acta Psychol.* (Amsterdam), Vol. 26, 1967, pp. 1–8.

J. S. Coleman, "Mathematical Models and Computer Simulation", in Robert E. Faris, Ed., *Handbook of Modern Sociology*, Chicago, Rand McNally, 1964.

23. The modern theory of "fuzzy systems" will play a major role in the study of feasibility. See

L. Zadeh, 1965, *op. cit.*

L. Zadeh and R. Bellman, 1970, *op. cit.*

L. Zadeh and R. Bellman "Outline of a New Approach to the Analysis of Complex Systems and Decision Processes", *IEEE Transaction on Systems Man and Cybernetics*, Vol. SMC-3, Jan. 1973, pp. 28–44.

A. Kaufmann, "Introduction à la Théorie des Sous-ensemble Flous 1. Eléments Théoriques de Base." Maisson et Cie, 1973.

26. The study of problems of this nature was inaugurated in 1934. See

W. R. Thompson, "On the Theory of Apportionment", *Amer. J. Math.*, Vol. 57, 1935.

A means of formalizing human preferences on the desired goals as well as on the decision-making process in simulations is discussed by

A. Lerner, "A Learning Approach to the Dynamic Modeling of Human

Planning and Decision-making Systems", *Technological Forecasting and Social Change,* Vol. 2, 1970, pp. 125–132.

See also:

R. Bellman, "Top Management Decision and Simulation Processes", *The Journal of Industrial Engineering,* Vol. 9(5), Sept.–Oct. 1958, pp. 459–464.

L. H. Rapoport, "Interpersonal Conflict in Co-operative and Uncertain Situations", *J. of Experimental Social Psychology,* Vol. 1, 1965, pp. 323–333.

Chapter 6

MATHEMATICAL MODEL
OF THE INITIAL INTERVIEW

1. INTRODUCTION

In the foregoing chapters we have discussed various aspects of the initial psychotherapy interview viewed as a two-person interaction process. In this chapter we wish to construct mathematical models which combine some of the mathematical ideas of Chapters 4 and 5 with the examination of various aspects of the therapy process as seen in Chapters 2 and 3. One of our major goals is an investigation of interviewing techniques with both training and research goals in mind. This theme will be repeated in subsequent chapters from different vantage points.

2. THE PATIENT AS A SYSTEM

Let us begin by reviewing some previous ideas. Our basic hypothesis is that the patient may be regarded as a responsive system describable in terms of the previously introduced notions of influences, responses, and states (Figure 1). The influence I in the patient diagram above corresponds to the responses of the therapist, both verbal and nonverbal; the response R denotes the responses of the patient, again both verbal and nonverbal. The state of the patient, S, together with the influence, I, determine the response R.

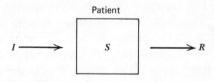

Figure 6.1

For our purposes it is important to employ a slightly more detailed model where I produces a change of state S to S_1 as well as a response R (Figure 2).

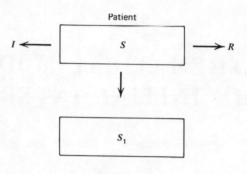

Figure 6.2

Subsequently we shall introduce the method we shall employ for specifying the state of the patient.

3. THE THERAPIST AS A SYSTEM

We hypothesize a similar abstract structure for the therapist. The situation, however, is asymmetric. Not only are the influences and responses of the therapist distinct in nature from those of the patient, but a different type of state will be employed; see Sections 6 and 7.

4. INTERACTION PROCESS

We view then the initial psychotherapy interview as a sequence of interactions between two systems, that of the therapist, S_T, and that of the patient, S_P (Figure 3).

The foregoing schematic is designed to indicate that the response of each system acts as an influence on the other, producing both new responses and corresponding changes of state. These influences and responses are the patient and therapist responses to each other.

We assume that the therapist controls his response to greater or less extent by conscious, rational choice—at least this is his aim—and that this becomes the influence on the patient system. We assume further that the response of the patient depends upon his state and the therapist's response. The dependence will be probabilistic rather than deterministic in our subsequent work. The reasons for this are discussed later in the chapter.

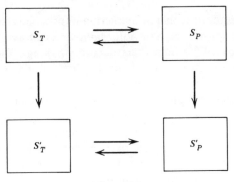

Figure 6.3

5. VERBAL AND NONVERBAL RESPONSES

In any two-person interaction process responses are of two principal types: verbal and nonverbal. We can indicate the fact that the response is a vector with at least two components by adding a few arrows to the schematic of the preceding section (Figure 4).

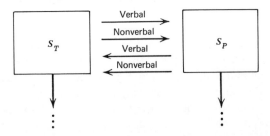

Figure 6.4

Recognition of these two types of responses provides a stimulus to the use of far more sophisticated structures for both patient and therapist than those given above. We shall briefly consider one possible configuration in Section 21.

6. INFORMATION PATTERN

Let us now recall the important term, information pattern. We take it to be the totality of patient data available to the therapist at any point in the interview. As the process continues, more and more data accumulate, producing a continuous change in the information pattern. One basic problem facing the therapist is that of extracting information from these accumulated data. Here we use the term *information* to denote that portion of the entire data set useful for immediate decision-making. What is information in the patient's responses then depends on what the therapist wants to accomplish and upon how he evaluates these responses.

Another fundamental problem, more so than that of data gathering and interpretation as far as an initial interview is concerned, is that of establishing lines of communication with the patient. An essential part of the decision-making process may be that of determining suitable means of communication. This again is an adaptive process. We shall explore this point in a later chapter and we emphasize it in our simulation processes.

7. STATES

With the aid of the foregoing we can now be precise about the term state that we used for both the therapist and patient systems, S_T and S_P.

We take S_T to be the information pattern described above. It is the basis for the therapist's response. With each response of the patient, both verbal and nonverbal, this information pattern is changed. This information pattern is interpreted according to the theoretical background and experience of the therapist. We take S_P to be the state of mind of the patient which determines whether he makes a convergent or divergent response, and the nature of this response, to a therapist response. With each response of the therapist and patient the relationship between therapist and patient, and therefore the state of mind of the patient, is affected. We shall discuss this in more detail subsequently where the nature of the probability of a convergent or divergent response is described.

8. MULTISTAGE DECISION PROCESSES

To recapitulate, each response of the therapist elicits a response from the patient. These response-response pairs, together with any patient history initially available, determine the sequence of therapist-patient states and thus the nature of the interaction process of the interview.

The therapist possesses a number of response options. He is thus confronted with a multistage decision process: How can he respond so as to achieve the specified goals of an initial psychotherapy interview?

9. OBJECTIVES OF AN INITIAL INTERVIEW

The therapist is faced with a patient he has never seen before, a patient with difficulties unknown to him at the start of their relation.

Furthermore, it is not clear how to communicate with the patient to obtain the information on which the interview depends. We have abstracted and simplified this problem to one of obtaining information concerning the states and responses of an unknown system. It remains to specify some criteria of performance.

Let us recall the major objectives of the initial interview:

1. Establish rapport, a working relationship, with the patient.
2. Obtain sufficient information to:
   a. Determine as far as possible the nature and severity of the patient's problems, and his motivation and capacity for therapy.
   b. Formulate a tentative clinical diagnosis, make a referral, or plan a treatment.
3. Reinforce the patient's desire for continuing therapy when this need exists.
4. Make the patient feel better by the end of the interview.

In the models that are constructed, and in the simulations, the computer vignettes, we have concentrated upon the first part of an initial interview and thus upon the first major objective, that of establishing rapport with the patient.

10. POLICY

An interviewing technique may be considered to be a combination of policy and method. The policy provides a scheme for interpreting the information pattern which leads to a decision for the therapist to respond in one way or another. In turn, this interpretation and its implementation depend upon the training and experience of the therapist.

There are a number of policies which can readily be described. Each has its advantages and disadvantages; each has appropriate times and modes of usage. Let us give some examples of common policies:

1. Make no verbal responses, or very few of them.
2. Ask a fixed sequence of questions independent of the verbal and nonverbal responses of the patient.
3. Explore a fixed sequence of themes (e.g., sex, marriage, job) regardless of the nature of the patient's responses.
4. Ask a series of random questions regardless of the responses of the patient.
5. Use key words taken from the patient's conversation to determine the therapist's next response.
6. Use principal themes in the patient's response to determine the next response of the therapist.

7. Use a "stream of consciousness" approach to allow the patient's words to trigger associated ideas in the therapist.

8. Follow a patient response containing material of unusual significance by a routine, or stall response which provides time for a longer consideration of the patient response.

9. Repeat every verbal response of the patient in the form of a question.

10. Concentrate on the patient's affect or emotion rather than the facts he presents.

11. Concentrate on the facts presented by the patient rather than the concomitant emotion.

12. Respond to the patient's nonverbal behavior rather than to the verbal content of his responses.

13. Allow his own affective response to the patient, rather than ideas, to determine the therapist's behavior.

14. Attend to the process of the interview, to the continuing interaction between them, rather than to either the patient's or the therapist's ideas or emotions.

11. DISCUSSION

Some of the foregoing policies are of adaptive type, which is to say they take account of the actual behavior or information given by the patient as well as taking into account the process of the interview, and some are not. The first, second, third, fourth, and ninth are nonadaptive. The fifth, sixth, and eighth are adaptive. The tenth, eleventh, twelfth, or fourteenth may or may not be adaptive.

The seventh and thirteenth are of adaptive type where we deliberately put intuition in charge. In complex intellectual processes this is often a fruitful approach, particularly when we consciously employ decision-making and evaluative abilities for monitoring purposes as an aid to intuition.

In practice, various combinations of these policies may be employed. How the therapist decides to shift from one type of policy to another is a very complex aspect of the overall adaptive decision process.

12. FEASIBILITY

If we had a precise criterion for evaluating an interview, we could seek to determine an optimal interviewing policy. However, in this context the concept of optimality is meaningless for at least two reasons. In the first place, it may not be possible to define any objective precisely enough to recognize what is meant by "best". Secondly, there are usually in any interview a number of incommensurable objectives in mind, again ruling out this concept.

Consequently, in this situation, as in other complex processes, we will employ the concept of feasibility rather than optimality. We are interested then in procedures which are reasonably effective, not most efficient. We have already commented on this. Nonetheless, this idea requires a good deal of further discussion; see Chapter 8.

Even if no explicit criterion function exists, we can meaningfully explore the effects of using various policies. It is this which explains our emphasis upon policy and our use of simulation processes to study policies. We shall amplify these ideas considerably in Chapter 7.

13. DESCRIPTION OF ADAPTIVE DECISION PROCESS

Let us now begin to define in precise fashion the adaptive decision process discussed in the foregoing sections. We are confronted with a psychologically disturbed patient, corresponding to a $[I, S, S_1, R]$ quadruple, to use the terminology of Section 10, Chapter 5. However, since the type and degree of disturbance are not known initially, the quadruple is not known.

It should be pointed out that certain background or collateral information concerning the patient may be furnished by physicians, other therapists, social workers, parents, family, or police to provide some basis for an *a priori* estimation of the structure of the patient's responses.

Using the response-response couplets of the exchange between them, the therapist has the dual task of discovering something of this structure and of using this derived knowledge to achieve the goals of the interview. The therapist responds or chooses to respond in a certain way, evaluates this response and the response of the patient, responds again himself, and so on. Observe that the solution to the problem of determining an interviewing technique is a policy, an algorithm for choosing responses dependent upon the information pattern and the therapist's goals. Let us note that henceforth when we use the terms patient or psychotherapist we are speaking of their counterparts in the mathematical model, not the actual people.

14. SPECTRUM OF ADAPTIVE DECISION PROCESSES

It is important to note that the foregoing represents only a step towards a desired precise description of the interaction process. The reason for this is that we have not yet specified how the patient responses are communicated to the therapist, and how much time is allotted for the decision-making processes of the therapist.

It follows that there are a wide range of possibilities. For example, the patient response, including verbal and some nonverbal aspects, may be presented in printed form on a typewriter or a video screen hooked into a computer. Thus, for example, a patient response might have the following format:

Patient:　I have not been sleeping well lately.
　　　　　(Worried expression; taps fingers on the desk.)

Within this format there remain a large number of options. We can, for example, allow the therapist to reread each response as often as desired, and also allow him access to the set of all previous response pairs. Alternatively, we can use a ticker-tape presentation, mimicking the transient nature of an actual conversation, or we can allow a fixed time for reading of the patient's response.

Although readily adapted to either a typewriter or a Cathode Ray Tube (CRT), the simulation processes described subsequently use the CRT. In a later chapter we shall discuss the possibility of more realistic communication involving the use of voice recorded responses and audio-visual devices.

Secondly, there is the question of how much the therapist should know about the structure of the $[I, S, S_1, R]$ quadruples. For research and training purposes we can go from one extreme, allowing complete knowledge, to the other, of giving no preliminary information. There are many intermediate stages which can be used as well.

Finally, let us examine the nature of the decision-making process. The actual process, the initial interview, takes place in real time. This means that the therapist must make his responses essentially at the pace of ordinary conversation. However, again for research and training purposes, we can go to an extreme position and allow the therapist unlimited amounts of time between responses. He can be permitted to take notes and even to repeat previous questions if he wishes. Taking notes is an important activity since it highlights the question of what is significant information, and how to discern it. In general, we can contemplate the use of all types of theoretical considerations by the student to study this adaptive decision process. We can provide for this by controlling the delivery of the responses.

15. ON-LINE DECISION PROCESS

Let us once again stress an essential feature of the initial interview, the on-line aspects; cf. Chapter 5. For the purposes of research and training, it is reasonable to construct models of adaptive decision processes in which varying amounts of time are permitted to elapse between patient and therapist responses. In the actual process, however, the therapist for various reasons cannot allow any considerable amount of time between his response and that of the patient. It follows that in a brief period of time, a time interval comparable to that in ordinary conversation, he must assimilate the patient's response, correlate it with what he has retained of previous response pairs, examine his reaction and his current estimate of the nature of the interaction process between himself and the patient, and then respond to the patient.

We have called this example of decision-making under time pressure an "on-line decision process". The mathematical and operational problems raised by processes of this nature are novel, and of exceptional interest and complexity. In particular, we face the difficult task of training people for this activity.

16. CATEGORIES OF MODELS

Since the initial psychotherapy interview is a complex interaction process, it is to be expected that research of significance in this area will involve some intricate mathematical models. On the other hand, since we are interested in training, we can identify a number of strong arguments for using simple models, at least initially. We can expect, then, that a number of models of different types and different levels of complexity will be valuable for different purposes.

A most interesting and important question is that of determining the levels of sophistication at which an experienced therapist operates in the initial interview. How much attention does he pay to the details of the patient's response? What features are significant in determining the responses that he makes? How does he identify the state of the patient? The simulation processes appearing in later chapters are aimed at providing partial answers to these questions.

17. DISCUSSION

We have discussed in general terms a multistage decision process of adaptive type as well as some of the many specific processes contained within this format. For a more precise study along mathematical lines, we require first the quadruple $[I, S, S_1, R]$ and, secondly, some techniques for a qualitative and quantitative evaluation of an interview resulting from a particular interviewing policy.

We shall begin with a consideration of the $[I, S, S_1, R]$ quadruple.

18. CAUSE AND EFFECT

To obtain the desired quadruple, we can envisage two approaches:

1. Development of a theory which predicts R and S_1 on the basis of I and S.

2. A listing of all possible $[I, S, S_1, R]$ quadruples using some combination of theory and the everyday experience of practicing therapists.

We rule out the first approach on the grounds that no reliable theoretical basis exists at the present time for determining rules which will enable us to predict S_1 and R, given I and S, and a patient with a particular set of problems. Some of the difficulties we meet are those encountered in pursuing the second, an enumerative approach; some are of even more fundamental nature.

While the enumerative approach which requires a listing of response-response couplets possesses certain attractive features, it founders on a characteristic obstacle, the dimensionality difficulty. Let us discuss this.

19. OPERATIONAL DIFFICULTY OF DIMENSIONALITY

If we do not possess a theory which predicts R and S_1, given I and S, an alternative is to list all allowable $[I, S, S_1, R]$ quadruples. Consider, however, the set of all possible therapist responses and all possible patient responses. There are of course an immense number of possible response-response couplets. For even a brief dialogue, how would we compile such a list? How would we store and retrieve all of the possibilities?

For example, if we allow only 100 verbal responses for the therapist and 100 possible responses for the patient, there are 10,000 possible response pairs at each stage. Consider then the number of possibilities for an interchange of 100 stages. This approach is hopeless.

Furthermore, the conceptual problem of modeling a conversation is extraordinarily complex. We have incomplete understanding at the present time of the role words play in an act of communication. Although a good deal of work has been done in connection with attempts to abstract semantic content from sentences, we shall not pursue this road.

The decision process as originally envisaged is not operationally sound. We cannot handle either *general* $[I, S, S_1, R]$ quadruples or a very large number of specific ones. Fortunately, borrowing some standard ideas concerning approximation from the domains of physics and engineering, we can introduce some modifications which yield an operational model.

20. COMPLEXITY REPLACED BY PROBABILITY

In Section 18 we pointed out, without attempting to justify the statement, that no existing theory of two-person interactions is capable of producing the desired $[I, S, S_1, R]$ quadruple. It is furthermore extremely unlikely that any comprehensive theory will exist in the near future. In order to circumvent this serious obstacle, lack of theory, we use a conceptual device previously discussed in Chapter 2; we replace the uncertainty of complexity with the uncertainty of probability.

Consequently, instead of creating a deterministic cause-and-effect relation, we introduce a suitable stochastic relation. This new relation has the form: if the therapist uses response A, there is a probability p_1 that the patient will make response B, a probability p_2 that the response will be C, and so on.

The original deterministic interaction has been replaced by a stochastic interaction. We have circumvented the lack of a precise cause-and-effect relation at the cost, however, of greatly increasing the size of the table of $[I, S, S_1, R]$ quadruples. Instead of a definite response, R, and a new state, S_1, we now have a set of associated responses and a set of associated states.

We have already discussed the serious dimensionality problems associated with an $[I, S, S_1, R]$ quadruple. What do we do now that the table has greatly increased in size?

21. REDUCED RESPONSE SPACE

In order to avoid the operational hazards raised by the use of quadruples, we begin by severely limiting the number of therapist and patient responses. In place of allowing the therapist to choose any appropriate response, we permit him only to choose from among a finite number of predetermined responses. These allowable responses are determined by the preceding patient responses. Similarly, we allow only a finite number of patient responses, determined by the therapist response and previous course of the interview. Initially, we use the smallest possible number allowing a choice, namely two.

Subsequently, in later chapters we will discuss some ways of increasing the dichotomy to a larger set of alternative responses, and even of restoring to the therapist the prerogatives of a completely free choice. To accomplish this last objective, we must introduce a new feature; see Chapter 8.

22. DISCUSSION

At the moment it would appear that this reduction from an unrestricted response set to one of two predetermined choices is rather confining and disturbingly artificial. Let us point out by means of a physical analogy that the situation is not so bad as it may appear at first glance.

Consider the problem of tracing a curve connecting two points, P and Q, in the plane shown in Figure 5. In order to trace any desired path, we need the capability of motion in any direction at any point on the path (see Figure 6).

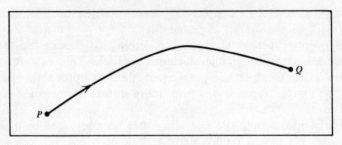

Figure 6.5

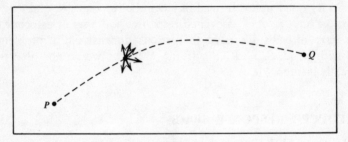

Figure 6.6

Suppose, however, instead of allowing this complete freedom of behavior, we allow only motion in three directions: up, down, and straight ahead; see Figures 7 and 8.

We can, despite this restriction, obtain an excellent approximation to the smooth path in Figure 6 by use of these three preassigned types of motion, provided only that the individual steps are sufficiently small.

In Chapter 2 we pointed out that quite complex processes can be described by means of vastly simplified states. Here we have indicated that complex interactions can be effectively replicated by a sequence of cause and effect relations of much more elementary type.

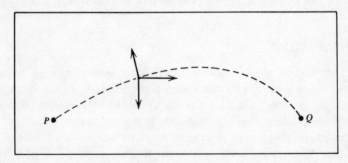

Figure 6.7

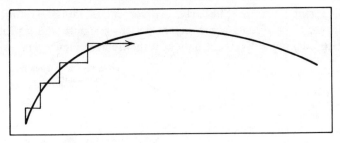

Figure 6.8

If we consider the possibility of 100 to 150 interchanges in the initial interview, and if we limit ourselves to interaction processes involving relatively small amounts of information at each stage, then the foregoing restriction to two possible responses for both therapist and patient need not be too confining. We will be able to obtain realistic approximations to an actual interview; see Chapter 9.

23. LOCAL SIMPLICITY VERSUS GLOBAL COMPLEXITY

We are employing a familiar principle of science: complex processes can often be effectively studied as combinations of far simpler processes. Sometimes, this involves some approximations, sometimes not. In the foregoing case (cf. Figure 9), observe that we can imagine that we are approximately to a policy which traces out a curved path. In place of continuous steering from P to Q, we allow at each point only a choice of turning in one of three possible directions.

Naturally, in each particular process, the validity of an approximation procedure of the foregoing type must be carefully assessed.

The use of simple approximate policies in initial training seems quite reasonable. As expertise is gained, steps can be combined to form more sophisticated policies. We shall discuss subsequently how we construct a hierarchy of simulation processes.

24. SIMPLIFIED QUADRUPLES

Using the foregoing ideas, we can drastically simplify the $[I, S, S_1, R]$ quadruple. Introducing the concept of *attitude* discussed in detail in Chapter 3, we may separate the therapist and patient responses into two categories: *convergent* and *divergent*.

We suppose that a convergent therapist response has probability p of producing a convergent patient response and a probability $1 - p$ of producing a divergent response. Similarly, a divergent therapist response has a probability q of producing a convergent patient response and a probability $1 - q$ of producing a divergent patient response (see Figure 9).

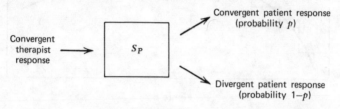

Convergent patient response
(probability p)

Convergent therapist response → S_P

Divergent patient response
(probability $1-p$)

Figure 6.9

In general, p and q will not be equal. The values of p depend upon the patient we are considering, and need not be the same at each stage for a particular patient. This question of a probabilistic response will be discussed in detail in Chapter 7.

25. PATIENT'S STATE OF MIND

What has been previously, and intuitively, called the patient's state of mind may now be defined precisely by the two probabilities above, p and q. As noted, these probabilities may change as the interview proceeds so that if the therapist is basically convergent, the chances of a convergent patient response will improve over time. If, on the other hand, the therapist is basically divergent, this fact will be reflected in a decrease of the probability of a convergent patient response. In other words, there should be cumulative effects of convergent and divergent therapist behavior on the developing attitudes of the patient.

In Chapter 8 we shall describe some simple ways of effecting the desired dependence.

26. DESCRIPTION OF NEW PROCESS

Let us return again to a description of the multistage decision process of adaptive type that we will be considering, taking into account the foregoing simplifications. We begin with a patient, a system possessing the properties described in Sections 24–25. At the first stage, the student (the term we shall henceforth employ for the person assuming the role of the therapist) is presented with a choice of two responses. Having chosen one of them, the patient's response is determined according to the assigned probabilities which reflect the attitudes of a hypothetical patient. This response is then communicated to the student. Associated with the response is another set of two therapist responses; as before, the student chooses one of these. The goals are as described previously.

Figure 10 indicates a situation in which the therapist selects the first of his two choices, receives the second of the two possible patient responses, and is about to choose one of the next two available responses.

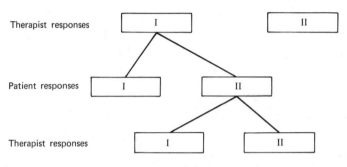

Therapist responses   I   II

Patient responses   I   II

Therapist responses   I   II

Figure 6.10

27. INITIAL INFORMATION PATTERN

To complete the description of the foregoing adaptive decision process, we must describe the kinds of preliminary knowledge of the process that may be made available to the student. There is a wide range of possibilities once again.

For example, we may:

1. Instruct the student to proceed as if he were conducting an interview with a real patient that he has never seen before and about whom he has no prior information.

2. Provide a detailed discussion of the mathematical structure of the process, including the values of the probabilities of the convergent and divergent responses but no patient information. The student would still have the task of determining which are the appropriate convergent and divergent therapist responses at each stage.

3. Provide a sketchy discussion of the mathematical structure of the process, but no information concerning the patient.

4. Provide a sketchy discussion of the patient, but no information concerning the mathematical structure of the process.

5. Provide some mixture of information concerning the patient and the structure of the process.

What we wish to emphasize is that a single skeletal structure fleshed out by various modifications of the initial information pattern can lead to a wide variety of possible adaptive decision processes.

28. OPERATIONAL DIFFICULTIES

Let us see what is required to store the total response set for the simplified process described in the previous pages. At the onset, the therapist has one of two choices. The patient's response to this choice may be any of two, and so on (see Figure 11).

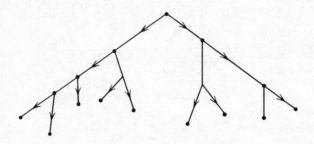

Figure 6.11

We see then that to complete one full exchange or stage, both therapist and patient responses, 4 possible patient responses are required. To complete two stages, 16 possible patient responses are required. Continuing in this fashion, to complete N stages, we see that 4^N possible patient responses are required. Since $2^{10} = 1024 > 1000$, we see that $4^{10} \cong (1000)^2 = 1,000,000$, an estimate of what is needed for ten stages. It follows that to complete twenty stages of this process more than 10^{12} (1,000,000,000,000) possible patient responses would be required.

One 50 minute interview can readily involve more than 100 stages as examination of the literature will disclose. Hence, even in an extremely simplified actual interview, we encounter numbers of response pairs which are impossibly large. Once again, we face the ogre of operational difficulty.

Fortunately, we possess a simple and effective device for keeping the total response set within reasonable bounds. This will be discussed in Chapter 8.

29. LIBRARY OF PROCESSES

It is clear that the response set of a patient will depend strongly upon the particular patient and his problems. Consequently, the response set of the therapist will depend strongly upon the responses of the patient, assuming, as we do, that we are concerned with an adaptive process. What is a convergent interviewing technique with one patient may be quite divergent with another, and conversely. Convergent and divergent are thus relative,

not absolute, terms. We will provide some examples of this in the computer vignettes of Chapter 9.

It follows that research of the foregoing nature will be more useful as
more processes of this nature are constructed. What is needed then is a
library of processes, each emphasizing certain characteristic problems faced
by therapists with different characteristic orientations. We will pursue this
interesting theme in Chapter 9.

30. MORE COMPLEX MODELS

Let us conclude the chapter by briefly indicating some of the ways in which
we can construct more complex mathematical models.

To begin with, in place of a simple schematic of Figure 1 for the patient
system, we can use the schematic shown in Figure 12.

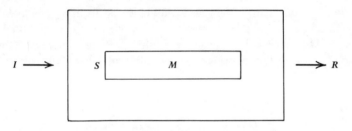

Figure 6.12

Here M denotes some internal structure, equivalent to a method for
producing responses from influences that reach it, while S denotes what
we can call the state of mind of the patient. As indicated, S acts as a filter
which may vary from catalyst to impenetrable wall and which determines
the nature of the actual response that reaches the therapist.

We can suppose initially that the mechanism M is fixed, but that S, the
state of mind, can be influenced and modified by the therapist's responses
as well as by the patient's own responses. Essentially what this means is that
M varies slowly by comparison with the variation of S.

We can penetrate a little more deeply. In place of the schematic of
Figure 12, let us employ the schematic shown in Figure 13.

We may think of the verbal and nonverbal responses of the therapist as
having an effect on both conscious (aware) and subconscious (or less than
fully aware) mechanisms of the patient, M_c and M_s. These independently
produce responses which are mixed in another component of the mind, K
(which we can call the censor), before passing through the filter, S, and
becoming the verbal and nonverbal responses observed by the therapist.

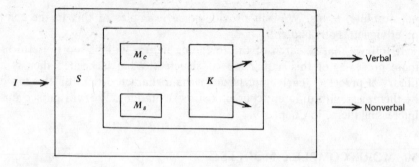

Figure 6.13

As we have already indicated, and shall discuss again, we face more than enough obstacles in treating the simpler model. Hence, we shall avoid the temptation to treat these more interesting models at any further length at this time. We do wish, however, to indicate the flexibility of the systems approach and some of the many ways in which the existing model can be extended. This means that it can be readily used to understand the interactions in terms of the theories of many different schools of psychotherapy.

NOTES AND REFERENCES

1. The work in this chapter is an outgrowth of ideas presented first in
   R. Bellman, M. B. Friend, and L. Kurland, *A Simulation of the Initial Psychiatric Interview*, R-449-RC, December 1966, The RAND Corporation.
   R. Bellman, M. Friend, and L. Kurland, "On the Construction of a Simulation of the Initial Psychiatric Interview", *Behavioral Science*, Vol. 11, 1966, pp. 389–399.
   R. Bellman, W. C. Hopgood, and C. P. Kell, "Computer Vignettes: A Research Tool for the Study of the Initial Psychotherapeutic Interview", *Journal of Cybernetics*, Vol. 1, 1971, pp. 19–27.

   For another computer-based approach to the problems of interviewing psychiatric patients, see:
   R. Stillman, W. Roth, K. Colby, and C. Rosenbaum, "An On-Line Computer System for Initial Psychiatric Inventory", *Amer. J. Psychiat.*, Suppl., Vol. 125(7), January 1969, pp. 8–11.

   See also:
   R. Bellman, "Psychodynamics and Mathematical Simulation of the Initial Psychiatric Interview", USCEE 221, University of Southern California, August 1967.

K. Colby, 1965, *op. cit.*

Rice and Rice talk about two parts in developing a mathematical model: "The first is the identification of the pertinent and important variables in the problem. The second is the identification of relationships between these variables and the solution of the problem."
Rice, 1969, *op. cit.*

See also:
S. Rosenberg, "Co-operative Behavior in Dyads as a Function of Reinforcement Parameters", *J. of Abnormal Social Psychology,* Vol. 60, 1960, pp. 318–333.

4. The Balints view the patient and therapist as interacting systems. They state that the aim of the interviewer is to assess the patient's mental state based on his contribution to the interaction between the therapist and patient. The patient comes to the interview with habitual ways of behaving; the therapist is responsible for managing the interview in such a way that the relationship becomes a cooperative one.
Balint, 1961, *op. cit.*

Alexander makes the point that the therapist should suit his treatment and manner to the specific needs of the patient and control his behavior.
F. Alexander, November 1963, *op. cit.*

6. The concept of information pattern is essential to the study of adaptive processes. See
R. Bellman, *Adaptive Control Processes,* 1961, *op. cit.*

7. In his paper, Dr. Lawson Lowrey says that the therapist, whether analyst, social worker or counselor, must accept responsibility not only for the patient's responses but for his own activities. See
L. Lowrey, "Counseling and Therapy", *American Journal of Orthopsychiatry,* Vol. 16, October 1946, pp. 615–622.

8. For some applications of dynamic programming to learning processes, see
W. Karush and R. Dear, "Optimal Stimulus Presentation Strategy for a Stimulus Sampling Method of Learning", *J. Mathematical Psychology,* Vol. 3, 1966, pp. 19–47.
W. Karush and R. Dear, "Optimal Strategy for Item Presentation in a Learning Process", *Management Science,* Vol. 13, 1967, pp. 773–785.
W. Karush and R. Dear, "An Optimal Procedure for an N-Stage Learning Process", *J. Siam Control,* Vol. 4, 1966, pp. 116–129.

10. See
L. Bellak and M. Smith, 1956, *op. cit.*
K. Colby, 1951, *op. cit.*
R. Ekstein and R. Wallerstein, 1958, *op. cit.*
A. Enelow and M. Wexler, 1966, *op. cit.*

J. Fleming and D. Hamburg, 1958, *op. cit.*

M. Pearson, 1963, *op. cit.*

B. Pope and A. Siegman, 1967, *op. cit.*

J. Ruesch in Fromn-Reichmann and Moreno, 1956, *op. cit.*

A. Siegman and B. Pope, 1966, *op. cit.*

H. Strupp, "The Nature of the Psychotherapist's Contribution to Treatment", 1960, *op. cit.*

H. Strupp, *Psychotherapists in Action,* 1960, *op. cit.*

H. Strupp, "Patient-Doctor Relationships: Psychotherapists in the Therapeutic Process", in A. Bachrach, 1962, *op. cit.*

S. Tarachow, 1963, *op. cit.*

H. Witmer, ed., 1947, *op. cit.*

11. According to Harry Stack Sullivan, intuition means only knowledge about something which isn't clearly formulated.
H. Sullivan, *The Interpersonal Theory of Psychiatry,* 1953, *op. cit.*

14. The importance of carefully thought out theoretical constructions is discussed by
H. Strupp, "Toward a Specification of Teaching and Learning in Psychotherapy", *Arch. Gen. Psychiat.,* Vol. 21, 1969, pp. 203–212.

20. It is necessary to remember that when we talk about probability, we must assume randomness, and talking about randomness, we assume probability. See
K. Colby, 1960, *op. cit.*

30. Clinically, "the terms conscious and unconsciousness ... (are) ... useful in denoting degrees of awareness".
F. Redlich and D. Freedman, 1966, *op. cit.*

Chapter 7

COMPUTERS
AND SIMULATION

1. INTRODUCTION

In the foregoing chapter we examined some of the difficulties encountered in the construction of a mathematical model of an initial psychotherapy interview. One of the most formidable of these is "dimensionality," the set of problems caused by the sheer magnitude of possible interactions in a two-person process. Fortunately, in a number of cases the digital computer can be used in various ways to circumvent this omnipresent characteristic of reality. In this chapter we shall continue the discussion of the previous chapter focusing on the model of the initial interview constructed in Chapter 6.

We shall begin by considering uncertainty due to complexity in a deterministic process, using the traditional, experimental approach to eliminate uncertainty. We are particularly interested, however, in the problem of learning to make decisions in the face of certain kinds of *uncertainty*. In order to understand the relevance of mathematics and computers to this class of problems we shall discuss at some length methods which might be used to study a card game. The game of Blackjack or Twenty-One will serve for illustration.

Finally, we will inquire into the technique of simulation, a most powerful experimental and research tool in the human sciences, and how this is carried out by computer.

2. UNCERTAINTY DUE TO COMPLEXITY

As we have noted, we are primarily concerned with decision-making, and more precisely, decision-making under conditions of uncertainty. Let us begin, however, with simpler questions connected with the descriptive aspects of systems. As a point of reference let us consider a system S with a number of component systems $S_1, S_2, \ldots, S_N$ (Figure 1).

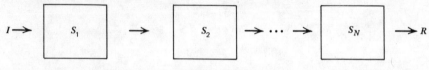

Figure 7.1

To begin with, let us suppose that the behavior of each individual system is known in the sense that we possess the required *ISR-table* (input-state-response) for each subsystem $S_1, S_2, \ldots, S_N$. These may be of deterministic or stochastic nature.

We are interested in the case where there are a large number of these subsystems, although some of these subsystems may be the same system at different times. We do not, however, necessarily assume that their structure is as uncomplicated as that illustrated in Figure 1. For example, the actual structure may have the form as shown in Figure 2. Furthermore, the structure examined may be of far greater complexity.

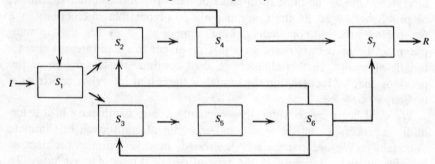

Figure 7.2

Despite the fact that the behavior of the individual components is well documented, the complicated structure of the system may prevent us from readily predicting what R will ultimately result as a consequence of the initial influence I. In many investigations of this nature, we face the fact that the state of mathematical and scientific skill is not sufficient to use the available information concerning local interactions to determine global effects. We thus possess no useful rule which permits us to predict R, given I. This is a typical example of uncertainty due to complexity.

3. EXPERIMENTAL APPROACH

A standard approach for overcoming this barrier is the use of experiment. To find out how a system operates, we propose to observe it closely, identifying sets of variables and watching to see what the overall response is to various inputs.

Occasionally, it is convenient to observe the performance of the actual system. In general, however, we wish to determine the behavior of the system under a wide range of influences and operating conditions. Hence, if possible, small-scale replicas are devised to facilitate the experimentation; sometimes, however, large-scale models are necessary. To test these models, large or small, one uses such devices as towing tanks and wind tunnels, and many analogous structures.

The idea is readily carried over to man-machine systems. To determine how a telephone exchange might operate under peak load conditions, a typical telephone exchange complete with operators is constructed, tested, and subjected to characteristic demands for service. Many illustrations of this natural and fruitful idea can be given. To study reality, we observe reality or useful replicas of reality.

4. ADVANTAGES

There are many obvious advantages to the experimental approach. Many of the approximations inherent in any theoretical model are bypassed in this fashion. Furthermore, most of the difficulties associated with a mathematical model, consequences of our intellectual limitations, disappear in a direct examination of the actual system. The (I, S, R) tables may be constructed on the basis of direct experimentation.

5. DISADVANTAGES

Unfortunately, it is also true that the experimental approach possesses some serious disadvantages.

To begin with, it may be impractical, or even impossible, to build a useful replica of the system of interest. Although we can study the actual behavior of a transportation system or a chemical factory by direct observation, we may not, however, be able to perform a number of important experiments without seriously interfering with normal operation. An automobile manufacturer can build a prototype of a new automobile, but it hardly qualifies as experimentation to build an ocean liner or a hospital complex. Despite the fact that it is desirable to understand the effects of a particular interviewing policy in an initial interview, there are reasons why we may prefer not to use an actual patient.

Secondly, there is the question of cost in time. It may not always be desirable to operate in real time. For example, it is essential to determine in some fashion the effect of a fiscal policy to be pursued for one year in a national economy without spending one year in the process of study. It is desirable to study within a relatively short time patients with certain presenting problems that might ordinarily be encountered only occasionally in a five-year or ten-year period: for example, patients with terminal illnesses.

Thus, there can be serious costs in resources (human and nonhuman), or time, or both, when the experimental method is employed.

6. DESTRUCTIVE TESTING

In some cases performing experiments may be dangerous to the experimenter, as witnessed by early experiments with Roentgen rays and nuclear reactors. In other cases, testing is destructive to the machine, or to the system, or to the individual, as, for example, experimentation with new drugs.

This is a particularly serious point in the practice of psychotherapy. One takes a critical view of experimentation with people already suffering.

7. IDENTIFICATION

Let us briefly consider the question of observation. In studying a real system, there is the problem first of all of isolating cause and effect. Determining all of the influences actually operating on a particular system is never simple and, as a matter of fact, rarely completely feasible. In vivo a system is subject to many different kinds of influences, some beyond our control, and some possibly beyond our current comprehension. Hidden variables, or non-specifics as they may be termed, can result in serious difficulties in the interpretation of observed results and, ultimately, in the formulation of correct principles.

The history of science shows very clearly that the observer, the scientist, is strongly bound by his culture, his philosophy, and his training. There is much to observe in any real system and thus considerable choice in the selection of what to observe and the length of time that it is observed. It is well to note that no observation takes place without implicit or explicit theory guiding the selection of observables, the use of measuring devices, and the listing of data. There are no critical experiments, only critical experimenters.

It follows that before observing real systems we would do well to practice on simple idealized systems.

8. IDENTIFICATION USING EXPERTS

One way to overcome the obstacles involved in this type of learning situation is to employ experts as guides and interpreters to teach us to identify and extract information from data. Let us recall that we classify information, as in earlier chapters, as that part of data useful for decision-making and learning. For example, the trainee learns to conduct an interview under the supervision of an experienced therapist. There are, however, obvious drawbacks to this procedure, necessary as it is, since an observer can have a serious effect upon the behavior of both patient and therapist.

9. MOTIVATION

The preceding considerations make it clear that it would be highly desirable to possess techniques that would enable us to observe some cause and effect relations and to test some policies without any use of the actual system. Furthermore, we want to introduce the novice to a complex system under carefully controlled and limited conditions. A suitable combination of mathematics and digital computers enables us to go quite far in this direction in a number of important situations. How far depends both upon the nature of the system and what we wish to accomplish.

10. MATHEMATICAL SIMULATION OF COMPLEXITY

Let us return to the phenomenon of uncertainty due to complexity discussed in Section 2. We have agreed that the behavior of the subsystems is known, along with their interactions. Nonetheless, we may possess no usable theoretical technique for determining R, given I.

We can, however, laboriously trace the effect of the specific influence I through the system. Thus, using the simpler schematic of Section 2 we have the schematic shown in Figure 3. By this schematic we mean, as usual, that I influences S_1 to produce an influence I_1, which in turn becomes an influence to S_2, which produces I_2, and so on. Thus, by a direct enumeration of cases we can determine the IR relation for the entire system, first for a particular I and then for the set of all admissible I's.

The idea is conceptually sound, if not particularly elegant in thought or execution. We are merely imitating, or simulating, the behavior of the actual system. The computer, which can run through an incredibly large number of procedures of the foregoing type in a reasonable amount of time, makes the foregoing idea operational in many cases.

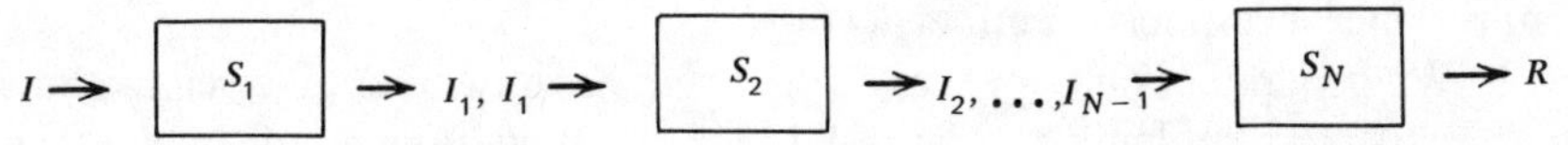

$$I \rightarrow \boxed{S_1} \rightarrow I_1, I_1 \rightarrow \boxed{S_2} \rightarrow I_2, \dots, I_{N-1} \rightarrow \boxed{S_N} \rightarrow R$$

Figure 7.3

11. DETERMINISTIC PROCESS

Prior to our discussion of certain simple properties of the computer, let us illustrate the foregoing ideas in a bit more detail. Suppose that we are given a set of influence-response tables for the individual systems (see Figure 4).

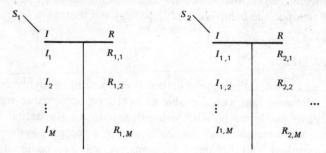

Figure 7.4

If we want R, the response of the entire system due to particular influence I_1 (see Figure 4), we can proceed systematically to obtain it by means of the following steps:

1. Using the influence-response table for the component S_1, we find that an influence of I_1 produces a response of $R_{1,1}$;

2. Using the influence-response table for the component S_2, we find that an influence of $R_{1,1}$ ($I_{1,1}$ for S_2) produces a response of $R_{2,1}$; and so on.

To make the procedure operational we require a specification of the initial influence together with the set of influence-response tables. We can then step-by-step trace the path of the initial influence through the system and describe its effects, both local and global, internal and external.

12. ILLUSTRATION: STOCHASTIC PROCESS

Let us consider next a case of particular interest to us where the influence-response table for each component S_i is stochastic. Thus, for example, for S_1 it may have the appearance shown in Figure 5.

If we ask for the set of possible end results of the influence I_1, we can then proceed as in the following fashion:

1. Using the influence-response table for S_1, we find that an influence I_1 can produce a response of either R_1 or R_2.

2. We generate a random event which can have two possible realizations with respective probabilities p_1 and $1 - p_1$, e.g., we toss a coin which can land heads with probability p_1 and tails with probability $1 - p_1$.*

* How a digital computer tosses coins will be discussed in detail in Section 36.

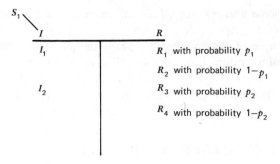

Figure 7.5

3. If the coin shows heads, we choose the outcome R_1; if tails, the outcome R_2.

4. The particular outcome is used as the influence on the next stage, and we continue in this fashion.

We thus have a branching of possibilities shown in Figure 6. This branching creates several kinds of problems, both theoretical and operational, which no amount of mathematical sophistication or computer capability can totally eliminate. We can, however, hope to reduce the difficulties somewhat by various techniques.

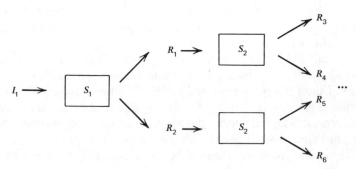

Figure 7.6

13. SAMPLING

In order to obtain a representative idea of the effect of a specific influence, I_1, upon a system with stochastic features, the process described above involving the systematic tracing of effects will necessarily have to be repeated many times. Although the probability is very small that a complex stochastic system will react the same way two times in a row, nonetheless, the probability is very high that there will be a regularity of response in some average sense if the influence stimulus is repeated a large number of times.

The technique of determining the properties of a stochastic system by repeatedly using certain influences is called sampling. Although the basic idea is simple, successful use requires considerable thought and experience.

All of the fundamental ideas of science are elementary. It is their operational use which requires a great deal of care, thought, and ingenuity.

14. INCORRECT, ILLOGICAL, IRRATIONAL

In terms of the foregoing model of a complex system, it is interesting, as an aside, to analyze what we might mean by the common terms *incorrect, illogical,* and *irrational.*

We can obtain an *incorrect* result from the operation of a system in the following ways:

1. Use of an influence I_2 instead of the actual influence I_1.
2. Use of the influence-response table for a different system rather than that for S_1.
3. Reading response R_1 as response R_2.

An incorrect result can, in principle at least, be corrected by going through the process again, step-by-step. Thus, we often make mistakes in arithmetic which can be corrected by repetition of the process. However, we can also make mistakes in the checking process, which considerably complicates the whole procedure.

We can call the solution process of a person *illogical* if he refuses to accept evidence that the influence I_1 produces the response R_1 despite the existence of the *I-R* experiments and tables. In other words, *logical* means acceptance of standardized rules of deducing effects from causes; responses from influences; illogical means deviation from these algorithms. Operationally, incorrect and illogical behavior may both produce the same erroneous results. However, illogical behavior is readily repeated and not as easily corrected. It represents a deeper and more persistent level of error.

We call a behavior *irrational* when we don't understand the *IR* mechanism of a particular subsystem. The procedure, however, may nevertheless be perfectly correct and logical as far as the individual himself is concerned. As we have already pointed out, this is particularly the case in decision processes where one individual may possess a criterion quite different from another's. The behavior of each then appears irrational to the other.

How to recognize and distinguish between incorrect, illogical, and irrational behavior in real time when they occur in various combinations, particularly in stochastic and adaptive processes, is not an easy matter.

15. FEASIBILITY OF MATHEMATICAL SIMULATION

It is clear that the mathematical simulation method described above can handle processes of some degree of complexity. Can it, however, handle processes of a high degree of complexity, and, if so, what factors limit its applicability to any type of process?

There are three considerations we must keep in mind when studying this question:

1. Can we reduce a particular process to a sequence of influence-response operations of the foregoing type?
2. Can we keep track of all of the instructions contained in the influence-response tables?
3. Will a simulation process of the type described above consume too much time?

Any answers we provide to these questions are clearly conditional ones, highly dependent on the properties of contemporary science and digital computers, and on current mathematical theory. Note that these are two different kinds of questions. The first is conceptual, the second and third operational. The line of demarcation, however, is not clear-cut. To use a theory, we must be operational; to be operational requires a theory.

16. PORTRAIT OF THE DIGITAL COMPUTER AS A GLORIFIED FILE CLERK

Let us now turn to an examination of certain simple properties of a digital computer. The actual physical principles and mechanisms which enable these operations to be carried out, principles of mechanical, electrical, or pneumatic nature, are of no particular consequence to us here. We may if we wish, however, conjure up a picture of a large office, replete with filing cabinets, reference books, and telephones, staffed by a very large number of energetic elves. Some sit at telephones giving and taking messages, some scurry about either taking material out of files and reference books, or putting it in. What we wish to emphasize is that what we will discuss involves only concepts implied by the foregoing imagery.

We require for our purposes a device that can perform the following tasks:

1. Store a set of symbols;
2. Retrieve some of these symbols at command;
3. Store sets of ISR-triplets; or, more generally, ISS_1R-quadruples;
4. Use these triplets, or quadruples, to determine the consequences of a particular influence;

5. Follow a set of instructions to employ these results in a sequence as described above.

6. Provide and display intermediate and final responses, as specified, upon request.

The set of symbols ordinarily used are the integers 1, 2, 3, . . . , 9, and 0, whence the name *digital computer*. Nonetheless, the particular set of symbols used is of no significance for our work. We are interested in storing words and sentences in connection with the verbal and nonverbal aspects of the two-person interaction in an initial psychotherapy interview. There are simple ways of using one set of symbols for another, e.g., assign a number to each of the 26 letters, for example: $A = 1, B = 2, C = 3, . . . , Z = 26$; $I = 1, II = 2$, etc. In other words the alphabet employed is of no fundamental influence. There are, however, aspects of convenience to employing one rather than another.

The set of instructions which tells the computer how to handle an influence, what symbol manipulations to perform and in what order, and what is desired as an output is called the computer program. It may be written in any of a number of computer languages, for example Fortran, Algol, Simscript, and others which are now available.

17. SCIENTIFIC COMPUTING

For the purposes of much of science and mathematics, fundamental skills of the computer are the abilities to perform the four basic operations of arithmetic—addition, subtraction, multiplication, and division; to follow instructions to perform these operations according to a computer program; and to store the results of past operations so that they may be combined suitably with current operations.

We shall have no need of the computer's arithmetic ability in what follows, and therefore we shall say no more about it here.

18. OPERATIONAL ASPECTS

In contemplating the use of a digital computer for purposes of research, it is incumbent upon us to ask ourselves two questions:

1. Can the computer meet our needs?
2. Is the computer necessary?

The tasks described in the foregoing sections can all be performed by human beings. Furthermore, file clerks may be cheaper, sometimes far easier to communicate with, and may possess remarkable learning abilities.

In addition, they are, on the whole, far more satisfying to have around than electronic consoles. Let us see then if we can justify our desire to employ a currently fashionable, therefore automatically suspect, device.

19. STORAGE FACILITIES

Let us begin with an examination of the capabilities of the digital computer as far as storage and retrieval of data are concerned. There are three types of storage associated with a digital computer:

1. Rapid access storage
2. Slow access storage
3. Tape

They are distinguished by the amount of data they can hold and the speed with which a number can be located and read (access time). Rapid access storage in large commercially available computers can currently handle about one million ten-digit numbers. Access time is about 10^{-5} seconds; i.e., 100,000 numbers can be located and dispatched somewhere else in approximately one second. Slow access storage increases the capacity by a factor of about ten at the expense of decreasing the access time by a factor of about ten. These times are changing year by year and are cited here merely to give the reader some estimate of the capabilities.

On the other hand, there is essentially no limit to the quantity of data that can be stored on tapes. Naturally, however, the retrieval time increases considerably as the quantity of data increases.

20. MEMORY

The introduction of digital computers about 25 years ago created an enormous burst of enthusiasm. Some of this overflowed into both mysticism and anthropomorphism. Such terms as "giant brain", "thinking machine", and "memory" were consequently thrown about with abandon and a number of rash predictions were made concerning the eventual dethroning of human intellect.

One result of this was that rapid access storage was called "fast memory" and slow access storage was called "slow memory". Even today, the term "memory" is occasionally applied to what is storage capacity.

It is useful, as we have previously noted, to think of the present-day computer as a low-level filing system operated by a group of fast, but totally unimaginative, clerks. Table look-up is thus rather difficult and cross-indexing, i.e., associative activities, even more so. For problems of moderate size, we can readily replace understanding with speed. In treating problems of realistic complexity, however, we face serious obstacles when attempting to use such pedestrian techniques. We shall describe some of these obstacles below.

On the other hand, the very lack of imagination of a computer is perhaps its greatest asset. A computer does not get bored and the thousandth repetition of an operation differs in no way from the first. It thus permits absolute reproducibility, an ideal asset for experimentation.

21. DESIRABILITY OF SLOWNESS

In scientific computing, speed is usually essential. For our purposes, however, since we are interested in simulating a two-person interaction process, speed is actually undesirable. As a matter of fact, if the patient response were communicated almost instantaneously to the student, we would have an element of artificiality which would then have to be counteracted. It would be necessary to introduce a time delay to provide a realistic interval between student and patient responses.

By varying the rapidity with which the patient responses are given, and the rate of the response itself, we can introduce two further important parameters into the simulation process we discuss in the following chapter.

22. TERMINALS

One of the most important contemporary developments is the use of terminals connected with computers. Terminals provide two advantages:

1. Convenient access to a centrally located computer.
2. Simultaneous use of a computer by a number of different persons.

This is an important consideration for the library of short simulation processes which we have constructed. It means that many people in a class, or even in different schools, can simultaneously use these processes. This is significant pedagogically.

23. SIZE OF INFLUENCE-RESPONSE TABLES

Having given some brief idea of the storage and retrieval capacity of the computer, the only need we shall have for it, let us turn to an examination of whether this expensive device fits our needs.

Returning to the simple schematic shown in Figure 7 we would like to store ISS_1R-quadruples. Clearly we cannot store *all* possible therapist responses and *all* possible patient responses, since we cannot even conceive of them in entirety.

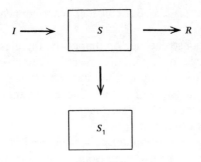

Figure 7.7

This observation, however, does not particularly dismay us. After all, even a logarithm table does not provide the numerical value of the logarithm of *every* number. It furnishes values of representative numbers with the supposition that we can use these values in a systematic fashion to supply any desired value. This presentation of representative values, together with an interpolation procedure, is a standard mathematical-scientific device for storing data.

Let us attempt the same idea here. We can agree initially to eliminate alternative grammatical constructions, linguistic flourishes, and the overwhelming redundancy and overlapping of the English language, and to reduce responses to certain essentials:

Verbal: semantic content, emotional content.
Nonverbal: vocal responses, facial expression, postures, and changes in posture.

We can imagine that the therapist might wish to ask a question, or make a comment, in one of several different areas: Sex, Love, Marriage, Job, Mother, Father, Son, Daughter, Family, Friends, Age, Health, Philosophy of Life.

Some of these can be combined; some can be further differentiated. The point, however, is that within each category there are a number of different kinds of questions which can be asked.

Further, we can allow different tones of voice, say, friendly, neutral, hostile, and three body attitudes, say, alert, neutral, relaxed. There are a large number of combinations of the foregoing characteristics.

We see then that the task of cataloging even a part of the total set of responses of the therapist is a formidable one.

Turning to the patient, we can envisage a number of possible responses to each therapist response, with these responses further influenced by his mood. The ISS_1R quadruple table is excessive when we consider only a single stage of the interview. But consider what happens when we examine the multistage process.

The patient's response depends on that of the therapist; the next response of the therapist depends upon this response-response pair; the second patient response depends upon the first response pair and the second response of the therapist; and so on. The branching rapidly gets out of hand. We have already discussed the arithmetic of this in a simplified case in Section 28 of Chapter 6.

It is clear then that the computer cannot be used in any routine fashion. But it can be used fruitfully with some combination of sophistication, ingenuity, and experience.

24. USE OF THEORY

Considerations of the foregoing type begin to make us appreciate having a theory to use. In this case, theory would provide us with a rule, an algorithm, for calculating S_1 and R, given I and S. It is clearly very much more convenient to store the algorithm than to store the entire ISS_1R table.

What do we do, however, when theory does not exist, or only a partial theory exists?

25. PROCRUSTEAN FITS

We frequently encounter this frustrating branching phenomenon in applications of mathematics to physical processes. Indeed, it is the rule rather than the exception. To overcome it, we perform a Procrustean fit, trimming the response tree to the capabilities of the computer.

There are two principal methods of trimming in the simulation of an initial interview:

1. Limiting the number of patient and therapist response options.
2. Limiting the amount of branching of possible exchanges.

We have already discussed one aspect of the first method in Chapters 5 and 6. In Chapter 8 we shall continue the discussion and introduce a procedure for the second. Let us emphasize that each process requires its own careful consideration. In the construction of mathematical models, there is no uniform procedure to be followed that bypasses the dimensionality problem.

26. DECISION PROCESSES AND FEASIBILITY

We have considered a decision process to consist of the following components:

1. A set of choices concerning influences on the system.
2. A table of influence-state-response relations.
3. A set of observations of the state and response of the system.
4. A method for evaluation of the process.

We can then envisage the following possibilities:

1. Determination of optimal policies by theoretical means.
2. Determination of optimal policies by testing a set of possible policies. Furthermore, we possess a new option:
3. Testing feasible policies which are not necessarily optimal.

In practice, optimal policies generally play a role subordinate to feasible policies as we have noted before. Optimality in fact should be regarded as a mathematical device for handling the really important problem, that of feasibility.

27. GAME-PLAYING

Let us illustrate the foregoing ideas in the familiar terms of a card game. If we are interested in improving our play, or learning to play initially, there are several alternatives we can contemplate:

1. Detailed mathematical analysis leading to a determination of optimal play; i.e., derivation of a set of rules which yield the greatest average amount of winnings.
2. An examination of tens of thousands of actual hands to determine optimal play based on the experience of people playing the game.
3. An examination of tens of thousands of computer-dealt hands to determine optimal play by simulated experience.
4. An examination of tens of thousands of actual hands to study the use of simple approximate rules of play.
5. An examination of tens of thousands of computer-dealt hands to study the use of simple approximate rules of play.

28. BLACKJACK EXPLICATED

To illustrate some of the methods that can be used, let us consider a simplified version of the card game, Blackjack, often called Twenty-One.
Let us recall the way in which the game is commonly played.
Using a bridge deck, the dealer gives the player two cards face down and himself two cards, one face up. The cards have associated numerical values, Ace through Ten as indicated, Jack, Queen, and King each counting 10. To simplify some subsequent discussions and diagrams, we shall

ignore the important point that in the actual game the Ace can also count as 11.

The player looks at his cards and then makes the first decision. He can decide to draw a card or not. If he does not draw, the decision passes to the dealer and the player has no further options. If the dealer has a total of 16 or over, he cannot draw. Play is ended and the totals of the two hands are compared. If the dealer's total exceeds the player's, the dealer wins; if the total is less, he loses; if equal, it is a draw.

If the dealer has a total of 15 points or less, he must draw a card. If his total with three cards is over 21, he automatically loses. If his total is between 16 and 21, inclusive, the game is decided as before by comparison of the two totals, the player's and the dealer's. If his total is still under 16, he must draw another card, and so on.

If, on the other hand, the player decides to draw another card, he loses automatically if his three-card total exceeds 21. He automatically wins if he achieves a total of 21. If he does not obtain either 21 or over, he has the option of stopping, or drawing another card. Once he stops, the game proceeds as described above with the options now up to the dealer.

The game is an excellent example of a multistage stochastic decision process. We have simplified it leaving out inessential details. This is of no great conceptual concern since many versions exist. The variations are, however, of significance in determining whether the game is favorable to dealer or player.

29. TESTING A SIMPLE POLICY

As we have previously observed, the state of available knowledge is not sufficiently advanced to warrant a detailed mathematical analysis of optimal policies in an initial psychotherapy interview. Furthermore, the term "optimal" is usually not well defined in processes involving human beings. Hence we have studiously avoided the term "optimal". We are, nonetheless, interested in the study of various reasonable interviewing techniques. Before seeing how we might go about this in a mathematical model of a psychotherapy interview, let us look at how we would pursue this theme in a simpler model of a far simpler process with a computer at our disposal. We will continue to illustrate these ideas with the game of Twenty-One. With the aid of the computer, thousands of experiments can be performed with only a small initial effort on our part.

Let us suppose we wanted to test the following simple policy for the player: "Never draw a card if there is any chance of ending up with a total exceeding 21, regardless of what the dealer has."*

* In practice, this is not a bad policy. It loses slowly.

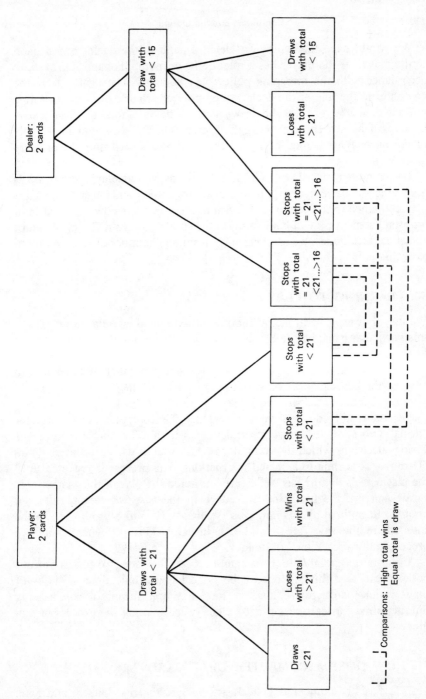

Figure 7.8

We would have the computer "deal" a hand to the dealer and a hand to the player. If the player has a total of 12 or more, his hand is frozen, in accordance with the foregoing policy, i.e., he stops. The dealer (i.e., the computer in the role of the dealer) then proceeds to draw or not according to preassigned house rules: he draws a card if he has a total of 15 or under; he stops if he has 16 or over. If the player (i.e., the computer in the role of the player) has a total of 11 or less, he draws a card until 12 or more is attained.

The computer records the win, loss, or tie, as well as playing both hands according to the assigned policies. It follows the simple instructions for play contained in the computer program. The process is now repeated until we attain some feeling of confidence in the statistical results. Using standard statistical techniques, we can determine a suitable number of plays required to evaluate this policy.

30. LEARNING TO PLAY

We may, however, be in the position of an individual who has never played this particular game before. In this case, he will certainly not know enough to possess a theory of play, i.e., a policy. Before fixing on a method of play, he will want the chance to play the game a number of times and to observe the consequences of various decisions. In other words, he would like an opportunity to learn the game.

He can readily do this, playing against the computer. The computer "deals" two cards to the player and two to itself. The player then makes various decisions which the computer records and to which it reacts, again, of course, according to assigned instructions. The process is repeated until the player feels that he has sufficiently mastered the play of the game.

We can use the foregoing procedure in the case where the rules are known but optimal play is not. Observe that we can also use it even in the case where the rules are *not* known initially. This is then an adaptive process in our preceding terminology.

An important point is that the computer can be instructed to test various policies and that this testing can be done in electronic time, millions of times faster than actual. Thus, we have a simple means of compressing time required for learning or, equivalently, accelerating the process in real time.

31. HOW DOES A COMPUTER DEAL CARDS?

Let the cards be numbered 1, 2, 3, . . . , 13, with Jack, Queen, and King assigned the numbers 11 through 13 respectively, the Ace assigned the number 1, and the others as indicated by their numbers. The computer picks two of these numbers at random for the player's hand and two for the dealer's hand. The player is then told, for example, "You have been dealt two cards, a 4 and a Queen. The dealer has been dealt two cards, one unknown and a 10 showing." Note that the picture cards have the uniform value of 10 in the game although they are numbered 11, 12, 13 for identification purposes.

This information may be printed out in a typewriter, or displayed on the screen of a television set. If we are using a television screen, we can even picture the hands, imitating what occurs at a casino.

The player now must make one of two decisions:

1. Stop; i.e., draw no cards.
2. Draw one card.

If the player decides not to draw, following, for example, the simple policy described above in Section 30, the computer has two possibilities:

1. If the hole card, the unknown card, is 6 or above, it stops.
2. If the hole card is 5 or below, it must draw a card; i.e., choose a third random number, and so on.

The decisions of the player are communicated to the computer by pushing buttons, using typewriter keys, or using a light pen. When the computer stops, comparison of the hands is made. In this case where the player has 14, 17 or more for the dealer is a win for the dealer.

If the computer draws a card, the new dealer total is computed. The decision to stop or draw is made as before, or an automatic loss is tabulated if the dealer total is over 21.

A schematic of the process is shown in Figure 9.

The computer dealer begins its play only after the player has terminated his play.

The essential point is that a decision by the computer is equivalent to the selection of a number according to a preassigned rule.

32. GENERATION OF RANDOM NUMBERS

We have in the foregoing pages referred constantly to the ability of the digital computer to perform certain types of random actions. For example, it can produce the numbers from 1 to 13 with equal probability, corresponding to the dealing of a card. This, however, poses a disturbing question. How does the digital computer, a completely deterministic device, generate a random number following a prescribed program?

There are two different types of ways in which this can be done. In the

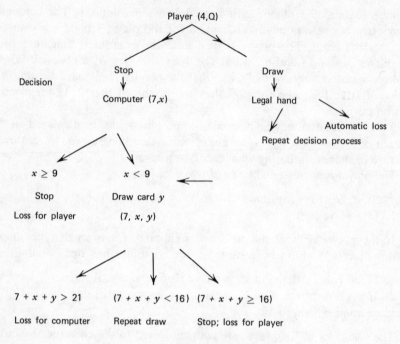

Figure 7.9

first place, we can at our leisure record sequences of random physical events and store these records for subsequent use. Thus, for example, suppose our hypothetical fair coin were tossed repeatedly, yielding the sequence

$$\text{HTTTHHTHHTTHTTHHH} \dots$$

Figure 7.10

Here, H denotes heads and T denotes tails. For digital computer purposes, let us replace H by 1 and T by 0, thus obtaining the sequence

$$1\ 000\ 11\ 0\ 11\ 00\ 1\ 00\ 111 \dots$$

Figure 7.11

There are now many ways of converting a random sequence of 0's and 1's into sequences of random integers between 0 and 13. For example, we can take groups of four consecutive digits,

$$1000\ 1101\ 1001\ 0011 \dots$$

Figure 7.12

and think of these as expressions in the scale of two. Thus

$$1000 = 1(8) + 0(4) + 0(2) = 0(1) = 8$$
$$1101 = 1(8) + 1(4) + 0(2) + 1(1) = 13$$
$$1001 = 1(8) + 0(4) + 0(2) + 1(1) = 9$$
$$0011 = 0(8) + 0(4) + 1(2) + 1(1) = 3$$

and so on. We can accept the integers 1, 2, 3, . . . , 13, and reject the values 0, 14, 15 which can also be produced in this way; e.g., 1111 = 1(8) + 1(4) + 1(2) + 1 = 15. Alternatively we can use some other simple method for obtaining only the integers 1, 2, . . . , 13 from strings of 0's and 1's.

Applying techniques of this nature, extensive general tables of random numbers have been prepared and can be used for the foregoing purposes. If a certain number of random events are to be simulated, say 100, we can use a string of 100 of the numbers in a table of this nature. This set is stored inside the computer available for use as requested.

Thus, for example, if we were dealing the first hand of a game of Twenty-One as previously described, using the first four numbers above, we would give the player an 8 and a 13 (King), with the dealer having a 9 face down and a 3 face up.

In place of using an existing table of random numbers, however, we may prefer to generate our own as we need them. There are many ways of doing this. One way, for example, is the following. Let us take a nine-digit number, e.g., 123456789, and square it, obtaining 15241578750190-5100. Take the middle nine digits, 157875019, square, and extract the middle nine digits of the product, and so on. It is to be expected that if we repeat the process a sufficient number of times, say 100, we will obtain a nine-digit number with the numbers 0, 1, 2, . . . , 9 appearing in a random order.

A number of simple rules of this type permit the computer to generate random numbers as needed. These numbers will not, of course, really be random since they are calculated according to assigned rules. However, they will appear so according to all reasonable statistical tests. They avoid systematic bias, and thus they are appropriate for our purposes.

33. EVALUATION OF A STOCHASTIC DECISION PROCESS

In a deterministic decision process the decision-maker has complete control of the outcome. In a stochastic decision process the outcome is determined by a combination of specific decisions and random events. How do we disentangle the two effects? How does one distinguish between a sound decision cursed by bad luck and a bad decision blessed with good luck? This is a basic question that confronts anyone attempting to develop effective methods for stochastic and, particularly, adaptive decision processes.

Consider, for example, the case of a person wishing to learn optimal play in the game of Twenty-One using the computer simulation described in the previous pages. How does he go about this?

There are a number of different questions contained in the foregoing:

1. Does "optimal play" have a meaning?
2. Do explicit rules for the determination of optimal play exist?
3. Are there experts who can recognize optimal play and use this knowledge to improve the play of a beginner without the use of explicit rules?
4. Is it possible for an individual to observe his own play and to improve it without reference to the play of others?
5. How does one use the experience of others to deduce a pattern of optimal play?
6. Is it worth the effort to learn optimal play as opposed to feasible play?

Let us discuss these questions in turn.

34. WHAT CONSTITUTES OPTIMAL PLAY?

We have previously agreed that in a process involving stochastic elements decision-making is to be evaluated in terms of *average* behavior. For example, in the game of Twenty-One, we may wish to play to win as often as possible on the average. If, however, we are allowed to wager different amounts on different hands, we may wish instead to play so as to make the long-term average gain as large as possible.

The average, whichever one used, is evaluated in the expected fashion. The decision process is carried out a certain number of times with a tabulation of the results, say, wins and losses in the Twenty-One game. In this way, a frequency of wins is calculated. How many plays are required in order to provide a firm basis for judgment is usually a delicate matter. In general, if possible, it is best to err on the side of conservatism, and repeat the process until stabilization of the calculated frequency is clearly observed.

If we are accepting the simple arithmetic average as a criterion, an optimal policy is one which yields the greatest frequency of wins. It is clear, however, that use of an optimal policy cannot guarantee a win on a particular play, or even in any fixed sequence of plays. Every card player, every person who has engaged in a game with stochastic elements, can testify to this. The best of play can be vitiated by the vagaries of chance.

Many examples exist of the occurrence of events of vanishingly small probability.

Risk is thus one price of uncertainty. We can diminish the price by repetition of the process a large number of times and by conservative action on any particular play, but we cannot eliminate risk entirely. Many perplexing questions remain as to the proper course of action in stochastic situations where we do not possess the luxury of repetition.

This is, of course, a particularly serious problem in the medical field where the cost of a wrong treatment is so high.

35. RULES FOR OPTIMAL PLAY

Let us suppose that we have agreed upon a specific criterion and seek to learn optimal play, which is now a well-defined concept. If rules for optimal play exist, which they do in a number of simple processes, it becomes a matter of recognition of the situation and implementation of the decision. Sometimes these are simple, often not. As a simple example, consider the game of Tic-Tac-Toe a deterministic process.

The rule is for the first player to occupy the center square (Figure 13). If the second player makes an incorrect response, say an O where indicated in Figure 14, the first player should choose a corner, since he now has a forced win, by means of, say, the occupation of the lower right-hand square, no matter what move the second player makes (Figure 15). Observe that

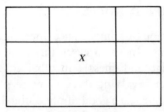

Optimal first move

Figure 7.13

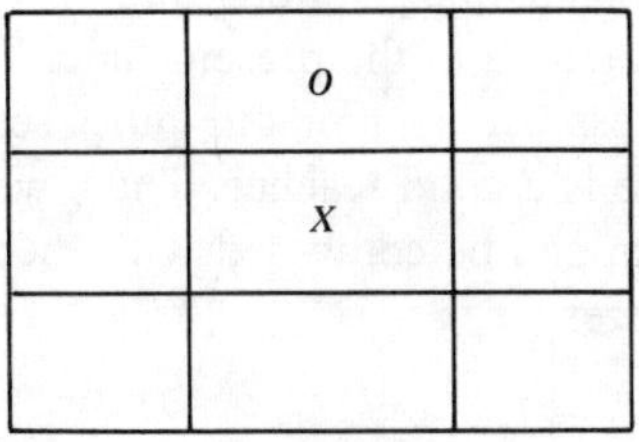

Incorrect second move

Figure 7.14

An optimal second move

Figure 7.15

occupation of the lower left-hand square would be just as good. This illustrates the important point that optimal moves need not be unique. In many situations there are a number of alternate courses of equally effective action. In most complex situations there is a large set of feasible policies which for all practical purposs have outcomes which are indistinguishable. This blurring of fine detail is what makes the operation of large complex systems possible.

Very seldom can we evaluate a situation in such simple terms as making a correct move to guarantee a desired outcome. This means, as stated above, that risk-taking is an essential part of the important processes of life. In other words, stochastic decision processes are the rule rather than the exception.

36. LACK OF CODIFIED RULES

In a number of situations of importance there are no codified rules for optimal decision-making. In some cases this is due to the complexity of the process (e.g., bridge and chess); in other cases it is due to inherent ambiguities (e.g., poker involving three or more players, or medical diagnosis). How then does one learn good, if not optimal, play?

The answer is that one learns good play by some mysterious combination of theory, teaching by experts, and personal experience. How the human mind learns to perform complex actions and to cope with genuine complexity is not well understood at the present time. We do observe, however, that this learning process occurs. For our purposes, then, we shall accept the fact that experience is a good teacher. Thus, we strive to provide some artificial experience that can be combined with theory. This is the basis for using simulation processes.

37. EXPERTS

In previous discussion we have questioned the meaningfulness of the concept of optimal policy in connection with an initial psychotherapy interview since we cannot provide an explicit criterion for evaluation. Intuitively, however, we accept the concept of some more and some less effective policies. But how are we to evaluate a particular interview or a computer simulation?

One answer lies in the use of experts. Some psychotherapists on the basis of theory, experience, and innate ability have learned how to conduct initial interviews in excellent fashion. They may not be able to describe completely what standards they are employing as they go along, but they can judge in a particular interview how well someone else has performed. They can point out appropriate and inappropriate therapist responses, and explain to a great extent why these are of this nature; they can identify patient states and types of behavior.

As is true of experts in all fields, they can evaluate a situation when they see it, without necessarily being able to analyze the elements involved, or being able to anticipate what they expect to see.

An expert, or a group of experts, is equally capable of examining a particular computer simulation and evaluating its various components and range of policies.

On the basis of the previous discussion, it is clear then that experts are required to construct meaningful simulation processes. We shall discuss this further in the following chapter. Are they, however, needed after the simulation process has been constructed? The answer depends critically on the level of the simulation process. If, as in the game of Tic-Tac-Toe, it is easy to learn from computer experience, no supervision of the trainee is needed. In the game of Twenty-One, although no supervision is needed to learn optimal play, it is reasonable to believe that the learning experience can be substantially accelerated using the analysis of an expert player.

We have previously considered the problem of learning from experience. In a complex process, of course, there is always the danger that incorrect, as well as correct, behavior will be acquired since one may be unaware of correct behavior. This is a well-known effect in tennis or golf, and other games as well. Particularly in an intellectual process limited experience can readily lead to faulty conclusions. One can reach equilibrium at an undesirable plateau.

Experts are thus vitally needed to discuss and interpret the sequence of decisions. A simulation process is designed as a research tool and as a teaching aid, to supplement—not to replace—the experienced instructor.

38. CAVEAT SIMULATOR!

Having discussed the need for simulation at the beginning of the chapter, it is appropriate at the end of the chapter to indicate what is perhaps the principal danger of simulation. This consists of a tendency to confuse reality with the mathematical model constructed. The model is man-made, simpler, controllable, and therefore, ipso facto, psychologically more appealing. It becomes seductively easy to believe that optimal decision-making in this model of reality, abstracted and simplified, is actually optimal decision-making in the real world. The student must thus constantly be reminded of the many simplifying assumptions inherent in any simulation. This is one of the functions of the expert. Indeed, the search for these may be one of the most important pedagogical aspects of a simulation process.

NOTES AND REFERENCES

1. For a very much more detailed discussion of the theory of simulation, see R. Bellman, et al, "On the Construction of a Multi-Person, Multi-Stage Business Game", *Operations Research*, Vol. 5, 1957, pp. 469–503.
   J. R. Greene and R. L. Sisson, *Dynamic Management Decision Games*, New York, Wiley and Sons, 1959.
   E. M. Babb and L. M. Eisgruber, *Management Games for Teaching and Research*, Chicago, Educational Methods, Inc., 1966.
   H. Barko, Computer *Applications in the Behavioral Sciences*, Englewood Cliffs, New Jersey, Prentice-Hall, 1962.
   H. Guetzkow, Ed., *Simulation in the Social Sciences, Readings*, Englewood Cliffs, New Jersey, Prentice-Hall, 1962.

7. On science and the observer: "The practice of medicine, like scientific method, begins with observation. *How* the clinician observes, as well as *what* he observes, determines the kind of information he will obtain." Enelow and Wexler, 1966, *op. cit.*

9. It has been hypothesized, evaluated, and statistically accepted that a medical student may better learn certain interviewing techniques from interacting with a programmed learning film than from a class discussion of his own filmed interview with an actor-patient. This last is a highly regarded pedagogical technique. Both methods are examples of introducing the novice to a complex situation under limited and controlled conditions.
   Enelow and Wexler, 1966, *op. cit.*

13. The sophisticated study of this mathematical technique is called the "Monte Carlo" technique. See
    J. Halton, "A Retrospective and Prospective Study of the Monte Carlo Method", *SIAM Review*, Vol. 12, 1970, pp. 1–63.

15. See
W. Reitman, *Cognition and Thought,* New York, Wiley and Sons, 1965 for a detailed general introduction to design and uses of simulation models. An evaluation of the place of such models in psychiatry is also included.

16. Starkweather and Decker have provided a means for processing verbal content for individual patients to show shifts, the individual lexicon, etc. See
J. Starkweather and J. Decker, "Computer Analysis of Interview Content", *Psychological Reports,* 1964, Vol. 15 (3) pp. 875–882.
See also
J. Starkweather, "Computer Simulation of Psychiatric Interviewing", in N. Kline and E. Laska, 1968, *op. cit.*
and
J. Starkweather, "Computest: A Computer Language for Individual Testing, Instruction and Interviewing", Psychological Reports, Vol. 17, 1965, pp. 227–337.
Newell and Simon are early pioneers in using information processing models in psychiatry. See
A. Newell and H. Simon, "Programs as Theories of Higher Mental Processes", in R. Stacy and B. Waxman (eds.) *Computers in Biomedical Research,* Vol. 2, 1965, New York, Academic Press, pp. 141–172.
The following list represents some interesting computer uses in related areas and valuable evaluative discussions.
Computers in Psychiatry, Supplement to the American Journal of Psychiatry, Vol. 125 (7), January 1969, pp. 1–36.
K. Colby, S. Weber, F. Hilf, "Artificial Paranoia", Stanford University, Computer Science Department, Artificial Intelligence Project Memo AIM-125, July, 1970.
K. Colby and H. Enea, "Machine Utilization of the Natural Language Word 'Good'", Stanford University Technical Report No. CS 78, September 1967.
K. Colby, F. Hilf and W. Hall, "A Mute Patient's Experience with Machine-Mediated Interviewing", Stanford University, Computer Science Department, Stanford Artificial Intelligence Project Memo AIM-113, March 1970.
W. Cooley and P. Lohnes, *Multivariative Procedures for the Behavioral Sciences,* New York, Wiley, 1962.
B. Eidusun, S. Brooks, R. Motto, A. Platz and R. Carmichael, "New Strategy for Psychiatric Research, Utilizing the Psychiatric Case History Event System", in N. Kline and E. Laska, 1968, *op. cit.*
R. Fowler, Jr., "Computer Interpretation of Personality Tests: The Automated Psychologist", *Compr. Psychiat.,* Vol. 8, 1967, pp. 455–467.

B. Glueck, Jr. and M. Reznikoff, "Comparison of Computer-Derived Personality Profile and Projective Psychological Test Findings," *Amer. J. Psychiat.*, Vol. 121, 1965, pp. 1156–1161.

B. Glueck, Jr. and M. Rosenberg, "Automation of Patient Behavioral Observations", in N. Kline and E. Laska, 1968, *op. cit.*

D. Gorham, "Validity and Reliability Studies of a Computer-Based Scoring System for Ink-Blot Responses", *J. Consult. Psychol.*, Vol. 31, 1967, pp. 65–70.

F. Hilf, K. Colby, D. Smith and W. Wittner, "Machine-Mediated Interviewing", Stanford University, Computer Science Department, Stanford Artificial Intelligence Project Memo AIM-112, March 1970.

W. Slack, G. Hicks, C. Reed and L. Van Cura, "A Computer-Based Medical-History System", *New England Journal of Medicine,* Vol. 274, 1966, pp. 194–198.

W. Slack, B. Peckham, L. Van Cura, W. Carr, "A Computer-Based Physical Examination System", *The Journal of the Amer. Med. Assn.*, Vol. 200(3), 1967, pp. 224–228.

N. Kline and E. Laska, 1968, *op. cit.*

P. Meehl, *Clinical Versus Statistical Prediction,* Minneapolis, University of Minnesota Press, 1954.

P. Meehl, "Wanted—A Good Cookbook", *Amer. Psychol.*, Vol. 11, 1956, pp. 263–272.

J. Pearson, H. Rome, W. Swenson, "Development of a Computer System for Scoring and Interpretation of Minnesota Multphasic Personality Inventories in a Medical Clinic", Ann. N. Y. *Acad. Sci.,* Vol. 126, 1965, pp. 684–695.

Z. Piotrowski, "Digital-Computer Interpretation of Ink-Blot Test Data", *Psychiat. Quart.*, Vol. 38, 1964, pp. 1–26.

M. Rosenberg and B. Glueck Jr., "Future Developments in Automation of Behavioral Observations on Hospitalized Psychiatric Patients", *Compr. Psychiat.*, Vol. 8, 1967, pp. 468–475.

M. Rosenberg, B. Glueck Jr., W. Bennett, "Automation of Behavioral Observations on Hospitalized Psychiatric Patients", *Amer. J. Psychiat.*, Vol. 123, 1967, pp. 926–929.

M. Rosenberg, B. Glueck Jr., and C. Stroebel, "The Computer and the Clinical Decision Process", *Amer. J. Psychiat.*, Vol. 124, 1967, pp. 595–599.

M. Rosenberg, M. Reznikoff, C. Stroebel, R. Ericson, "How Patients Feel About Computers", *Hospital and Community Psychiatry,* Vol. 18, 1967, pp. 334–336.

W. Sanders, G. Breitbard, D. Cummins, R. Flexer, K. Holtz, J. Miller, G. Wiederhold, "An Advanced Computer System for Medical Research", in *Proceedings of the Fall Joint Computer Conference,* New York, American Federation of Information Processing Societies, 1967, pp. 497–508.

R. Spitzer and J. Endicott, "Automation of Psychiatric Case Records", in J. Aronson, 1970, *op. cit.,* pp. 604–621.

R. Spitzer, J. Endicott, J. Fleiss, "Instruments and Recording Forms for Evaluating Psychiatric Status and History: Rationale, Method of Development and Description", *Compr. Psychiat.*, Vol. 8, 1967, pp. 321–343.

S. Stroebel, W. Bennett, P. Ericson, B. Glueck Jr., "Designing Psychiatric Computer Information Systems: Problems and Strategy", *Compr. Psychiat.*, Vol. 8, 1967, pp. 491–508.

G. Ulett and I. Sletten, "A Statewide Electronic Data Processing System", *Hospital and Community Psychiatry*, Vol. 20, 1969, pp. 74–77.

D. Veldman, "Computer-Based Sentence Completion Interviews", *J. Couns. Psychol.*, Vol. 14, 1967, pp. 153–157.

J. Weizenbaum, "Eliza", Department of Electrical Engineering, M.I.T., August 1965.

17. Elementary discussions of the computer from technical to theoretical will be found in the following references:

W. Dorn, "Computers in the High School", *Datamation*, Vol. 13, February 1967, pp. 34–38.

E. Feigenbaum and J. Feldman, *Computers and Thought*, New York, McGraw-Hill, 1963.

B. Caller, *The Language of Computers*, New York, McGraw-Hill, 1967.

D. Halacy, *Computers, the Machines We Think With*, New York, Harper and Row, 1962.

D. McCracken, *Digital Computer Programming*, New York, Wiley, 1957.

W. Orr, *Conversational Computers*, New York, Wiley, 1968.

J. K. Rice and J. R. Rice, 1969, *op. cit.*

S. Rosen, *Programming Systems and Languages*, New York, McGraw-Hill, 1967.

S. Ulam, "Computers", *Scientific American*, Vol. 211(32), September 1964, pp. 202–208.

P. Wegner, *Programming Languages, Information Structures and Machine Organization*, New York, McGraw-Hill, 1968.

F. Young, *The Nature of Mathematics*, New York, Wiley, 1968.

The development of parallel processing computers will drastically revise the previous time and capacity estimates. See the expository article:

D. L. Slotnick, "The Fastest Computer: ILLIAC IV", *Scientific American*, July 1970, pp. 76–87.

18. See

R. Bellman, "Mathematical Models of the Mind", *Math. Biosci.*, Vol. 1, 1967, pp. 287–304.

20. It is important to emphasize that the use of the term "memory" in connection with a digital computer is quite misleading. To begin with, we have only a feeble understanding of the mechanisms of the brain and the mind. How ideas and images are created and stored, how data are filed, processed, and retrieved by the brain remains a mystery, probably the most outstanding of the many fascinating ones that currently confront us.

We do know, solely on the basis of observation, unfortunately, that the brain does possess powerful associative methods, ways of cross-indexing and correlating. If these mechanisms were understood, really spectacular computers could be constructed.

23. It is possible to construct computer programs which will scan responses for semantic and emotional content, but these require very difficult and complex analysis. Progress in this area has been slow. See
K. Colby, et al, "Artificial Paranoia", 1970, *op. cit.*
J. Starkweather and J. Decker, 1964, *op. cit.*

31. See
R. Bellman and D. Blackwell, "Red Dog, Blackjack and Poker", *Scientific American,* Vol. 184, 1951, pp. 44–47.
E. Thorp, *Beat the Dealer,* New York, Random House, 1966.

32. See
"One Million Random Numbers and Standard Deviates", Santa Monica, California, The RAND Corporation, 1949.
B. Jansson, *Random Number Generators,* Stockholm, Sweden, Victor Pettersons Bokindustri AB, 1966.

38. See
M. Apter, *The Computer Simulation of Behavior,* New York, Hillory House Pub., 1970.

Chapter 8

A COMPUTER SIMULATION
OF THE INITIAL
PSYCHOTHERAPY INTERVIEW

1. INTRODUCTION

In Chapter 6 we provided a conceptual framework for a mathematical model of an initial interview viewed as a multistage decision process of adaptive type. In Chapter 7 we discussed some of the ways in which a digital computer could be used in the study of processes of this nature. In this chapter, emphasizing methodology, we wish to combine some of the ideas of these two chapters and examine the details of the construction of a simulation of an initial interview. In the following chapter we will discuss the construction of short simulations (which we call computer vignettes), and provide some response trees.

It is interesting to note that the construction of a simulation of an initial psychotherapy interview has many features in common with the writing of a play or a scenario. There is a beginning, a middle and an end; there are two characters; there is the tension or conflict which arises when strangers meet, and there is a resolution of this conflict. One feature, however, which is quite different is the problem of interpretation and evaluation of the process.

2. DESCRIPTION OF SIMULATION PROCESS

Let us now describe the format of the simulation process. We shall begin with a stripped-down version and add various embellishments as the chapter continues.

The process begins with the person taking the role of therapist, hereafter referred to as "student", given specific information concerning the patient, together with a certain amount of time to read and interpret it. As previously noted, this data can range from detailed reports of social workers or perhaps other psychotherapists to none at all. Furthermore, the time allotted for preliminary scanning of this material can be varied. In any case, the student is told to proceed as if he were conducting an interview with an actual patient.

To begin the interview, he is presented with an opening remark by the therapist and a patient's response. For example, the following statements may appear on a CRT screen in front of the student:

Therapist: Mrs. Jones? I'm Dr. Brown. What can I do for you?
Patient: I expected to see an older person.

From this point on, the student is given a choice of two responses (Figure 8.1).

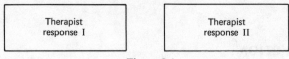

Figure 8.1

One of these responses is convergent, one is divergent. This fact, of course, is not told to the student, nor is he necessarily even informed that there are value judgments attached to the responses. The student is given an amount of time to read these responses and to choose one of them. Again, this is a period of time which may vary in a number of ways dependent upon the objectives of the simulation. This point has been discussed previously.

Suppose that the student selects Response *I*. Associated with this response are two patient responses, as indicated in Figure 8.2.

The student need not know how many possible responses there are, nor the mechanism by which they are chosen. One of the foregoing responses is convergent, one, divergent with respective probabilities, p and $1 - p$, of being chosen by the computer. Similarly, the second response available to

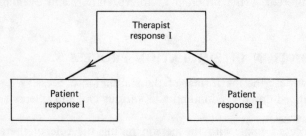

Figure 8.2

the student has two possible responses with the associated probabilities, q and $1 - q$. If I is the convergent therapist response, p is greater than q, otherwise, the reverse.

The student is shown the patient's response together with a set of two possible continuations (Figure 8.3).

Again, one of these therapist's responses is convergent, one, divergent. The order in which these appear is randomized at each stage so that the student does not readily perceive any unintended relationship in the order of presentation. The student chooses one of the two responses offered and then receives a patient's response.

Alternatively, giving rise to a simulation process of quite different nature (which we shall not discuss to any further extent) the possible responses can be shown one at a time until the student chooses one. Using the technique described in Section 13, we can ensure a very large supply of possibilities at the expense of little additional effort.

The process continues in this way until its termination.

3. EXAMPLE

Before proceeding further, let us give an example of the response sets.*

Therapist: Mrs. Jones? I'm Dr. Brown. What can I do for you?

Patient: I expected to see an older person.

After having been shown this opening interaction, the student is presented with two possible continuations and is expected to select one of them.

Therapist: (1)   I'm not as young as I look.

              (2)   I'd like to help you. Let's talk and see if we can work together.

Let us assume that the first possibility is chosen, (actually a divergent therapist response) and that the patient's next response is:

_____

* This dialogue is taken from the first computer vignette of the succeeding chapter, "The Young Psychiatrist".

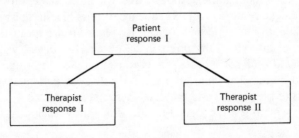

Figure 8.3

Patient: I certainly hope not.

Again, two possible continuations are presented to the student for his selection. The process grows in this fashion, branching rapidly as the therapist and patient interact.

4. TERMINATION

There are a number of options for ending the simulation. We can allow a fixed number of stages within which the student attempts to achieve the goals of the initial interview; see Chapter 5. Or, we can follow the lead of the actual process and allow a fixed time within which the therapist-patient interaction takes place.

In the short simulation processes of the next chapter, the computer vignettes, we terminate the process as soon as certain preliminary goals are attained.

5. DISCUSSION

Before coming to grips with the problem of the dimensionality difficulty emphasized in the preceding two chapters, let us examine the construction of the response set. There are several problems we face.

1. The response must be plausible, both in style and content.
2. Any sequence of responses must be logically consistent and bear a reasonable resemblance to an actual dialogue between a therapist and a patient.

The first condition means that we have a specific patient in mind and that the patient's response might reasonably be expected as a consequence of a specific response by the therapist. The therapist's response must also be of a nature that might be encountered within the community of therapists practicing today. These are not particularly difficult conditions to meet.

The second condition, on the other hand, is much more difficult to satisfy. In constructing the response tree we must make sure that *every* possible dialogue resulting from a sequence of possible therapist and patient responses is both plausible and logical. By *plausible* we mean that it reads like an actual interview, the point made above. By *logical* we mean that the therapist at each stage bases his responses only on information actually available to him at that point, and similarly that the patient responds only on the basis of the present and previous therapist responses.

The only way to test the logical nature is to follow each possible branching. While this may be done by hand, in the construction of a simulation the computer can be used to great advantage in displaying these branchings.

6. CONSTRUCTION OF RESPONSES

To construct the response set we used a combination of experience and theory. Let us consider the construction of the therapist responses first. There are two approaches we can use. To begin with, we can bypass theory, explicit theory, that is, and at each stage ask an experienced therapist, or group of therapists first, "How might you respond at this point in the interview?" and then, "What would some inappropriate responses be?"

Secondly, we can construct a theoretical structure of convergence and divergence, as described in the previous chapter, and determine sets of possible responses along these lines. After this has been done, it is still essential, considering the tentative nature of existing theory, for an experienced therapist to look over the response tree so constructed and evaluate the individual responses on the basis of his training, experience, and intuition.

There are three possible ways to construct the set of patient responses.

1. Use of an actual interview to provide the trunk of the response tree. (May be combined with 2 or 3 below);

2. Use of experienced therapists to provide possible patient responses. (May be combined with 1 above);

3. Use of theory plus experience to provide the set of possible patient responses.

At various times, each method has been employed. In the beginning, before a detailed theoretical structure was available, we employed the first and second method. More recently, we have used the third method exclusively. We wish to emphasize that, in any case, the final evaluation of a response tree rests upon a combination of theory and experience.

7. INTERPRETATION DEPENDENT UPON THEORY

It is essential to keep in mind that the terms convergent and divergent are dependent upon a specific underlying theory of psychotherapy. A different theory might easily result in an interchange of these labels for patient and therapist responses alike and, thus, would lead to the construction of an entirely different response tree.

We aim for consistency within the particular theoretical structure we employ. Our basic intent, however, is to develop a methodology for con-

verting a theory of psychotherapy into various research and training procedures using some of the nonquantitative methods of mathematics, rather
than promote any specific theory. Hence, the methods we have employed
for the construction of simulations of the initial interview will work equally
well for a range of theories of psychotherapy.

8. USE OF AN ACTUAL INTERVIEW

Let us elaborate on the use of an actual interview in the construction of a
simulation process. We choose an interview which provides a great deal
of data concerning a patient and preferably one which has an associated
patient history and interpretation of the responses. A number of recorded
interviews of this nature exist in the literature. Let us suppose that this
interview is an ideal one in which both the therapist and the patient make
only convergent responses (see Figure 8.4).

We begin by considering ways of modifying or changing actual patient
responses to obtain divergent responses which might tend to lead an
inexperienced therapist astray. There are several simple ways of doing this:

1. Replace the actual response by some noncommittal remark such as
"May I smoke", or a stalling comment, "I don't feel like talking about
that";

2. Delete a significant part of the actual response;

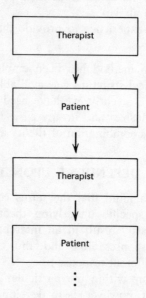

Figure 8.4

3. Add some comments which tend to conceal the significant content and emphasize relatively unimportant aspects.

Using these, or other techniques (see Chapter 5), we are led to a response tree of the form shown in Figure 8.5. It is now necessary to provide

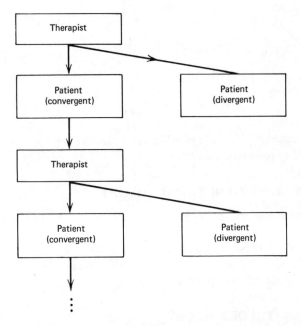

Figure 8.5

some divergent therapist's responses. In Chapter 5 we explained how to construct divergent responses. Some simple ways of converting convergent to divergent therapist responses are:

1. Add some anxiety producing elements to the convergent response.
2. Replace the actual response by a form of questioning which suggests answers.
3. Remove those elements which show concern and interest in the patient and his problems.

We now have a response tree of the type shown in Figure 8.6.

At this point it is necessary to decide upon the set of patient responses to a divergent therapist response. One simple method that may be employed is to use the same response set as to the convergent therapist response with a lower probability of a convergent response. After a while, however, new

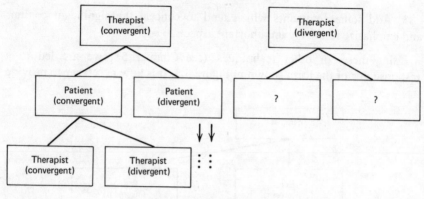

Figure 8.6

responses based upon the available facts concerning the patient and his history will have to be constructed.

9. USE OF EXPERIENCE AND THEORY

In place of using an actual interview, we can start with a hypothetical patient and use a combination of experience and theory to decide upon hypothetical responses for both patient and therapist. This is the method used in the next chapter. This method enables us to focus upon characteristic types of patient-therapist encounters.

10. USE OF THEORY ALONE

With a somewhat different view we can construct a model of a patient as a system with an $I\text{-}S\text{-}S_1\text{-}R$ table. The patient's problems, personality, symptoms and behavior would be described according to standard psychiatric classification and these would determine S_1 and R, given I and S. Similarly, we could form the input responses of the therapist. We feel, however, that at this time it is preferable to confine ourselves to the simpler and less rigid models appearing in the following chapter.

11. LOOPING

As discussed previously in a number of places, the number of possible response pairs increases in alarming fashion as the number of stages increases. In order to circumvent this serious problem of dimensionality, we employ the basic device of looping.

Let us begin a discussion of this technique with the observation that time is a fundamental constraint in most psychotherapy interviews. Whatever occurs must take place within a fixed time period, usually a bit less than one hour. Accepting this principle of time constraint, we consider it appropriate to evaluate a simulated initial interview in terms of the time required to achieve certain goals.

It follows then, as a reasonable consequence, that the selection of divergent therapist's responses be penalized by a loss of time in obtaining information and in achieving a working relationship with the patient. One way to accomplish this objective, which simultaneously helps avoid the dimensionality barrier, is to use as a divergent response a patient response at an earlier stage in the interview and to continue the process from there. Specifically, what happens is that when a student selects a divergent therapist response several times in a row, the patient response which appears may be the same one the patient gave earlier. The interview process has looped back and no progress has been made. In this way we constantly prune the divergent branches of the response tree and thus prevent an unmanageable expansion. The convergent branches may be trimmed, and the topics limited, by horizontal pruning, i.e., by using as a convergent response one of another branch at the same level.

The response tree of the branching interview may then have the appearance shown in Figure 8.7.

In the following chapter we shall give some examples of this technique. Using looping, we can obtain the equivalent of thousands of possible hour interviews with only a few hundred responses, and hundreds of short interviews of ten or fifteen minute duration with a response tree of less than one hundred entries.

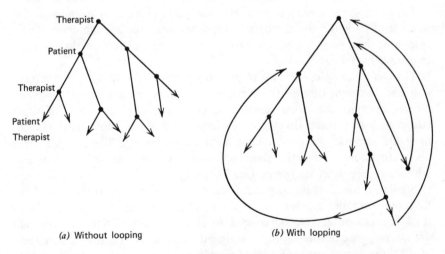

(a) Without looping   (b) With lopping

Figure 8.7

12. CYCLING

One of the difficulties associated with the foregoing method of looping is the introduction of *cycling* if there is a moderate probability that the patient will respond in a divergent fashion and that the therapist will not be consistently convergent. By this we mean that we can readily encounter a sequence of the form:

> Therapist Response II
> Patient Response I
> Therapist Response II
> Patient Response I

Figure 8.8

in which the two therapist responses and the two patient responses are identical. In other words, the therapist response selected by the student leads to a patient response which had appeared earlier in the interview. This in turn is linked for choice selection to two therapist responses which had been offered previously. The next divergent therapist response selected by the student again leads to the same earlier appearing patient response followed again by the same two therapist response options for choice. Exact repetition of this nature is obviously undesirable.

13. INCREASE IN RESPONSE POSSIBILITIES

One simple way to avoid the foregoing phenomenon, and simultaneously to introduce greater realism into the simulation process, is to increase the number of patient's and therapist's responses available at each stage. These responses, however, are equivalent as far as their linkages in the response tree are concerned.

Thus, for example, in place of providing two responses, one convergent and one divergent therapist's response, we can offer four additional possibilities, two at each node of the response tree, to give a total of three convergent and three divergent responses. All three convergent choices have the same set of associated patient responses and likewise all three divergent choices have the same set of patient responses. We shall call additional responses *alternates* (see Figure 8.9).

Similarly, the convergent patient responses may be any of three, and the divergent response may be any of three. Thus the procedure is the following: The computer is programmed to choose a convergent or divergent patient response according to an assigned probability. Then it chooses one of the three equivalent responses of a set in rotating order (see Figure 8.10).

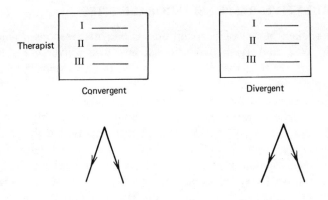

Figure 8.9

With the storage capacity of contemporary computers, this figure of three can easily be increased to five or fifty with the only effort that of composing the responses. The constraint on this construction is that the responses must be equivalent as far as emotional and logical content is concerned within the context of the particular simulation.

14. AVOIDANCE OF THE APPEARANCE OF CYCLING

Once we have constructed the alternates we can more easily avoid the appearance of cycling caused by exact repetition of words. After a response has been chosen, whether therapist or patient response, it will not be immediately available again in the course of a particular simulation. This is not a difficult instruction for the computer program.

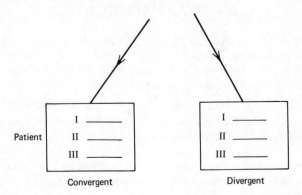

Figure 8.10

15. CUMULATIVE RESPONSE PROBABILITIES

We have spoken before of probabilities of patients' responses where the probability of a convergent patient's response to a convergent therapist's response is greater than that of a convergent patient's response to a divergent therapist's response.

Let us go one step further. The effect of both convergence and divergence on the part of the therapist in the initial interview is clearly cumulative. A patient has memory. We can take account of this fact in the simulation process by having the probability of a convergent patient's response dependent upon what has previously occurred in the interview.

There are several ways of doing this. To begin with, we can make the probability dependent on both the current response and the previous one, two, or three, etc., therapist's responses. Alternatively, we can keep track of the entire interview.

Suppose, for example, we wish to take account only of the present and previous therapist's responses. If the probability of a convergent response is p, we can move it in the direction of 1 if the last therapist's response was convergent, and in the direction of 0 otherwise.

In the first case we might change p into $p + (1 - p)/10$; in the second case p might be transformed into $9p/10$. We can also introduce levels above and below which the probabilities cannot go. Again these are simple tasks for the digital computer.

If we wish to use the entire set of previous interactions, we can carry out similar alterations in terms of the total numbers of past convergent and divergent responses.

NOTES AND REFERENCES

1. R. Bellman, M. Friend and L. Kurland, *A Simulation of the Initial Psychiatric Interview*, 1966, *op. cit.*
R. Bellman, M. Friend and L. Kurland, "On the Construction of a Simulation of the Initial Psychiatric Interview", 1966, *op. cit.*

R. Hillman speaks of the computer as a valuable tool for teaching psychiatric interviewing. Its major advantages are that it allows comparison and repetition and circumvents the moral problem of "practicing" on a patient. See
R. Hillman, *Teaching of Psychotherapy Problem by Computer*, Technical Report. ACME Computer Facility at Stanford Medical Center, Stanford, California, 1970.

Rather than simulate a patient, Stillman et al have simulated a psychiatric

interviewer. They constructed an on-line branching computer system to interview patients. Specifically, the computer requests and records mental status, psychometric and personal history information. The branching program is based on the traditional diagnostic method of a therapist; i.e., questioning in certain areas in greater depth depending on the patient's previous response. See
R. Stilman, et al, 1969, *op. cit.*

Related and intended as a training device for psychiatric trainees, is:
F. Hilf, et al, 1970, *op. cit.*

The Spitzer and Endicott program simulates the diagnostic process used in clinical practice. See
R. Spitzer and J. Endicott, "Diagno: A Computer Program for Psychiatric Diagnosis Utilizing the Differential Diagnostic Procedure", *Arch. Gen. Psychiat.,* Vol. 18, 1968, pp. 746–756.
R. Spitzer and J. Endicott, "Diagno II: Further Developments in a Computer Program for Psychiatric Diagnosis", *American J. Psychiatry,* Supp., Vol. 125(7), January 1969.

Another, earlier language branching program for interviewing was constructed by Starkweather. See
J. Starkweather, "Computest . . .", 1965, *op. cit.*

With a computer-based interviewing technique itself based on a branching diagnostic technique, the computer carries on a dialogue with the patient. While it cannot use non-verbal information, neither does it bias the patient's response by conveying non-verbal information to him in the manner of presentation of questions and other responses. Dr. W. Slack and L. Van Cura have found that the computer is at its best and sometimes better than physicians in areas other than that of primary interest to the physician. The specialist in his own area is superior to the computer as an interviewer. See
W. Slack and L. Van Cura, "Computer-Based Patient Interviewing, Part I", *Postgraduate Medicine,* Vol. 43(3), March 1968, pp. 68–74 and "Part II," Vol. 43(4), April 1968, pp. 115–120.

Dr. Slack et al have also prepared programs which obtain physical exam data directly from the examining physician. The collection, storage and retrieval of data functions of the computer are all used. In addition, a summary of the findings is printed out in phrase form for the immediate use of the physician. See
W. Slack et al, 1967, *op. cit.*

For additional references see the following:
K. Brodman, A. Van Woerkom, A. Erdmann, Jr., and L. Goldstein, "Interpretation of Symptoms with a Data Processing Machine", *Arch. Intern. Med.,* Vol. 103, 1959, pp. 776–782.
M. Collen, L. Rubin, J. Neyman, G. Dantzig, G. Baer and A. Siegelaub,

"Automated Multiphasic Screening and Diagnosis", *Am. J. Pub. Health,* Vol. 54, 1964, pp. 741–750.

M. Kamp and J. Starkweather, "The Electronic Computer as an Interviewer", *California Mental Health Research Digest,* Vol. 3(3–4), 1965, pp. 103–104.

G. Hicks, M. Gieschen, W. Slack and F. Larson, "Routine Use of a Small Digital Computer in the Clinical Laboratory", *JAMA,* Vol. 196, June 13, 1966, pp. 973–978.

J. Overall and D. Gorham, "A Pattern Probability Model for the Classification of Psychiatric Patients", *Behav. Sci.,* Vol. 8, 1963, pp. 108–116.

J. Overall and L. Hollister, "Computer Procedures for Psychiatric Classification", *JAMA,* Vol. 187, 1964, pp. 583–588.

W. Slack et al, 1966, *op. cit.*

W. Smith, "A Model for Psychiatric Diagnosis", *Archives Gen. Psychiat.,* Vol. 14, 1966, pp. 521–529.

5. For the use of similar techniques in the composition of music, see
W. Mozart, *The Dice Composer,* Koechel, 294D, A. Laszlo (ed.).

7. For additional discussion of the relationship of the terms convergent and divergent to the theory which underpins their definitions, see
R. Bellman, C. Kell, W. Hopgood, 1970, *op. cit.*

8. In our initial work, we used the "nurse interview" in M. Gill et al, 1954, *op. cit.* The simulation there is that of an hour interview.

9. An interesting example of a patient formed by a combination of theoretical considerations and experience is found in the paper by
K. Colby, "Artificial Paranoia", 1970, *op. cit.*

10. The classification we have in mind is, for example,
Diagnostic and Statistical Manual of Mental Disorders, 2nd Ed., 1968, *op. cit.*
It is as it stands however not a sufficiently definitive work.

Chapter 9

COMPUTER VIGNETTES

1. INTRODUCTION

In previous chapters we have examined an initial psychotherapy interview from a number of vantage points. Our basic premise is that this complex process can profitably be considered a multistage decision process of adaptive type. Within this conceptual framework we have discussed ways in which computer simulations of a one-hour initial interview could be constructed, a process which can be used for research and training purposes.

Considering the time factors imposed by both construction and use of full-length simulations, we have focused on developing a library of shorter simulation processes to provide a variety of interaction experiences. Each of these shorter processes, intended to represent the first fifteen to twenty minutes of initial interviews, illustrates certain common patient-therapist interactions which cause the inexperienced therapist some anxious moments. This anxiety would both hamper his own efforts and, communicated to the patient, further impair his effectiveness to the extent that the patient's confidence and favorable expectations are affected. We call these brief computer simulation processes, Computer Vignettes.

In this chapter we shall present three vignettes, "The Young Psychiatrist", "The Silent Patient", and "The Telephone Interview". This will give us an opportunity to provide some specific examples to accompany the general methodology of the preceding chapters.

2. SIMULATIONS

In the simulations which follow, the student may be given some or all of the following information. Most likely he will be given a minimal amount, such as that presented in selections 4, 6, and 8 describing the problem and the patient.

In addition, the student will be asked to make the following assumptions: He is a professional therapist. The patient, presented to him via a computer display, has voluntarily come to him for help with his difficulties. This is an initial interview in which he and the patient meet for the first time.

As the therapist, he must determine in the course of the interview how he will help the patient. In particular, he must establish a meaningful communication link. Essentially, he is being asked the following question: If you were the therapist, how would you interview this patient?

If the therapist achieves his goals in a specified time, the interview is considered successful; otherwise, not. These goals have been discussed in previous chapters.

3. CONVERGENCE AND DIVERGENCE

Let us briefly recall some fundamental ideas. We distinguish two principal types of responses, convergent and divergent. In general terms, a convergent response is one tending to facilitate communication, enlarge the information pool, and achieve the goals of most interviews which take place at the beginning of treatment or evaluation for disposition of a case. Briefly, the goals for a therapist are described as follows: to establish a therapeutic relationship and begin treatment and, without adding to the patient's burden of pain, to obtain the necessary information to assess the present functioning of the patient and, tentatively, to formulate a plan for treatment or referral. A divergent response is here taken simply to be one which is not convergent. These terms are relative, rather than absolute, dependent upon the patient and the state of the interview itself. For example, responding to a divergent therapist, a convergent patient's response will not contain as much information as one made in response to a convergent therapist. A patient's response in this situation may contain some elements of divergence or relatively few convergent elements.

The construction of responses is described by the third method cited in Section 6 of the preceding chapter.

4. COMPUTER VIGNETTE I—THE YOUNG PSYCHOTHERAPIST

Our first vignette centers about a young psychotherapist and a patient older than he. She is hostile to youth in general and in this case fearful that a young, relatively inexperienced therapist will not be able to help her.

There is a strong possibility that they will reinforce each other's insecurities. The therapist must be careful to avoid this if he is to achieve a therapeutic relationship with the patient.

The patient is a middle-aged woman of average intelligence. She is a business college graduate who has been employed by an insurance company for sixteen years, first as a secretary and, more recently, as the supervisor of a secretarial pool. She has been married for fourteen years to a man several years her senior. He had been married before and has grown children by his first marriage. The patient and her husband have no children together. The patient never got along too well—or too badly—with her step-children.

She feels, however, vaguely threatened by youth, by her step-children, as well as by the ambitious young secretaries who work under her direction.

Except for a brief romantic episode leading to marriage, the patient has a history of emotional deprivation. She has had some previous psychotherapy.

5. POLICY FOR CONSTRUCTION OF RESPONSES

In the present vignette the patient's divergence is expressed principally by focusing on the youthfulness of the therapist. She uses this characteristic as a basis for attacking and hampering him. The therapist, in turn, is divergent if he allows her to continue, or worse yet, enters into a parallel discussion of youth and inexperience in general. In this simulation, a divergent patient is hostile to the therapist or therapy situation. A divergent therapist over-intellectualizes and is more concerned with his own role than he is in the helping relationship. The therapist is convergent when he works persistently at achieving the goals of the interview and is concerned for the patient and interested in her problems. The patient is convergent when she gives information and permits the development of a therapeutic relationship.

Construction Principles, Convergent Therapist

1. The therapist offers to help the patient with her problems, persistently, if necessary.

2. The therapist accepts the patient's feelings, including negative ones, and remains non-judgmental and matter-of-fact.

3. The therapist forms questions which encourage narrative replies, rather than simple agreement or disagreement, and does not suggest either answers or modes of answering.

Construction Principles, Divergent Therapist

1. The therapist concentrates on the patient's account of events rather than feelings about them, or on a problem not yet adequately established.

2. The therapist takes an overactive or underactive role in the therapy situation and is ingratiating, judgmental, argumentive, threatening, or punitive.

3. The therapist forms questions which allow simple agreement or dis-

agreement, or which do not give leads for exposition, or which are confusing by asking for more than one kind of information in one request or abruptly changes subject or suggest answers or modes of answering.

Construction Principles, Convergent Patient
1. The patient admits her problems.
2. The patient gives information about her problems.
3. The patient expresses willingness to continue with the therapy situation.

Construction Principles, Divergent Patient
1. The patient denies having problems and her need for help; she is argumentive.
2. The patient gives too little information about her problems. She is verbose, yet talks about facts and gives data rather than about her feelings, or she is too brief and deals in generalities; or she is silent, or irrelevant, or tangential.
3. The patient expresses dissatisfaction with the therapy situation, or with the therapist personally.

6. COMPUTER VIGNETTE II—THE SILENT PATIENT

We next consider a situation where the therapist sees a patient, a student, in a college health center for the first time. The patient is apparently shy, clearly distrustful, and emotionally disturbed. Is the emotional disturbance serious or not?

This is a particularly difficult recognition problem for the inexperienced therapist since the patient tends to be silent. The therapist hopes to achieve the general aims of an initial interview, to establish rapport with the patient, to obtain some information from him, and to give him some comfort and support. Yet, initially, he must proceed in slow stages—the patient will give no response if he does not feel at ease. To begin with, the therapist must in some way obtain the patient's confidence. Then, he must elicit sufficient information to formulate both a tentative diagnosis and a plan for treatment. The vignette will end when the patient is communicating more or less freely, thus allowing the nature and extent of his problems to be recognized.

The patient is a nineteen-year-old college student whose academic interest is theoretical physics. His two roommates, having found him increasingly uncommunicative, believe that he needs psychotherapy and have convinced him to seek aid at the student health center. Their concern had become pressing because for the past week the patient had stopped attending classes and had, in fact, only left their room for occasional meals in the dormitory's dining room.

Although he had always tended toward solitary pursuits, the patient has been feeling himself progressively shut off from people. His manner is shy and distrustful, yet is not overtly hostile. He is self-absorbed, rather unresponsive, and emotionally flat. His behavior is occasionally inappropriate, and his responses are frequently unrelated to the responses of the therapist.

7. POLICY FOR CONSTRUCTION OF RESPONSES

We have taken a psychodynamic approach which postulates underlying conflict of some type as the source of the patient's present disturbance. We have attempted to illustrate how a therapist with this orientation might be expected to function in terms of this particular theoretical position.

For example, we assume that the patient has made schizoid retreats from the world because his feelings are so overwhelming. The therapist wishes to establish rapport with him and finds this very difficult because the patient is suspicious and withdrawn. The therapist wishes also to assess the functioning capacity of the patient. He tries, gently, to find out something of the patient's insight and degree of ego disorganization.

Patient responses are considered convergent if they allow the development of a working relationship with the therapist and give some information. Even silence may be considered convergent if coupled with some appropriate nonverbal expression such as shifting in his chair, nodding, or other significant postural or facial movements. Intellectualizing is a strength—the patient's defense—as well as a symptom. This the therapist will accept and use during the interview. The patient's divergence is expressed by unresponsiveness or simple, generalized ngativism.

The manner and behavior of the convergent therapist is patient and accepting. Whenever possible, his questions make use of information disclosed by the patient. He is direct, remains firmly in command, and is strongly supportive throughout the entire interview. If he finds it necessary to probe for information, he is careful to be supportive at the same time.

Since we assume anger, together with his fear of expressing this anger, as the probable cause for the patient's silence, we consider those responses by the therapist divergent which tend to increase patient anxiety and thereby evoke these feelings. According to our theoretical assumptions, too early involvement with his emotions is to be avoided since it is likely that the patient has not sufficient ego strength at this time. Any behavior, in fact, which the patient perceives as threatening would be considered divergent. In general, divergent therapist responses are anxiety producing and would tend not to achieve the desired result—to establish a working relationship with the patient and to maximize the information obtained in the interview. Instead, they would probably lead to his further withdrawal and cause him to become even less communicative.

Construction Principles, Convergent Therapist

1. The therapist offers to help the patient with his problem, persistently, if necessary, and is strongly supportive.

2. The therapist accepts the patient's responses with non-judgmental and matter-of-fact manner.

3. The therapist frames direct, concrete and simple questions which offer structure for controlled responses from the patient yet do not put words into his mouth.

4. The therapist, after several successful exchanges, tries to discover whether the patient has feelings or unreality or depersonalization, whether his thoughts follow a meaningful chain of ideas or are disconnected, whether his judgment of external events is impaired, whether his behavior is disturbed, and whether he seems emotionally impoverished.

Construction Principles, Divergent Therapist

1. The therapist questions about thoughts or feelings and probes without simultaneously offering support.

2. The therapist's verbal responses are judgmental, or show surprise or irritation. They are nonaccepting.

3. The therapist frames questions which do not furnish leads for exposition, or which call for simple agreement or disagreement.

4. The therapist takes an underactive role, not one offering a firm guide to the patient; or follows the patient's lead down nonproductive, tangential paths; or responds with silence.

Construction Principles, Convergent Patient

1. The patient responds appropriately in content or form to direct questions.

2. The patient directly expresses something of his problems or sensations which may have informational value.

3. The patient admits that he has some serious difficulties.

Construction Principles, Divergent Patient

1. The patient does not respond, verbally or nonverbally, to direct questions.

2. The patient responds to direct questions without expressing anything of informational value.

3. The patient verbally denies his need for help; he is argumentive, or personally hostile to the therapist.

8. COMPUTER VIGNETTE III—THE TELEPHONE INTERVIEW

The psychotherapist is telephoned at 11 a.m. by a patient who says she is desperate and must see him immediately. She has not been in treatment with him previously but has been referred by a friend.

The caller sounds mildly hysterical. She almost shouts at times. She seems to be very frightened; she reports symptoms of increased heart and breathing rates. She says that she feels she is suffocating and fears she may be having a heart attack.

The psychotherapist's schedule is full for the day. He needs to assess the degree of crisis in order to determine the urgency of this situation and to ease the patient's distress. Then, he will be able to decide whether he wishes to use his rest and lunch hour, always an option in an emergency, to see this patient today, whether he might safely postpone seeing her for a short time to fit her into his regular schedule, between the regularly scheduled patients, or after hours.

The patient is an unmarried woman of about thirty-five years of age. She has been living alone since the death of her widowed mother a year ago. Two months have passed since an engagement of four years ended—almost casually, without recriminations or regret. She had not been emotionally involved in the relationship for some time prior to the breakup.

The patient is now having an acute anxiety attack, her first such attack. She has called the family doctor and told him that she feels terribly upset and does not know why. She also told him that the mild tranquilizers he had prescribed at the time of her mother's death did not help her. Her doctor suggested she see a psychotherapist.

The patient followed this advice after a sleepless night and telephoned a psychiatrist whose name was among those given her by the family doctor. This psychiatrist attempted to allay her fears by telling her that nothing was seriously the matter with her, that she was feeling tense and nervous, and that in the interim, before he could see her, she could ease her upset state by exercising and taking a hot bath before retiring at night. This psychiatrist wished to make an appointment to see her during his first free time, six days from then.

The patient at first agreed to the time set for an appointment but shortly afterwards, her agitation increased and she became quite frightened again. She was also angry and determined now to improve her plight. She called a friend who gave her the name and number of the psychiatrist with whom she is now in contact.

9. POLICY FOR CONSTRUCTION OF RESPONSES

The therapist quickly identified the caller's symptoms of acute anxiety. The signs are unmistakable. The therapist wishes to find out more about the patient's fears and how to ease her tensions and discomfort.

A convergent therapist will ask the patient a number of questions, especially factual questions. Yet, he frames questions in such a way that he does not put words into her mouth. The therapist knows that anxiety tends to diminish and disappear if a patient becomes involved in a series of rational, easily grasped exchanges. He knows that talking about anxiety eases the anxious state.

A divergent therapist tends to be overly reassuring as a way of avoiding the situation and covering up the patient's anxiety. He is too supportive and authoritarian, preventing the patient from expressing the extent of her anxiety and thus reducing it. At the same time he prevents himself from assessing the patient's present state of functioning to determine the immediacy of her need to see him.

A convergent patient will accept and follow the lead of a convergent therapist, a divergent patient will not.

Construction Principles, Convergent Therapist

1. The therapist frames questions or responses which offer structure to the patient and encourage controlled or factual responses about her symptoms and problems.

2. The therapist accepts the patient's responses in a matter-of-fact manner.

3. The therapist shows concern and interest in the patient and her problems and a willingness to help her immediately; he attempts to ascertain the nature and severity of her problems.

4. The therapist attempts to reinforce the patient's wish to establish a therapeutic bond and to meet with him for at least an initial interview.

Construction Principles, Divergent Therapist

1. The therapist is authoritarian and controlling; he directs the patient without allowing her sufficient responsibility or freedom.

2. The therapist is overly reassuring about the patient's feelings of anxiety; he doesn't allow the patient to ventilate her fears.

3. The therapist is nonaccepting of the patient's responses, or is judgmental and ignores the information given to him by the patient about her feelings, symptoms or problems.

4. The therapist frames responses which do not give leads for exposition, or which call for assent with the therapist's views, or which do not offer structure to encourage controlled responses from the patient about her problems.

Construction Principles, Convergent Patient

1. The patient talks about her symptoms; she gives information about her problems.

2. The patient responds to the therapist's questions and suggestions directly, and in a cooperative manner.

3. The patient expresses willingness to enter into a therapeutic relationship, rather than only demanding an immediate appointment.

Construction Principles, Divergent Patient

1. The patient gives responses of no informational value about her symptoms or problems.

2. The patient repeatedly requests or demands an immediate appointment but does not talk about the reasons for her demand.

3. The patient threatens self-injury, yet at the same time avoids entering into a therapeutic relationship with the therapist; she ignores the therapist's questions or suggestions.

10. SOME SAMPLE DIALOGUES

The following three pairs of dialogues are based on the responses constructed for the three vignettes discussed in this chapter. They are presented to give the reader an idea of the types of dialogues which might occur.

For the sake of example, in the first dialogue of each of the three pairs, the probability of the patient responding convergently was set at 0.5, i.e., so that the patient would respond convergently fifty percent of the time. It was further assumed that the therapist would make convergent responses one hundred percent of the time. In the second dialogue of each of the pairs, it was assumed that *both* patient and therapist would make convergent responses fifty percent of the time. Random responses were generated from number tables. Dialogues, if not concluded naturally, were cut off after eighteen exchanges.

CASE 1. The Young Psychiatrist

Patient: 50% Convergent

Therapist: 100% Convergent

Th: Mrs. Jones? I'm Dr. Brown. What can I do for you?

Pt: I expected to see an older person.

Th: I'd like to help you. Let's talk and see if we can work together.

Pt: I really wanted an older man with lots of experience to treat me. I've had this problem for so long . . .

Th: Can you tell me about your problem?

Pt: Well, it goes back a long way. Where shall I begin?

Th: Wherever you wish.

Pt: Well, it's a pretty serious problem. And I'm not so sure I want to discuss it with someone as young as you.

Th: It's natural for you to want the best kind of help for your problem, and to feel that an older person could understand you better. I would like to help you. Let's talk see if we can work together.

Pl: But that's the point. I'm not sure I want to talk about my problem with you. You just seem so young.

Th: You feel that an older person might understand you better. That seems natural to me. Yet I would like to help you. Let's see if we can talk together about your problem.

Pt: But this problem that I have has been bothering me for much too long already and I want the best help I can get. You don't look old enough to have had enough experience for that.

Th: I'd like to help you with your problem if you could tell me about it.

Pt: I wish you could help me figure out where to start. I've had the problem for so long now.

Th: Why don't you start with whatever is bothering you right now.

Pt: For about the last ten years I've been having terrible spells whenever I'm in a large crowd. When I go to a movie I have to sit on the aisle. It's so embarrassing. (Patient goes on discussing her problems.) END

CASE 1A. The Young Psychiatrist

Patient: 50% Convergent

Therapist: 50% Convergent

Th: Hello. My name is Dr. Brown. What brings you to see me?

Pt: You look so young; I'm not sure you can help me.

Th: I've had a lot of experience. I'm not really as young as I look.

Pt: I certainly hope not.

Th: Have you had some troubles with younger men particularly?

Pt: I had a friend who went to a young psychiatrist. And she's worse than before. It cost her thousands of dollars and she's worse than she ever was.

Th: Don't you think we're losing time now? Why don't we get down to important matters?

Pt: But it's important to me.

Th: Can you tell me about your problem?

Pt: Well, it goes back a long way. Where shall I begin?

Th: Suppose you begin by telling me why you wanted an older man.

Pt: But my problem is so difficult—I've had it for so long. I think an older man with more experience could help me better.

Th: It's natural for you to want the best kind of help for your problem and to feel that an older person could understand you better. I realize that I seem young, but I have had enough experience and training to have helped a lot of people already.

Pt: I would just rather be seeing an older man.

Th: Would you like to tell me about your problem?

Pt: I've had the problem for so long now; where shall I start?

Th: Wherever you wish.

Pt: I'm not sure how to tell you, but whenever I'm in a large crowd I start to feel faint and as if I can't breathe. (Patient continues talking about her distressing symptoms.)
END

CASE 2. The Silent Patient

Patient: 50% Convergent

Therapist: 100% Convergent

Th: (Greets patient at door.) I'm Dr. A. Won't you come in? (Motions toward chair.) How can I help you?

Pt: (Walks into office, looks at diploma from Texas University, sits down in proffered chair, casts eyes to the floor and is silent.)

Th: What can I do for you?

Pt: My roommates thought I should come.

Th: Can you tell me why your roommates thought you should come?

Pt: No.

Th: How can I be of help?

Pt: (Shakes head "no"; remains silent.)

Th: Is there some way I can help you?

Pt: My head feels full. I feel confused.

Th: How long have you felt this way?

Pt: Since that party I went to and had too much to drink.

Th: Can you tell me what's troubling you?

Pt: Things seem so strange and unreal. And it's hard not to do something wrong when I can't think clearly.

CASE 2A.   The Silent Patient

Patient: 50% Convergent

Therapist: 50% Convergent

Th: (Greets patient at door.) I'm Dr. A. Won't you come in? (Motions toward chair.) How can I help you?

Pt: (Walks into office, looks at diploma from Texas University, sits down in proffered chair, casts eyes to the floor and is silent.)

Th: What can I do for you?

Pt: (No response.)

Th: Have you some problem you'd like to discuss with me today?

Pt: (No response.)

Th: Are you here because someone else thought you should come?

Pt: (Nods "yes".)

Th: Could you tell me why you've come here?

Pt: My roommates thought I should come.

Th: Can you tell me why your roommates thought you should come?

Pt: No.

Th: How can I be of help?

Pt: (Shakes head "no".)

Th: How do you feel about coming?

Pt: I have no feelings about it.

Th: Tell me why you've come—I'd like to help you.

Pt: Why would anybody come? You're the expert.

Th: Yes, but we're talking about you.

Pt: (No response.)

Th: Can I do something for you?

Pt: I've come because my roommates thought I should.

Th: How did it make you feel—to come here?

Pt: (No response.)

Th: Is there some way I can help you?

Pt: (No response.)

Th: What can I do for you?

Pt: It's my roommates—they thought I should come.

Th: Do you know why your roommates thought you should come?

Pt: I don't know.

Th: You don't know? I'd like to help you.

Pt: I'm having trouble concentrating. I don't know what I mean.

Th: Do you believe you should have come? I'd like to help you.

Pt: First, I have to help myself. I have to straighten things out in my mind.

Th: Can you tell me what's troubling you?

Pt: (Shakes head "no"; remains silent.)

CASE 3. The Telephone Caller

Patient: 50% Convergent

Therapist: 100% Convergent

Th: Hello. This is Dr. Ramsey. Can I help you?

Pt: Doctor, I've got to see you, or somebody, right away. I must see you.

Th: You must be feeling that you are in a very difficult situation. Can you tell me something about it?

Pt: It started several days ago. I've just got to see you today.

Th: I'll be glad to help you. Can you tell me how you're feeling?

Pt: Of course. That's why I want to see you right away.

Th: This must be very upsetting to you. Has it been going on for a long time?

Pt: I feel like this all the time lately. I must talk to you immediately.

Th: You must be feeling that you are in a very difficult situation. Can you tell me something about it?

Pt: I have a feeling something awful is going to happen. I'm afraid I'm going to have a heart attack. When did you say you could see me?

Th: Have you felt this way before?

Pt: Can't you see me today?

Th: I'd like to help you. Can you tell me more? Also, I'd like to know how long you've been feeling this way.

Pt: What's that got to do with it? I just want an appointment to see you.

Th: How long has this been going on—your feeling this way?

Pt: It seems very long, but I guess it has only been two days. I feel as if I just woke up from a nightmare.

Th: Can you tell me more about how you're feeling?

Pt: Well, actually my heart is pounding less than it was. But I'd rather see you now. When can I come in? I don't know what to do.

Th: I'd like to see you when we can spend a reasonable amount of time together. Can you continue whatever you've been doing for yourself until now and come in tomorrow at 11?

Pt: I've been taking some sedatives my family doctor prescribed for me once, but I've practically run out of them. I must see you.

Th: Can you continue what you've been doing to make yourself feel a little better? And then come in tomorrow? We can talk the whole thing over and I can be of more help then.

Pt: Yes. I can come in on Tuesday. What time did you say? Actually, talking to you has made me feel a little better already.

Th: I'd like to see you at 11. If you should want to call me before then, I'll be here.
END

CASE 3A.   The Telephone Caller

Patient: 50% Convergent

Therapist: 50% Convergent

Th: This is Dr. Ramsey. What can I do for you?

Pt: You don't know me but I must see you right away.

Th: You must be feeling that you are in a very difficult situation. Can you tell me something about it?

Pt: I have a feeling something awful is going to happen. I'm afraid I'm going to have a heart attack. When did you say you could see me?

Th: Have you ever felt this way before?

Pt: Can't you see me today?

Th: Can you tell me more about how you're feeling?

Pt: Well, actually, my heart is pounding less than it was. But I'd rather see you now. When can I come in? I don't know what to do.

Th: I'd like to see you when we can spend a reasonable amount of time together. Can you continue whatever you've been doing for yourself until now and come in tomorrow at 11?

Pt: I've been taking some tranquilizers my family doctor gave me. They don't help much. I hate to wait for so long to see you.

Th: You know, the best advice may be to do nothing until we get together. Can you come in tomorrow at 11?

Pt: I feel as if I'm so out of breath and dizzy. When can I come in for an appointment?

Th: I would say let's not do anything until tomorrow and come in then, at 11. Can you do that?

Pt: I suppose I can. But I'd rather see you now. When can I come in?

Th: Can you get along until tomorrow at 11 a.m. and come in then?

Pt: If you were really interested, I'm sure you could manage to see me.

Th: I'd like to help you. Can you tell me more? Also, I'd like to know how long you've been feeling this way.

Pt: I've been feeling this way for nearly two days. I can't sleep at night and I feel so frightened.

Th: Can you tell me about how you feel?

Pt: My heart keeps beating so fast and my breathing isn't right. I know I'll feel a lot better when I can come in to see you.

Th: It would be best to hold off and do nothing until tomorrow when I have some free time. I'd like to spend some time with you tomorrow at 11.

Pt: Well, actually, my heart is pounding less than it was. But I'd rather see you now. When can I come in? I don't know what to do.

Th: I have some time tomorrow at 11. But, in the meantime, what can you do to make yourself feel a bit better?

Pt: Couldn't I possibly come in before then? I don't know what to do.

Th: Anybody would be upset in your situation, feeling the way you do. Do tranquilizers help you?

Pt: Well, you could help me if you gave me an appointment.

Th: I'd really like to tell you to come in but my schedule is so full today. I can't see you right away. We can arrange an appointment now though.

Pt: You really can't see me today?

Th: I could fit you in tomorrow at 11. Can you come then?

Pt: I suppose I can if I live that long. What do you expect me to do in the meantime since I can't see you?

Th: It really wouldn't be wise for me to try to help you over the phone. You might just continue what you've been doing until now.

Pt: Well, I've been taking some tranquilizers and some other pills—stronger ones. Nothing helps though. And I don't know what to do now.

Th: How long has this been going on—your feeling this way?

Pt: What's that got to do with it? I just want an appointment to see you.

Th: Of course you are upset if you feel so nervous. Have you taken anything to make yourself feel better?

Pt: I suppose it's too much to expect that you would be interested in a patient you don't know.
END

NOTES AND REFERENCES

1. One of the most important factors in psychotherapy may be the patient's desire to change or at least to be helped to feel better. In this regard, the optimism of the therapist conveyed to the patient is extremely important. Wilbur in Burton, 1965, *op. cit.*
J. Frank, 1968, *op. cit.*

Anxiety is a problem common to both the patient and the inexperienced therapist in the initial interview. Colby has this to say about the patient's discomfort: "every patient has some anxiety related to talking for the first time to a psychiatrist".
K. Colby, 1951, *op. cit.*

In discussing the need to relieve a patient's anxiety during an interview, Kolb says: "It is the function of the psychiatrist ... to arrange and conduct the interview in such a way that the patient ... is relieved of as much anxiety as possible." Only in this way will the examiner be able "to provide the information needed to reconstruct and understand the patient's illness." See
L. Kolb, 1968, *op. cit.*

See also:
R. Bellman, et al, *A Simulation of the Initial Psychiatric Interview*, 1966, *op. cit.*

R. Bellman, M. Friend and L. Kurland, "A Simulation of the Initial Psychiatric Interview: Revised and Expanded Version", University of Southern California, USCEE-240, December 1967.

R. Bellman, et al, "On the Construction of Vignettes", 1970, *op. cit.*

R. Bellman, *Psychodynamics and Mathematical Simulation of the initial Psychiatric Interview,* August, 1967, *op. cit.*

2,3.

R. Bellman, et al, "On the Construction of Vignettes", 1970, *op. cit.*

4. R. Bellman, C. Kell, W. Hopgood, *Computer Vignettes—I: The Young Psychiatrist,* University of Southern California, USCEE 69–19, October 1969.

M. Pearson, 1963, *op. cit.*

L. Wolberg, 1967, *op. cit.*

P. Nathan, 1967, *op. cit.*

M. Gill, et al., 1954, *op. cit.*

P. Polatin, 1966, *op. cit.*

L. Kolb, 1968, *op. cit.*

6. See cited references in section above plus

R. Laing, *Self and Others,* 2nd Ed., New York, Pantheon Books, 1969.

R. Bellman, C. Kell, W. Hopgood, *Computer Vignettes—II: The Silent Patient,* University of Southern California, USCEE 70–13, March 1970.

S. Arieti, "Psychotherapy in Schizophrenia", in S. Arieti, Ed., *American Handbook of Psychiatry,* Vol. 1, New York, Basic Books, 1959.

G. Blaine, Jr. et al., *Emotional Problems of the Student,* New York, Appleton-Century-Crofts, Inc., 1961.

J. LeValley, "Health Services and the Counseling Center", in P. Gallagher and G. Demos, *The Counseling Center in Higher Education,* Springfield, Charles C. Thomas, 1970.

A. Ichikawa, "Observations of College Students in Acute Distress", *Student Med.,* Vol. 10, Part 2, 1961.

8. See references cited in Section 4 above plus

R. Bellman, C. Kell, W. Hopgood, *Computer Vignettes—III: A Telephone Interview,* University of Southern California, USCEE 70–40, August 1970.

H. Eysenck, *The Dynamics of Anxiety and Hysteria,* New York, Praeger, 1957.

Chapter 10

TEACHING, TRAINING, AND RESEARCH

1. INTRODUCTION

Our aim in the foregoing chapters was to illustrate how mathematical ideas can be used to study the structure of the communication and decision processes of an initial psychotherapy interview. In this concluding chapter we wish to review the basic ideas and unify and simplify some of the discussion of the previous pages. Our interest is in understanding, teaching or training, and research.

2. UNDERSTANDING

As we have indicated, the initial psychotherapy interview may be viewed as a process involving a series of interactions, verbal and nonverbal, between a patient and a therapist. We have shown that a description of this process can be given first in abstract terms, then in more concrete terms, using such mathematical concepts as "system" and "multistage decision process".

This concise description of the interview can be used for understanding the nature of the process by many types of people, the clinical therapist as well as the patient, the teacher as well as the student. The systems approach provides a language which serves some classical functions. It focuses thinking and thus guides it; it allows communication between specialists and between the professional and layman.

It is important to note that mathematics furnishes languages for describing a variety of processes in the human sciences. Other languages are provided by psychiatry, anthropology, and sociology. This redundance and overlap are highly desirable. As we have discussed earlier, we do not believe it is possible to understand all of the complexities of existence from any single viewpoint. It would ideally be desirable to possess a philosopher's stone, a single all-embracing theory, but we do not expect to uncover one. We are required by the exigencies of life to be eclectic and multifaceted. Hence, it is desirable to construct as many languages and theories as possible to cover the spectrum of human consciousness. There will be overlapping, but always some new ground covered that was previously embarrassingly bare.

3. TEACHING

Very much in the same vein, we know far too little about the processes of teaching and learning. We do know that different methods are required for different people at different times. At the present time, there are three principal methods, all traditional, for teaching the practice of clinical interviewing. These are directed reading, the use of case seminars, and individual supervision of the student by an expert. Other didactic methods frequently used fall part-way between reading about therapy and the practice of therapy with actual patients.

A variety of mechanical devices are being used to increase understanding of the therapy interaction. Students may observe a clinical encounter behind a one-way vision screen or jointly conduct a real interview with the instructor who is behind a screen, giving instructions via earphones. Students may read or listen to taped interviews, both methods thought to be superior to reconstructed accounts of therapy sessions. They may view filmed interviews, which have the further advantage of allowing the student to watch as well as listen to what occurs.

Some newer approaches include writing therapy, watching a therapist conduct a mock interview with an actor playing the role of patient, or allowing the student to conduct one himself with an actor, followed sometimes by class discussion. These interviews may be video-taped or not.

Certain of the newer methods of teaching clinical therapy have been modified by some of the techniques of programmed instruction. It is widely believed that the best conditions for instruction force the learner to engage actively with the learning materials. Following this precept, instructional films of a therapist interviewing an actor-patient have been prepared which allow a student periodically to interact with the sequence of an interview in the role of therapist. He is allowed to choose his preferred response from a selection of three possibilities. After deciding how he would respond to the filmed patient, he may then see the film branch one stage to find out how the patient might respond to his choice of response as well as to the others, one of which is identified as "preferred". These newer approaches are related to the type of process described in the foregoing pages in that they provide a means of controlling the process and a method for introducing the student to patient behavior under limited conditions. Both are important teaching and research objectives. The major differences between the instructional film and the computer-based simulation are that the instructional films were designed to apply some of the principles of programmed learning such as receiving immediate knowledge of the appropriateness of the student's choice, rewarding the student with the film instructor's approval for a correct response, and being allowed to follow only the approved path to achieve the goals of the particular interview filmed. The simulations presented here diverge from these principles in that the interaction occurs in real time, a principle which will be discussed more fully in the next section. In adddition, the student does not receive immediate feedback as to whether a particular response is "correct" or "incorrect". Instead, trends emerge in the interaction as a result of the behavior of the participants. While their immediate responses to each other are related, this relationship is not exclusive, and responses are also related to all that has occurred in the therapy interview up to this point. Thus, the total picture is affected and shaped by the continuing interaction between student-therapist and the simulated patient.

4. ON-LINE DECISION-MAKING

To the presently used mechanical methods of aiding the understanding of clinical therapy, we have added one which possesses the features of individual responsibility and on-line decision-making. We present a replica of a patient to a student in such a way that he will be engaged in a dialogue which simulates an actual dialogue along the important axis of real time. Each time the patient "responds" to the therapist, it becomes the therapist's turn to continue the verbal interaction. In addition, instead of following only a single path, a number of alternate routes lead to achieving the goals of the interview or, if the student consistently responds in a divergent manner according to our theory of "good" interview policy or technique, the route will circle repetitively.

There are a number of different ways of displaying the patient response at each stage. This provides a family of processes which enable us to assess the significance of the information pattern. The most static of these is that which allows the student to read the patient response for as long as he wishes and even to review the previous responses. The most dynamic, in the format described above, permits only a single reading on a ticker tape, or the television screen (CRT) before it goes blank.

A training program of the type we describe below would gradually progress from static to dynamic processes as the student gains experience.

5. LIMITATIONS OF SIMULATION

The cardinal principle of the theory of simulation is that the only accurate simulation of reality is reality itself. Neither a text, no matter how lucid and encyclopedic, nor a simulation process is able adequately to describe a human relationship.

The test of a simulation as a teaching device is not so much what it leaves out, as what of importance it includes. The construction of a simulation process requires the ability to cut Gordian knots in much the same manner as they are sliced through in real situations. No ancillary such as a simulation process can do more than help prepare the novice for the experience of internship and residency in which he will be involved in a face-to-face relationship with a patient.

With these caveats, let us describe some of the ways in which we can readily add more realistic features to the vignettes presented in the preceding chapter.

6. REALISM AND REFEREES

The first way to add realism is a direct one in which additional patient and therapist responses are added. This means that the response tree will contain more branches leading to many more possible dialogues. Secondly, we can provide a large set of responses which are verbally different, but equivalent according to our norms, and thus which may be linked to the same smaller set of responses used at present. These two techniques have already been discussed.

Nevertheless, no matter how wide-ranging the set of questions, it is constricting to force a student to the rigid format of a fixed set of possible responses at each stage. To circumvent this situation to some extent, a referee or umpire can be employed in the following fashion. The student is permitted to make any response he wishes. The referee compares this response with one of the allowable responses in the vignette and chooses one which in his opinion corresponds most closely along a convergent or divergent path. If none of the allowable responses is sufficiently close, a stalling patient response is selected, such as "I don't understand", or "May

I smoke?" Presumably, after a certain number of responses of this nature the student will try another, more productive, tactic.

The student can be informed of the presence of an umpire or not. Otherwise, he can be told that the computer is using a scanning and matching program of some type which translates his response into an acceptable computer response and thus produces a patient response.

The fact that this new process is a three-person process (student-referee-patient) clearly has disadvantages. For example, a great deal of subjectivity is involved which rules out complete reproducibility. On the other hand, in return, using students as referees has pedagogical value and provides some further interesting training as well.

7. NONVERBAL ASPECTS

We have previously discussed the combined verbal and nonverbal nature of the communication between patient and therapist. Let us consider some of the ways in which such nonverbal and nonsemantic signals as appearance, gestures, and speech characteristics can be utilized in a simulation of the sort we have been describing.

There are several ways in which we can proceed. To begin with, we can display in addition to a response such additional behavioral information as:

"Patient puffs nervously on cigarette."
"Patient self-consciously crosses her legs and rearranges her skirt."
"Patient begins to cry."
"Patient picks at nails while speaking, does not look at therapist."

A significant part of nonverbal communication can be conveyed in this fashion.

Added nonsemantic, vocal information can be conveyed by the following:

"Patient speaks hesitatingly in a low voice."
"Patient is sarcastic."

There are still other methods by which the realism of the simulation can be increased. The responses can be recorded with a variety of tones and attitudes. By using a type of "juke box" hookup to the computer, the vocal response acts as an electronic button, and thus the trainee would be able to hear spoken responses by the patient. We can also employ techniques of electronic reconstruction of voice responses stored in the computer in place of a juke box of records. Along these lines, let us note that if we return to the rigid format of a fixed set of allowable responses, we can permit the trainee to address a vocal response directly to the computer by a slight amount of ingenuity in the program.

With current technology it is not difficult to extend the foregoing idea to the use of video tape along with the audio tape discussed above. The patient's responses are recorded on film and displayed on a television screen at the same time that his voice is heard. With the aid of professional actors, a large set of responses which employ both verbal and nonverbal elements can be made available.

8. AIMS OF THE SIMULATION PROCESS

As we have noted, one aim of our simulated initial interview is to serve as a device for student practice and for testing policies. An inexperienced therapist, apt to be anxious because of his inexperience, is likely to increase the anxiety of an already disturbed patient. As the quality of a patient's communications correspondingly decreases, as more distortion appears or less valuable information results, a novice therapist may become yet more anxious by the increasingly difficult interviewing situation. Thus, added to his problems of creating a working relationship with his patient and of securing helpful knowledge, is his own lessened personal effectiveness.

As a bridge between the classroom and the clinic, a simulated patient-therapy interview may provide useful practice in continuous verbal interaction, some familiarity with important problems that arise in professional practice, some preliminary knowledge of patients whose problems are rooted in taboo topics, and valuable experience dealing with initial patient resistances such as those expressed in the form of questioning the therapist about his age, experience and training, sex, religion, fees, or, perhaps, professional identification. Such experience in verbal interaction may help an inexperienced clinician when in an actual interview he wishes to attend very closely to *how* a patient speaks, or to the other nonverbal communication which may, more than semantic content, express how a patient feels.

9. FURTHER RESEARCH AND TESTING

The simulation processes described above will be administered to selected groups of psychiatrists, psychologists, medical and pre-medical students, counseling students, social workers, and clinic intake personnel for the joint purpose of analysis of various interviewing policies and techniques and improvement of the simulations.

At the same time a comparative study can be made of experienced vs inexperienced interviewers, and of interviewers of different training and theoretical orientation.

Eventually, we wish to explore other important dimensions of therapist and patient behavior and background and learn how these affect the interviewing situation. Previous studies have indicated, for example, that greater therapeutic success might result from better therapist-patient matching, such as minimizing social class or cultural differences. It has been noted that even favorable prognostic expectancies seem strongly to affect therapeutic outcome. Bare,* in a paper presented at the 1966 convention of the American Psychological Association, finds evidence that similarity in some traits and dissimilarity in others improves a counselor's ability to understand and therefore help his client. Considered here are such personality characteristics as independence, vigor, and cautiousness. Clara Thompson* has written that during her own early years as an analyst she believed that any well-trained analyst could work well with any "analyzable" patient. Later she came to the conclusion that because of temperament and even personal experience, one analyst could work more effectively with a patient who has a particular type of problem rather than another because he would be able to understand some patients particularly well. It has been observed that experienced psychotherapists practice increased selectivity and that therapists successful with one type of patient may not be with others. Frank* notes that different types of patients respond differently to different techniques.

Use of a simulation library will enable students to gain familiarity with patients who exhibit particular problems and to gain effective skills for the purposes of treatment or referral to specialists especially well suited to work with them.

Since each choice and response is recorded, rated, and charted, item analysis as well as pattern analysis will be available. Divergent responses common to certain groups, for example, psychiatrists, analysts, social workers, or medical students, can be sorted out from those due to an individual tendency; consistently divergent responses can be separated from more random ones.

10. PURPOSE OF THE SIMULATIONS

While full-scale use of the simulations awaits results of some of the research studies described above, the simulations can be used at present in a number of ways. As we have discussed earlier, the immediate purpose of the vignettes is to provide a student with a variety of on-line, decision-making

* See the references cited at the end of the chapter.

experiences related to some of the more difficult verbal interactions commonly encountered in the early years of a therapist's practice.

There will be no attempt to provide all of the conceivable difficult situations which may be encountered. It is important to emphasize that the simulation process is not viewed as a method for teaching students "correct" responses in particular situations. The focus of training is on concepts and policies rather than specific responses to be learned. This is accomplished by identifying the variables which influence the interaction in order to understand the process itself and to predict its outcome under various conditions. The emphasis then is on the adaptive aspects of a stochastic decision process.

Different models of disorders and pathologies can be incorporated into the system in order to allow the student to experiment in a way that might be painful—or even irreversibly harmful—to a person already suffering. A student would thus be allowed the question: "What would happen if I did this rather than that?" A possible result is that he would learn to foresee some of the contingent patient responses which could be expected when, as an interviewer, he asks certain questions or comments in a certain way. He may also learn to predict when the course of an interview begins to take a certain undesirable path—a hostile one, for example. Anticipating a difficulty, he may be able to avoid an unpleasant and possibly unproductive or even damaging encounter.

11. TRAINING POSSIBILITIES

Let us indicate some of the ways that the student-machine interaction can be used specifically for teaching purposes:

1. Students can examine their contributions to the interaction of the interview in detail to determine how they influence the course of the dialogue. The computer is readily instructed to print out the complete dialogue.

2. Students can be taught the elements of convergent therapist responses, and later can grade themselves, or be graded, on their proficiency in selecting such responses.

3. The speed of response by a student to a patient can be measured and evaluated. In this way a student can learn a normal range of response times.

4. Student and patient responses can be analyzed couplet by couplet and new, logically contingent therapist and patient responses constructed to deepen understanding of both patient and therapist behavior.

5. A profile of individual student progress in selecting convergent responses can be constructed.

6. Students may be allowed to experience an interview which has gone

sour, which is unproductive, and where the primary objective of the development of a therapeutic climate has not been successful. In this way he may be helped to recognize some of the convergent and divergent trends which lead to this situation.

7. Students may interact with an essentially divergent patient in order to experience the need to steadfastly continue the policies which guide their own responses and patiently pursue the goals of the interview.

The simulations can be made available for individual student use, for classroom demonstration and discussion, or for instruction of either one individual, or two or three students simultaneously.

12. CRITERION OF SUCCESS OF THE SIMULATION

The object of the simulation is to create a program which, within a designated range, is flexible enough to adapt to changes in the environment and so simulate to some extent the constantly balancing, shifting interplay of forces in an interview. We need first of all to judge whether we have succeeded in creating a model which closely enough mirrors the actual system. Then we will need to assess the level at which the model corresponds to reality, to determine whether the vignettes are in fact too simple or too complex to be useful.

Success in the vignette interaction hinges upon the selection of convergent rather than divergent responses and on the length of time that is taken to bring the vignette to a conclusion. If the vignettes are properly constructed an expert therapist will, in general, select more convergent than divergent responses and thus take less time to conclude the interview.

If, however, an expert consistently selects divergent responses, it may be deduced that he is using a different theory to approach the patient.

A simulation of a clinical interaction can also be tested by empirical matching. For example, do experienced clinicians agree that the patient and therapist responses in the program are something like what might be expected in a therapeutic situation? Another method would be to ask clinicians to judge which responses come from the program and which, using a recorded interview, from a person. Still another suggested by Dr. Colby is to match a program response with a clinician's prediction of a possible response.

13. HYPOTHESIS TESTING

The simulation can be used to test various hypotheses. For example, it is conjectured that with greater familiarity with patient and policy, a student would improve his performance with a particular vignette interaction. To test this hypothesis we can measure the student's success with the vignette interaction under different conditions. We can vary and measure the amount of patient information which is given to him, the sequence in which the information is made available, and whether or not he is treated to a discussion of the policy guiding the particular interview.

A special study, for example, may be designed which directs a student to interact with a computer program in the following sequence:

Vignette Interaction
Patient History Printout
Vignette Interaction
Response Construction Policy Printout
Vignette Interaction

The convergent/divergent response ratio and the amount of time it takes the student to bring the vignette to a conclusion can be calculated at each stage for comparison after all of the stages have been completed. Our hypothesis may be supported by the results of test experience. On the other hand, the information which is given to the student—in part or in toto—in any sequence, may have no effect whatever on his success with the computer interaction.

14. STATISTICAL EVALUATION

Questions of validity of the simulation process may be studied by comparing the computer vignette scores of professional therapists with those of students, of students at different stages of their academic careers, from beginners to advanced, of students with non-students, of students from both related and unrelated disciplines.

Results, if significant, could be used to measure the academic progress of students and, insofar as the verbal interaction of the computer vignettes is a valid indicator, to predict clinical competence in initial interview techniques.

Using statistical techniques we can present a profile of an interview to be used for various comparative purposes.

15. SIMULATIONS AND TRANSFER OF LEARNING

A question that arises in the use of simulation techniques in any field is whether a person learns to operate well within the confines of the simulation process or whether he really learns something about the process which has been modeled. In other words, does a transfer of learning take place so that any simulations are of value in dealing with reality?

At the present time it is impossible to answer this crucial question about the theory of simulation in a definitive fashion. One can, however point to many fields where simulation techniques are now widely accepted and used and express a personal opinion of their probable value and importance. There is growing evidence to support the belief that simulations are playing an increasingly popular role as well as serving an increasingly valuable purpose.

NOTES AND REFERENCES

3. The problems and limitations of the traditional didactic methods are reviewed in
R. Chessick, *How Psychotherapy Heals,* New York, Science House, 1969.
See also:
L. Wolberg, 1967, *op. cit.*

Verbatim recordings were introduced to improve teaching methods as long ago as 1939 by Felix Deutsch at Washington University Medical School in St. Louis. See:
F. Deutsch and W. Murphy, *The Clinical Interview, Vol. I: Diagnosis,* New York, International Universities Press, 1955.

For a further discussion of the superiority of transcripts over student reconstructed interviews, see:
Gill, et al., 1954, *op. cit.*
A. Enelow and L. Adler, "Natural History of a Postgraduate Course in Psychiatry", *Psychosomatics,* Vol. VIII(5), 1967, pp. 185–192.

Dr. Wilmer comments on the usefulness of video tapes in teaching the interview. He also talks about learning the various aspects of interviewing technique such as learning to listen and absorb verbal and nonverbal information. If learning does not always proceed equally on all fronts at once, these component skills may be learned and practiced to some extent independently of each other.
H. Wilmer, "The Role of the Psychiatrist in Consultation and Some Observations on Video-Tape Learning", 1967, *op. cit.*

A discussion of writing therapy is found in
E. Phillips and D. Wiener, 1966, *op. cit.*

See also:
P. Miller and J. Tupin, "Multimedia Teaching of Introductory Psychiatry", *The American Journal of Psychiatry,* Vol. 128 (10) April 1972, pp. 39–43.

R. Bellman, C. Kell and W. Hopgood, "Computer Vignettes: A Research Tool for the Study of the Initial Psychotherapeutic Interview", *J. Cybernetics*, Vol. 1, 1971, pp. 19–27.

K. Bennett and H. Barrows, "An Investigation of the Diagnostic Problem Solving Methods Used by Resident Neurologists", *Mathematical Biosciences*, Vol. 15, 1972, MB 418.

L. Chester, A. Hershdorfer and T. Lincoln, "The Use of Information in Clinical Problem Solving: A Framework for Analysis", *Mathematical Biosciences*, Vol. 8, 1970, pp. 83–108.

R. G. Hillman, "Teaching of Psychotherapy Problems by Computer", *Arch. Gen. Psychiatry*, Vol. 25, Oct. 1971, pp. 324–329.

Description and evaluation of programmed film instruction is found in

L. Adler, J. Ware, and A. Enelow, *Evaluation of Programmed Instruction in Medical Interviewing*, Postgraduate Division Department of Psychiatry, University of Southern California, School of Medicine, 1969.

J. Ware, H. Strassman, and D. Naftulin, "A Negative Relationship Between the Understanding of Medical Interviewing Principles and Performance in Actual Interviews", Pre-publication copy—property of *Journal of Medical Education*.

J. Ware, H. Strassman, and L. Adler, "The Use of Programmed Film to Teach Interviewing to Medical Students", paper read at the 122nd Annual Meeting of the American Psychiatric Assn., Miami Beach, Florida, May 5–9, 1969.

Related to the above films were the specially developed movies with delayed comments used to test differences among interviewers of different schools. See:

H. Strupp, *Psychotherapists in Action: . . .*, 1960, *op. cit.*

Excellent discussions of teaching machines as a training device are found in the several articles in

K. Austwick, Ed., *Teaching Machines and Programming*, New York, Macmillan, 1964.

See:

Leslie Reid, "Linear Programming and Learning", in *ibid*.

for a discussion of the relationship of the learner to the instructional materials.

Gordon Pask makes a distinction between factual knowledge and skill which is the ability to make use of knowledge. Different procedures are therefore found suitable for teaching factual material and skills. See:

G. Pask, "The Adaptive Teaching System", in *ibid*.

Until recently rules for medical decision-making were drawn up loosely from the examples of particular cases—it was considered education by apprenticeship and anecdote.

L. Chesler, A. Hershdorfer, and T. Lincoln, 1970, *op. cit.*

While it is a common view that clinical skills can be acquired only from

clinical experience, it is also reasonable to assume that many of the elements may come not only from personal experience alone but also from the accumulated clinical experience of predecessors. See:
P. Nathan, 1967, *op. cit.*

Colby says that one "learns to do therapy by following expert examples and thereby picks up the hidden decision rules of therapeutic algorithms and heuristics".
K. Colby, "Psychotherapeutic Processes", *Annual Review of Psychology,* Vol. 15, 1964, pp. 347–370.

There is need for improved training for clinical practice and for the introduction of structure in training and practice. See:
E. Hoch, A. Ross, and C. Winder, "Conference on the Professional Preparation of Clinical Psychologists: A Summary", *American Psychologist,* Vol. 21 (1), 1966, pp. 42–51.
E. Phillips and D. Wiener, 1966, *op. cit.*

Scheflen argues that there is need for "research strategies which avoid atomism, on the one hand, and purely intuitive search operations on the other".
A. Scheflen, "Natural History Method in Psychotherapy: Communicational Research", in L. Gottschalk and A. Auerbach, eds., *Methods of Research in Psychotherapy,* New York, Appleton-Century-Crofts, 1966.

See also:
A. Feinstein, *Clinical Judgement,* Baltimore, Williams and Wilkins, 1967.
H. Brainerd, S. Margen, and M. Chatton, *Current Diagnosis and Treatment,* Los Altos, California, Lange Medical Publications, 1968.
H. Harvey and J. Bordley, *Differential Diagnosis,* Philadelphia, W. B. Saunders, 1955.
A. Ginsberg and F. Offensend, *An Application of Decision Theory to a Medical Diagnosis-Treatment Problem,* Santa Monica, California, The RAND Corporation, P-3786, February 1968.
L. Lusted, *Introduction to Medical Decision-Making,* Springfield, Illinois, Charles C. Thomas, 1968.
J. Ultman, *Programmed Instruction in Clinical Pathology,* New York, Grune and Stratton, 1969.
D. Rutstein, *The Coming Revolution in Medicine,* Cambridge, Mass., MIT Press, 1967.
C. Kell, "Simulating The Basic Health Delivery System; The Doctor-Patient Interaction; A Systems Approach" Los Angeles. U.S.C. TR 72–11, February 1972.

4. A description of the computer programmed as a real-time interviewer involved in a multistage decision process is found in
G. Shure and R. Meeker, "A Computer-Based Experimental Laboratory", *American Psychologist,* Vol. 25 (10), 1970, pp. 962–969.

5. See:
   K. Colby, S. Weber, and F. Hilf, 1970, *op. cit.*

6. The use of umpires here is suggested by their use in the game of Kriegspiel, semi-blindfold chess.

7. Along with heart rate, the length of time to respond is considered a significant factor in the interviewing of patients by computer. Response latency communicated to the student via the program may be an easily communicated nonverbal element.
   W. Slack, "Computer-Based Interviewing System Dealing with Nonverbal Behavior as well as Keyboard Responses", *Science*, Vol. 171(8), 1971, pp. 84–87.

   According to Ekman and Friesen the importance of nonverbal information is not based on experimental evidence.
   P. Ekman and W. Friesen, paper presented at the third conference on "Research in Psychotherapy", Chicago, Illinois, May 31 to June 4, 1966.

   In his program, R. Hillman, 1970, (*op. cit.*) takes some non-verbal interaction into account by adding a choice of the therapist's emotional tone or manner to accompany his words. A description of the patient's emotional tone is similarly specified in the printout.

8. Basic to the value of the simulation process for trainee practice is the belief that a good interview technique is important. Balint, 1961, *op. cit.* has this to say: "A good interview technique is the crux of psychological diagnosis ... the whole of psychotherapy happens within the framework of the psychiatric interview which is, therefore, the indispensable vehicle for diagnosis as well as for therapy."
   And not only important, but most difficult.
   "Harry Stack Sullivan commented that the beginning student in psychiatry is put to work at the most difficult task, namely, that of getting the history of the psychiatric patient."
   See:
   K. Menninger, *A Manual for Psychiatric Case Study*, 1962, *op. cit.*

   See also:
   P. Sinfos, "Effects of a Shorter Psychiatry Course, on the Attitudes of Medical Students and Their Teachers", *The Psychiatric Quarterly*, Vol. 42(4), 1968, pp. 639–646.

   Reducing patient anxiety in the interview relieves the patient, improves the quality of his communications, reinforces the doctor-patient relationship.
   A. Enelow and M. Wexler, 1966, *op. cit.*

   A branching computer program is a very good device for collecting sexual data. It avoids the problem of the interviewer leading a patient by voice inflection, facial expression, and so forth in this sensitive conversational area. See:

W. Slack, "Computerized Data Collection in the Management of Uterine Cancer", *Clinical Obstetrics and Gynecology*, Vol. 10(4), 1967, pp. 1003–1015.

Also see:
Allport's Foreword in N. Farberow, *Taboo Topics*, Englewood Cliffs, N. J., Prentice Hall, 1963.

9. Interesting studies of experienced vs inexperienced therapists and of therapists of different theoretical orientations are
E. Dreyfus, 1967, *op. cit.*
F. Fiedler, "A Comparison of Therapeutic Relationships in Psychoanalytic, Nondirective and Adlerian Therapy", *J. Consulting Psychology*, Vol. 14, 1950, pp. 436–445.

See also:
A. Hollingshead and F. Redlich, *Social Class and Mental Illness*, New York, Wiley, 1958.
G. Seward, *Psychotherapy and Culture Conflict*, New York, Ronald Press, 1956.
A. Goldstein, "Therapist and Client Expectation of Personality Change in Psychotherapy", *Journal of Counseling Psychology*, Vol. 7, 1960, pp. 180–184.
J. Frank, 1968, *op. cit.*
C. Bare, "Counselor Sensitivity to the Counselor-Client Communication Process", *Proc. 74th Annual Convention of the American Psychological Association*, Washington, D. C., American Psychological Association, Inc., 1966, pp. 301–302.
C. Thompson, "The Role of the Analyst's Personality in Therapy", *Amer. J. Psychotherapy*, Vol. 10, 1959, pp. 347–359.
H. Strupp, "The Nature of the Psychotherapist's Contribution to Treatment", 1960, *op. cit.*
H. Strupp, "The Performance of Psychiatrists and Psychologists in a Therapeutic Interview", *Journal of Clinical Psychology*, Vol. 14, 1958, pp. 219–226.
J. Frank, 1959, *op. cit.*
C. Brownsberger, "Clinical vs Statistical Assessment of Psychotherapy: A Mathematical Model of the Dilemma", *Behavioral Science*, Vol. 10, 1965, pp. 421–428.

10. The definition of "learning" is crucial. It may be considered a combination of motor and intellectual changes such as in the acquisition of a skill such as playing a piano. It may refer only to concept formation such as acquiring insight into one's own behavior and emotions. It may be a visceral response with no intellectual component such as an intestinal habit formed in response to pain. See:
Porter, 1950, *op. cit.*

The goal of the simulation is not to teach a particular set of responses. Similarly, the experienced interviewer will not follow set procedure but

will use a spontaneous, deft, intuitive, flexible approach. See:
Gill, et al., 1954, *op. cit.*

11. The analytic value of writing a sequence for programmed learning is well known. It is also closely related to constructing a computer-based simulation. See:
K. Austwick, 1964, *op. cit.*

12. See:
K. Colby, "Computer Simulation of a Neurotic Process", in Stacy and Waxman, Vol. 1, 1965, *op. cit.*

For additional discussion of the evaluation of a model in relation to the modeled system, see:
K. Colby, S. Weber, F. Hilf, 1970, *op. cit.*
K. Colby, F. Hilf, S. Weber and H. Kraemer, "Experimental Validation of a Computer Simulation of Paranoid Processes", *Mathematical Biosciences,* Vol. 15, 1972, MB416.

14. See:
K. Colby, *ibid.*

The difficulties of evaluation of psychiatric interviews, because quantitative measurement is neither feasible nor practical in most cases, is discussed in
F. Redlich and D. Freedman, *The Theory and Practice of Psychiatry,* New York, Basic Books, 1966.

AUTHOR INDEX

Abelson, R., 96
Adler, L., 191, 192
Aldrich, C., 33
Alexander, F., 26, 33, 36, 117
Alexander, F., ed., 27, 33, 47, 50
Allport, G., 80, 195
Appel, K. E., 17
Applebaum, S., 33
A Psychiatric Glossary, 28, 34
Apter, M., 148
Arieti, S., 30, 80, 180
Aronson, E., ed., 96
Aronson, J., ed., 12, 14, 28, 146
Austwick, K., ed., 192, 196

Babb, E. M., 144
Bachrach, A., 38, 118
Baer, G., 161
Balint, E., 26, 39, 40, 47, 48, 49, 50,
    51, 52, 117, 194
Balint, M., 26, 39, 40, 47, 48, 49, 50,
    51, 52, 117, 194
Bandura, A., 37
Bare, C., 187, 195
Barko, H., 144
Barrows, H., 192
Barton, W., ed., 34
Bateson, G., 31, 80
Beck, A., 34
Bellak, L., 96, 117
Bellman, R., 11, 13, 34, 79, 80, 81, 96,
    97, 98, 116, 117, 148, 160, 162,
    180, 192
Bellman, R. et al., 14, 144, 179, 180
Bennett, K., 192
Bennett, W., 146
Berenson, B. G., 40
Berg, I., ed., 27, 39, 47, 53
Berger, M., 39
Berne, E., 14
Bernstein, A., 80
Birkhoff, G., 14, 35

Blacher, K., 39
Blackwell, D., 148
Blaine, G., Jr. et al., 180
Bochner, S., 11
Bordley, J., 193
Bower, G., 37
Boyd, R., 52
Boyer, C. B., 12
Brainerd, H., 193
Breitbard, G., 146
Bridgman, P., 35
Brill, H., 34
Brock, P., 13, 34, 80
Brodman, K., 161
Brooks, S., 145
Brownsberger, C., 195
Bryan, J., III, 81
Burton, A., 13, 31, 33, 38, 47, 179
Butler, J., 80

Caligos, L., 96
Caller, B., 147
Cameron, D. E., 35
Cameron, N., 37, 51
Campbell, R., 28, 34
Caplan, G., 26, 47
Carek, D., 27, 29, 49, 51
Carkhuff, R. B., 40
Carmichel, R., 145
Carr, W., 146
Chatton, M., 193
Chen, I., 11
Chesler, L., 31, 192
Chessick, R., 191
Chester, L., 192
Cohen, J., 96
Colby, K., 11, 14, 15, 26, 28, 47, 49,
    96, 116, 117, 118, 145, 146, 148,
    162, 179, 193, 194, 196
Cole, J. O., ed., 34
Coleman, J. S., 97

197

Coleman, R., 52
Collen, M., 161
Computers in Psychiatry, 145
Cooley, W., 145
Cummins, D., 146

Dantzig, G., 161
Davitz, J., 47
Davitz, J. et al., 39
Dawson, R., 80
Dear, R., 117
Decker, J., 145, 148
De Mascio, A., 52
Deutsch, F., 46, 48, 191
Diagnostic and Statistical Manual of Mental
    Disorders, 28, 34, 162
Dorn, W., 147
Dreyfus, E., 51, 195

Eidusun, B., 145
Eisgruber, L. M., 144
Ekman, P., 194
Ekstein, R., 96, 117
Endicott, J., 34, 96, 146, 147, 161
Enea, H., 145
Enelow, A., 33, 39, 47, 49, 50, 96,
    117, 144, 191, 192, 194
Erbaugh, J., 34
Erdmann, A., Jr., 161
Ericson, R., 146
Ewalt, J. R., 30
Eysenck, H., 180
Eysenck, H., ed., 32

Fairbanks, G., 39
Farberow, N., 195
Faris, R. E., ed., 97
Feigenbaum, E., 147
Feinstein, A., 193
Feldman, J., 147
Fiedler, F., 195
Fleiss, J., 96, 147
Fleming, J., 96, 118
Flexer, R., 146
Fodor, N., ed., 34
Foulkes, S., 48, 49
Fowler, R., Jr., 145
Frank, J., 12, 19, 26, 32, 52, 179,
    187, 195
Freedman, D., 27, 31, 32, 79, 97, 118, 196
Friend, M. B., 116, 160, 180

Friesen, W., 194
Fromm-Reichmann, F., 26, 27, 36, 118
Fromm-Reichmann, F., ed., 97

Gardner, E., 34
Gaynor, F., ed., 34
Gelder, M., 27
Gieschen, M., 162
Gildea, E., 29
Gill, M., 13
Gill, M. et al., 27, 29, 46, 48, 53,
    180, 191, 196
Ginsberg, A., 193
Giovacchini, P., 47, 51
Glover, E., 27
Glueck, B., Jr., 146
Goguen, J., 81
Goldhammer, H., 81
Goldstein, A., 195
Goldstein, L., 161
Gorham, D., 146, 162
Greenblatt, M., 52
Greene, J. R., 144
Greenson, R., 51
Group for the Advancement of Psychiatry,
    27, 46, 48, 49, 51
Grunebaum, H., 29
Guetzkow, H., ed., 144
Guntrip, H., 30

Halacy, D., 147
Haldane, J. B. S., 80
Haley, J., 27
Hall, W., 145
Halton, J., 144
Hamburg, D., 96, 118
Hargreaves, W., 39
Harrison, S., 27, 29, 49, 51
Harvey, H., 193
Hershdorfer, A., 31, 192
Hicks, G., 146, 162
Hilf, F., 145, 146, 161, 194, 196
Hilgard, E., 23, 37
Hillman, R., 160, 192, 194
Hinsie, L., 28, 34
Hoaglin, L., 39
Hoch, E., 193
Hoch, P., 35, 36
Hollingshead, A., 195
Hollister, L., 162
Holt, H., 39
Holtz, K., 146

Hopgood, W. C., 116, 162, 180, 192
Hurwitz, A., 6

Ichikawa, A., 180

Jahoda, M., 30
Jansson, B., 148

Kadis, A., 48
Kamp, M., 15, 162
Kanfer, F., 34
Karush, W., 117
Katz, M., ed., 34
Katz, M. et al., 35
Kaufmann, A., 97
Kell, C. P., 116, 162, 180, 192, 193
Kelman, H., 13, 47
Kelman, H. et al., 27
Kendon, A., 96
Kitagawa, T., 81
Klein, G., ed., 80
Kline, M., 12
Kline, N., 14, 96, 145, 146
Koch, S., 12
Kolb, L., 27, 30, 46, 51, 52, 179, 180
Korsch, B., 36
Korzybski, A., 35
Kraemer, H., 196
Kramer, K., 34
Krasner, J., 49
Krasner, L., ed., 27
Krech, D., 80
Krech, D., ed., 80
Kubie, L., 30
Kurland, L., 116, 160, 180

Laing, R., 48, 180
Larson, F., 162
Laska, E., 14, 96, 145, 146
Laszlo, A., ed., 162
Lazarus, A., 14, 28
Leifer, R., 29
Lennard, H., 80
Lerner, A., 97
LeValley, J., 180
Levine, M., 27, 33, 50
Lewis, Sir Aubrey, 35
Lieberman, M., 28
Liefer, R., 14
Lincoln, T., 31, 192
Lindzey, G., ed., 96

Lohnes, P., 145
Lowrey, L., 117
Luborsky, L., ed., 80
Lusted, L., 193

MacKinnon, R. A., 38
Mann, H., 31
Margen, S., 193
Marks, I., 27
Marmor, J., 27
Marshall, A., 81
Matarazzo, J., 27, 33
May, R., 96
Mayman, M., 27
McCracken, D., 147
McLean, P., 30
McQuown, N., ed., 80
Meeham, T., 12
Meehl, P., 146
Meeker, R., 193
Mehrabian, A., 38
Mendelson, M., 34
Menninger, K., 16, 27, 29, 31, 49, 51,
    80, 194
Michael, W., 37
Michels, R., 38
Miller, J., 80, 146
Miller, P., 191
Mock, J., 34
Monte, A., 15
Moran, P., 31
Moreno, J., 36
Moreno, J., ed., 97
Motto, R., 145
Murphy, W., 46, 48, 191

Naftulin, D., 192
Nathan, P., 33, 34, 49, 180, 193
Negrete, V., 36
Newell, A., 145
Newman, R., 13
Neyman, J., 161

Offensend, F., 193
Orr, W., 147
Orwant, C., 96
Osmond, H., 31
Overall, J., 162

Pask, G., 192
Patterson, C., 27, 32, 37

Pearson, J., 146
Pearson, M., 27, 47, 97, 118, 180
Peckham, B., 146
Pennington, L., ed., 27, 39, 47, 53
Percy, W., 35
Pfeiffer, E., 13, 30, 47, 53
Phillips, E., 29, 32, 191, 193
Pines, M., 53
Piotrowski, Z., 146
Platz, A., 145
Polatin, P., 27, 28, 48, 52, 180
Pollin, W., 34
Pope, B., 36, 52, 97, 118
Popper, K., 33
Porter, E., Jr., 37, 40, 195
Prestwood, A., 39
Pruyser, P., 27

Rado, S., 32
RAND Corporation, 148
Rapoport, A., 12, 14, 53, 96
Rapoport, D., 80, 97
Rapoport, L. H., 98
Rath, G. J., 97
Redlich, F., 13, 27, 31, 32, 53, 97,
 118, 195, 196
Reed, C., 146
Reese, W., 15
Reid, L., 192
Reitman, W., 145
Reznikoff, M., 146
Rice, J. K., 11, 12, 13, 117, 147
Rice, J. R., 11, 12, 13, 117, 147
Rice, L., 80
Rim, Y., 97
Rivera, J. de, 11
Robeck, M., 37
Roberts, J. M., 96
Rockland, L., 34
Rome, H., 146
Rosen, S., 147
Rosenbaum, C., 116
Rosenberg, M., 146
Rosenberg, S., 117
Ross, A., 193
Ross, H., ed., 27, 33, 47, 50
Roth, W., 116
Rubin, L., 161
Ruesch, J., 36, 39, 97, 118
Ruesch, T., 31
Rutstein, D., 193

Salzman, L., 28, 36
Sanders, W., 146
Saslow, G., 34
Schilling, J., 12
Sem-Jacobsen, C., 13
Seward, G., 195
Shannon, C., 79
Sharfstein, S., 29
Shostrom, E., 49
Shure, G., 193
Siegelaub, A., 161
Siegler, M., 31
Siegler, M. et al., 50
Siegman, A., 36, 52, 97, 118
Simon, H., 145
Sinfos, P., 194
Sisson, R. L., 144
Slack, W., 146, 161, 162, 194, 195
Sletten, I., 147
Slotnick, D. L., 147
Smith, C. (see Kell, C.)
Smith, D., 14, 146
Smith, M., 96, 117
Smith, W., 162
Solomon, H., 52
Sommers, M., 13
Spitzer, R., 34, 96, 146, 147, 161
Spotnitz, H., 96
Stacy, R., ed., 15, 196
Stafford-Clark, D., 47
Starkweather, J., 15, 39, 96, 145, 148,
 161, 162
Stein, M., ed., 32
Steinzor, B., 32, 36, 50, 53
Stillman, R., 116, 161
Stockhamer, N., 96
Stone, A., 33
Strassman, H., 192
Stroebel, C., 146
Stroebel, S., 147
Strupp, H., 30, 38, 97, 118, 192, 195
Strupp, H., ed., 80
Sullivan, H., 27, 29, 30, 39, 40, 53,
 118, 194
Sutton-Smith, B., 96
Swenson, W., 146
Szasz, T., 31

Tarachow, S., 97, 118
Teitelbaum, H., 35
The RAND Corporation, 148
Thompson, C., 12, 187, 195

Thompson, W. R., 97
Thorne, F., 36
Thorp, E., 148
Tupin, J., 191

Ulam, S., 147
Ulett, G., 147
Ultman, J., 193

Van Cura, L., 146, 161
Van Woerkom, A., 161
Veldman, D., 147
von Bertalanffy, L., 80

Wagstaff, A., 80
Wallerstein, R., 34, 79, 96, 117
Ward, C., 34
Ware, J., 192
Watkins, J., 27
Waxman, B., ed., 15, 196
Weaver, W., 79
Weber, S., 145, 194, 196
Wegner, P., 147
Weinstock, H., II, 35
Weizenbaum, J., 12, 147

Wexler, M., 33, 39, 47, 49, 50, 96,
    117, 144, 194
Whitaker, D., 28
Wiederhold, G., 146
Wiener, D., 28, 29, 32, 191, 193
Wigner, F., 12
Wilbur, 33, 38, 179
Wilmer, H. A., 47, 191
Wilson, J. et al., 37
Wilson, J., 37
Winder, C., 193
Winick, C., 39, 49
Witmer, H., ed., 47, 97, 118
Wittner, W., 146
Wolberg, L., 28, 38, 39, 46, 48, 51,
    97, 180, 191
Wolff, W., 19, 32
Wolman, B., ed., 33
Wolpe, J., 28, 38
Woolff, H., 27, 32

Young, F., 147

Zadeh, L. A., 50, 81, 97
Zubin, J., 35, 36

SUBJECT INDEX

Allergic reactions, 83–84
Alternates, 158
  see also Convergent and divergent
    responses
Anxiety, in initial interview, 51, 163,
    179, 194
  see also Psychotherapist, Psychotherapy
"As if" structures, 10
Average behavior, 76, 93
  see also Probability theory, Uncertainty

Blackjack, 133–140

Cause and effect relations, 5, 64, 107,
    110, 122
Classification, 22
  dangers of, 33
  in psychotherapy, 34, 35, 162
Coin-tossing, 77–78
Communication, in psychotherapy, 22, 28,
    35, 97
  by mathematics, 4, 13
  in simulation, 14, 185
  verbal and non-verbal, 23, 38, 39, 52, 101,
    185, 194
Computer, and simulation, 119–148
  in psychiatry, 96, 145–148
  in systems investigation, 68–69, 81
  properties of, 8, 127–130, 147
  vignettes, *see* Vignettes
Conscious, 40, 96, 118
Control process, 85
Convergent and divergent responses, 44–46,
    111–112, 150, 162, 164
  construction of, 152–156, 158, 160, 162,
    165, 167, 170, 180, 187
  see also Alternates, Simulation of
    initial interview, Vignettes
Cycling, 158–159

Data, 14, 123

Data (*Continued*)
  accumulation of, 66
Decision-making, 3, 17
  examining alternatives in, 82, 96
  theory of, 14
  under uncertainty, 92–93
  see also Decision process, Problem-
    solving, Uncertainty
Decision process, 7, 61, 83–98, 132
  adaptive, 95, 105–106
  feasibility vs. optimality, 89
  incorrect, illogical, irrational, 126
  multi-stage, 61–62, 90, 94, 102
  on-line, 24, 96, 106, 183, 188
  operational aspects of, 86
  stochastic, 92, 94, 124–126, 139
  structure of, 86
Deterministic system, 73–74
  see also Cause and effect relations,
    Stochastic systems
Diagnosis, in medicine, 193
  in psychotherapy, 49, 50
  see also Medical model, Mental illness
Dialogues, sample, 1
  The Young Psychiatrist, 171–173
  The Silent Patient, 173–176
  The Telephone Caller, 176–179
  see also Convergent and divergent
    responses, Vignettes
Dimensionality, 108, 114
  by branching, 132
  see also Looping
Disease model, *see* Medical model
Divergent, *see* Convergent and divergent
    responses

Evaluation, 186, 196
  of initial interview simulation, 189–191
  of stochastic process, 139–144
Experimental method, *see* Scientific
    method

Experts, 193
  for evaluation, 142, 153

Feasibility, 89, 97, 132
Fuzzy sets, 81

Game theory, *see* Simulation

Hidden variables, 73–74
  see also Observables

Idealized systems, 71
Influence-response analysis, 57–58, 65,
      79, 130
  of stochastic system, 76
Information, 14, 123
Information pattern, 95, 101, 113, 117
Initial interview, 9, 29, 39, 40–53, 116
  attitudes in, 44
  basic decision in, 43
  dyadic nature of, 43, 53
  importance of, 13, 25, 46
  objectives of, 41, 47–50, 102, 186
  patient attitudes and responses in, 45
  success of, 53
  therapeutic relationship in, 42, 50–52
  therapist attitudes and responses in, 45
  understanding of, 181
  see also Evaluation, Psychotherapy,
      Simulation of initial interview,
      Vignettes
Interaction process, interview as, 100, 117
  between systems, 60, 80
Interview, clinical, 52–53
  computer conducted, 145, 160–162,
      193, 194
  skills of, 33, 194
  see also Initial interview,
      Psychotherapy

Learning, 37, 95, 142, 195
  and dynamic programming, 117
  in psychotherapy, 36, 118, 144, 160
  see also Research in psychotherapy,
      Teaching/training in psychotherapy
Looping, 156–158
  see also Dimensionality

Mathematical method, 3, 5, 12, 71
  in investigation of systems, 66–67
  see also Rationality, Scientific method
Mathematical model, 9, 13, 98, 117

Mathematical model (*Continued*)
  see also Simulation, Simulation of
      initial interview
Mathematics, definition of, 4
Mental health, 17–18, 30, 32
  see also Mental illness
Medical model, 14, 17, 28, 31
  see also Diagnosis
Memory, computer, 129, 147
Mental illness, 21–22, 29, 30
  definition of, 17, 31
  diagnosis in, 31
  see also Diagnosis, Mental health
Model of initial interview, *see*
      Simulation of initial interview
Model-making, 63
  in psychiatry, 145
Monte Carlo technique, 144
Multi-stage process, *see*
      Decision process, multi-stage

Non-verbal, *see* Communication,
      verbal and non-verbal

Observables, 57, 76
  see also Hidden variables
On-line decision-making, *see* Decision
      process, on-line
Operational pressure, 7, 9, 17, 29, 127
Optimal play, 140
  rules for, 141

Patient, 53
  as malfunctioning system, 25, 100
  as system, 98
  definition of, 21
  degree of ill-health, 21–22, 30, 35
  goals of, 47
  see also Mental illness, Psychotherapist
      in simulation process
Policy, 87, 88–90
  determining by enumeration, 88
  feasible, 89, 104
  for constructing responses, 165, 167, 170
  interviewing, 10, 96–97, 103–104, 143
  optimal, 87, 133
Prediction, 34, 67, 79
  see also Mathematical method
Probability theory, 8, 78, 108, 118
  see also Uncertainty, Average behavior
Probelm-solving, 21
  in psychotherapy, 29, 32

Problem-solving (*Continued*)
  see also Decision-making,
    Decision process
Process, definition of, 59–60
Psychiatry, definition of, 16, 31, 53
  see also Model, Medical
Psychopathology, *see* Mental illness
Psychotherapist, 32, 51–52, 187
  as system, 100, 117
  definition of, 17–18, 21, 29
  goals of, 17, 47
  in simulation process, 149, 163
  techniques of, 117, 195
  see also Human systems, Psychotherapy
Psychotherapy, 3, 7, 16–40, 196
  as on-line process, 24
  as system, 100, 117
  classification in, 22, 31, 34, 35
  communication in, 23, 24, 35, 36, 38, 39
  definition of, 17, 18, 21, 29
  goals of, 17, 47
  initial interview in, 25, 39
  in simulation process, 149, 163
  operational view of, 17, 28
  problem-solving in, 21, 34
  techniques of, 117, 195
  theory in, 19, 20, 33, 34
  treatment in, 24, 31
  underlying conceptual structure of,
    25, 26, 39, 40
  see also Human systems, Patient,
    Psychotherapy

Random numbers, generation of,
    137–139, 148
Rapport, *see* Relationship, therapeutic
Rational behavior, 90, 93
Rationality, 3, 6, 10, 12, 72, 73
  in simulation, 97
  see also Mathematical method, Scientific
    method
Realism, 158, 184
Real time, 183
  see also Decision process, on-line
Referees, 184, 194
Relationship, therapeutic, 18, 28, 38,
    42–43, 47–48, 50–53, 97, 117
Reproducibility, 5, 70
Research, in psychotherapy, 13, 18, 186–196
  further testing and, 195
  hypothesis testing in, 189–190
  non-verbal aspects in, 185, 194

Research (*Continued*)
  statistical evaluation in, 190, 196
  testing by experts, 189, 196
  training possibilities using, 188, 196
  use of referees in, 184–185, 194
Response sets, *see* Convergent and
    divergent responses

Sampling, 125
Scientific method, 3, 11–12, 14, 120
  and observer, 122, 144
  in psychoanalysis, 79
  in systems investigation, 65–66
  objectives of, 69
  see also Mathematical method, Rationality
Simulation, 8, 13–15, 119–148
  decision-making in, 97–98
  feasibility of, 127, 145
  in human systems, 80, 145
  limitations of, 143, 184
  theory of, 144
  see also Model
Simulation of initial interview, 98–118,
    149–162
  aims of, 186–188
  construction of responses in, 153–154
  cumulative response probabilities in, 160
  description of, 149
  termination of, 152
  see also Evaluation, Initial interview,
    Simulation, Vignettes
State, of a system, 55–56
  of patient and therapist systems, 102
State-dependent analysis, 59
Stochastic process, *see* Decision-process,
    stochastic
Stochastic systems, 75–76, 79
  see also Decision-process, determinism
Structure, of system, 62–63
Systems, 5, 54–81
  description of, 55
  human, 79, 99, 100, 117
  idealized, 70–72
  investigations of, 56
  networks and hierarchies of, 73
  observation of, 122
  operation of, 82–83
  understanding vs. model-making, 63–64, 80

Teaching/training, in psychotherapy, 181–196
  see also Evaluation

Teaching/training (*Continued*)
  aims of simulation process, 186–188,
    194–195
  limitations of simulation, 184, 194
  on-line decision-making, 183–184
  transfer of learning, 190–191
Theory, 6, 9, 88
  in initial interview simulation, 153, 156
  in psychotherapy, 20, 22, 33, 80, 118
  in science, 65
  in systems analysis, 62
  operational value of, 14, 19, 33, 132
Therapist, *see* Psychotherapist
Therapy, *see* Psychotherapy

Uncertainty, 8, 91, 93–94, 119, 123
  see also Average behavior, decision-
    making, Determinism, Probability
    theory

Unconscious, 96, 118

Validation, *see* Evaluation
Variables, 14
Verbal, *see* Communication, verbal and
  non-verbal
Vignettes, 163–180
  response construction principles, therapist,
    165, 168, 170
  response construction principles, patient,
    166, 168, 171
  response construction policy, 165, 167, 170
  The Young Psychotherapist, 164–166
  The Silent Patient, 166–169
  The Telephone Interview, 169–171
  see also Simulation of initial interview,
    Convergent and divergent responses